W9-BZJ-168

DEMOCRATIZATION IN RUSSIA

Contemporary Soviet/Post-Soviet Politics

DEMOCRATIZATION IN RUSSIA

The Development of Legislative Institutions

 EDITED BY **Jeffrey W. Hahn**

M.E. Sharpe • Armonk, New York • London, England

Library of Congress Cataloging-in-Publication Data

Democratization in Russia : the development of
legislative institutions / edited by Jeffrey W. Hahn
p.   cm.— (Contemporary Soviet/post-Soviet politics)
Includes index.
ISBN 1-56324-719-4 alk. paper
ISBN 1-56324-720-8 (pbk).
1. Legislative bodies—Russia (Federation)
2. Democracy—Russia (Federation)
3. Russia (Federation)—Politics and government—1991–
I. Hahn, Jeffrey W., 1944–   . II. Series.
JN6697.D46 1995
328.47'09'049—dc20
95-24912
CIP

Printed in the United States of America

The paper used in this publication meets the minimum requirements of
American National Standard for Information Sciences—
Permanence of Paper for Printed Library Materials,
ANSI Z 39.48-1984.

BM (c)   10   9   8   7   6   5   4   3   2   1
BM (p)   10   9   8   7   6   5   4   3   2   1

Contents

List of Tables and Figures

Figures

Tables

About the Editor and Contributors

JEFFREY W. HAHN is a Professor of Political Science at Villanova University, where he specializes in Russian politics. His most recent book is *Local Power and Post-Soviet Politics* (1994) which he co-edited with Theodore H. Friedgut. He is currently completing a study of Russian political culture based on extended field research in Yaroslavl.

TIMOTHY J. COLTON is a Professor of Government and Russian Studies at Harvard University and Director of the Harvard Russian Research Center. He is the author of *Moscow: Governing the Socialist Metropolis* (Harvard University Press, 1995) and several other studies of Soviet and Russian politics.

JERRY F. HOUGH is a Professor of Political Science at Duke University. He is the author of numerous articles and books on Russian politics and foreign policy, including *Russia and the West: Gorbachev and the Politics of Reform*, the second edition of which appeared in 1990.

MICHAEL L. MEZEY is a Professor of Political Science and Dean of the College of Liberal Arts and Sciences at DePaul University in Chicago. He is the author of numerous scholarly papers, articles, and book chapters in the areas of American politics, legislative politics, and comparative legislative behavior. He has published two books: *Comparative Legislatures* (Duke University Press, 1979) and *Congress, the President, and Public Policy* (Westview Press, 1989).

LEV A. OKUNKOV is the Director of the Institute of Legislation and Comparative Law of the Government of the Russian Federation, located in Moscow. He is a specialist on comparative constitutional law. In addition to reviewing proposed legislation for the government, under his direction the institute is currently editing a collection of the world's constitutions.

ALEKSANDR E. POSTNIKOV is a Senior Researcher at the Institute of Legislation and Comparative Law of the Government of the Russian Federation, located in Moscow. He is specialist on legislation dealing with local government. He recently co-authored (with Vsevolod I. Vasiliev) a book entitled *Elections to the State Duma: Legal Issues* (1995).

THOMAS F. REMINGTON is a Professor of Political Science at Emory University. His recent publications include *Parliaments in Transition: The New Legislative Politics in the Former USSR and Eastern Europe* (1994) and a number of articles dealing with the development of parliamentary institutions in postcommunist Russia.

BLAIR A. RUBLE is the Director of the Kennan Institute for Advanced Russian Studies of the Woodrow Wilson Center in Washington, D.C. He is the author of two monographs and five co-edited volumes. His most recent book is *Money Sings: The Changing Politics of Urban Space in Post-Soviet Yaroslavl*, published in 1995.

LILIA SHEVTSOVA is a Senior Associate at the Carnegie Endowment for International Peace. Previously she was Deputy Director of the Institute of International Economic and Political Studies in Moscow and in 1994-95 she was a visiting fellow at the Woodrow Wilson Center. Dr. Shevtsova has published a wide range of articles in newspapers such as *Segodnya* and *Moscow News*. Her most recent article in English, on Russia's democratic transition, appeared in the *Journal of Democracy*.

KATHRYN STONER-WEISS is Assistant Professor of Politics and International Affairs at Princeton University. She holds a Ph.D. in political science from Harvard University and recently completed a comprehensive study comparing regional government performance in post-communist Russia. She is currently researching the political and economic aspects of Russian state decentralization in a comparative context.

YURII A. TIKHOMIROV is the Associate Director of the Institute of Legislation and Comparative Law of the Government of the Russian Federation, located in Moscow. He is a senior specialist on the development of legislative institutions in Russia and the author of numerous books and articles dealing with the soviets and with contemporary legislative institutions.

Preface

The genesis of this book can be traced to a conference held at the faculty club of Harvard University on October 29–31, 1993. The theme of the conference was to consider the prospects for democracy in Russia by focusing on the development of its legislative institutions at the local and national levels. The conference itself represented the culmination of a four-year research project begun in 1990 and involving American and Russian scholars, which was funded by the Carnegie Corporation of New York. The first and second sessions of the conference were devoted to reports by the principal participants in this project of their findings related to legislative development in Russia on the national and on the local level, respectively. The third session, however, was given to a roundtable discussion among the fifty or so specialists who had been invited to the conference and who were asked to comment on the findings presented earlier. These included not only experts in Russian studies, but political scientists from the field of legislative studies (a list of conference participants is appended). The goal of the third session was to explore how findings from the Russian case could be integrated into broader concerns of comparative political theory.

The organizers of the conference had no way of knowing that a few weeks before the date set for the meeting, Russian president Boris Yeltsin would abolish Russia's legislative institutions (then called "soviets," or councils). As it happened, on September 21, 1993, he dissolved the national parliament, the Supreme Soviet, and in early October he permanently suspended the authority of the local soviets.

Those who came to Harvard on October 29–31, 1993, expecting to discuss whether these institutions were becoming more democratic were suddenly confronted with the question of whether legislatures would continue to exist in Russia at all. As one Russian colleague pointed out, American political scientists specializing on the soviets had overnight become historians. In fact, it seems clear in retrospect that these events made a discussion of Russian legislative development more relevant, not less. Two reasons for this are worth mentioning here.

In the first place, the events of autumn 1993 set in motion a new stage in the transformation of the Russian political system from the authoritarian communist one which existed until 1990 to something else. However, in principle at least, the president's commitment to democratization continued. Even as he abolished the old system of the soviets, Yeltsin committed his government to holding new parliamentary elections in December 1993 and local legislative elections in the spring of 1994. While these institutions had new names and functioned differently from the old soviets in certain respects, like them they were to be the principal representative institutions of government responsible for legislation. Moreover, whatever their defects, the soviets of 1993 were far different entities than they had been before 1990. From the perspective of democratization many of the changes were positive and laid the groundwork for their successors. At the same time, there were obvious, and ultimately fatal, problems. What can be learned from an analysis of the legislative experience between 1990 and 1993 that can help us to assess whether stable democratic institutions will ultimately emerge in Russia? In this sense the present book represents something of a political autopsy.

A second reason for looking closely at the development of Russian legislatures between 1990 and 1993 is for what it can tell us about political transitions generally. The Russian experience provides us with a sort of living laboratory for testing theories about how and why democratic institutions get built (or fail to get built). There are really two related but analytically distinct theoretical issues to be addressed here: legislative institutionalization and democratization. As the literature on these subjects suggests, one can occur without the other. However, popular sovereignty without institutionalization is likely to be unstable, while the development of strong institutions without popular participation in the decision-making process is a prescription for authoritarian rule. For those interested in the development of democracy in Russia, legislatures are the logical place to concentrate since they are universally regarded as one of the principal institutions in democratic societies by which citizens communicate their preferences to those who govern. What can we learn by looking at the Russian experience with legislative development during 1990–93 about transitions to democracy? Conversely, what do theories of transition based on comparative research elsewhere have to tell us about what is happening in Russia? It is time to bring the study of Russia into the mainstream of research in the field of comparative politics.

The research project that generated the findings presented at the Harvard conference came about as the result of a telephone call by Blair Ruble (currently director of the Kennan Institute for Advanced Russian Studies in Washington, D.C.) to me in June 1988, a few days prior to my visit to Moscow to determine the feasibility of conducting survey research there. It was an exciting time for what was then known as Soviet studies. Gorbachev was about to deliver his historic address to the Nineteenth Conference of the CPSU outlining fundamental reforms of the Soviet political system, but the general shape of these momentous reforms was already known. Sensing what was under way, Blair suggested that I explore with some Russian colleagues the possibility of establishing a joint research project. This led to a conversation with Professor Georgii V. Barabashev, chairman of the department that dealt with legislative studies at Moscow State University (MSU), over a backyard barbecue at his dacha. He was enthusiastic and proposed that the Russian partners include the dean of the MSU Law Faculty, Mikhail N. Marchenko, and the director of the USSR Supreme Soviet's Institute for Research on Soviet State Construction and Legislation, Vsevolod I. Vasiliev. At that time, Vasiliev worked closely with Anatolii Lukianov, a Politburo member who became vice chairman of the USSR Supreme Soviet under Gorbachev a year later. Ruble and Barabashev were primarily responsible for launching this project.

After my return home, Blair Ruble and I were able to persuade professors Timothy Colton (Harvard) and Jerry Hough (Duke) to form the team of American participants. After lengthy negotiations in spring 1989 between the principal participants from both sides, a proposal for funding was submitted and approved by the Carnegie Corporation of New York as part of what was then known as its Cooperative Security Program. Beginning in January 1990, the two sides would send four scholars each to spend up to six weeks studying the other country's legislative system, locally as well as nationally. For the American team this led to an unprecedented opportunity to study the workings of Soviet local government. With the blessing of Lukianov, the team was allowed to conduct extensive field research in the province of Yaroslavl, some of which is reported in the chapters in this volume by Hahn, Ruble, and Stoner-Weiss. Equally remarkable were the opinion surveys of deputies conducted by Colton and Hough at the national level. The Russian team was especially interested in the experience of U.S. state and local governments, which they observed firsthand in a dozen states ranging from Alaska to North Carolina and from Massachusetts to California. Some of their findings shaped the legislation by which Russia is governed today.

The period covered by this project wrought changes more far-reaching than any of its original participants could possibly have foreseen. The communist system collapsed and a nascent capitalist democracy replaced it; what began as a Soviet-American project became a Russian-American one. Some of the participants changed as well. Sadly, Professor Barabashev died of cancer on March 23, 1993. The institute directed by Vasiliev became the Institute of Comparative Law and Legislation and is currently affiliated with the Russian government, not the parliament. Its director is Lev A. Okunkov, who led the Russian delegation at Harvard. Despite these alterations, the research continued. The first results of the joint project were reported at a conference held in Yaroslavl, Russia, in April 1992.[1] The return visit was held at Harvard in October 1993 and the results are reported in this book.

Most of the chapters are substantially revised versions of the papers originally prepared for the first Harvard conference. Only the chapter by Thomas Remington was not first presented at that time, although he participated in the conference. While they focus on Russian legislative development from 1990 to 1993, the authors were enjoined to indicate what relevance their findings might have for understanding the course of legislative development in Russia *after* the abolition of the soviets in October 1993. Most took advantage of the opportunity to update their contributions. The introductory chapter offers a theoretical framework for analyzing the development of legislative systems, along with an overview of the events of the entire period 1990–95. The concluding chapters by the editor and by Michael Mezey are explicitly addressed to the broader implications of this research for comparative political theory and for what happens next in Russia.

***

The editor of this book owes much to many. Institutionally, it is a pleasure to acknowledge the generous support of the Carnegie Corporation of New York without which this research could not have taken place. He would also like to thank Villanova University's Office of Research and Sponsored Projects for administering the grant from the Carnegie Corporation, and the vice president for academic affairs, the late Father Lawrence Gallen, for giving him a reduced teaching load throughout this period of time. Grants from IREX in 1988 and 1990 played a crucial role in the research reported here as did one from the National Council for Soviet and East European Research in 1992. The academic year 1990–91, spent as a visiting professor at the University of California–Berkeley, provided much food for thought. I also want to express my sincere gratitude to the city of Yaroslavl and especially to its mayor, Viktor V. Volunchunas, to the former chair of the City Soviet, Lev L. Kruglikov, and to its people for their cooperation and for the many kindnesses they showed to me and my colleagues.

The list of people to thank is long, but needs to begin with the principal participants: from the United States, Timothy Colton, Jerry Hough, and Blair Ruble; and from Russia, Georgii V. Barabashev, Vsevolod I. Vasiliev, Mikhail N. Marchenko, and Lev A. Okunkov. I appreciated their cooperation; I valued highly their insight and advice. Professors Daniel Berkowitz, Beth Mitchneck, and Susan Lehmann joined the project at various times and contributed much intellectual energy to it. The project benefited from the assistance of field managers who were drawn from the ranks of the best graduate students in the country and who looked after the project's affairs in Russia while they carried out their own research agendas. Chronologically these included: Josephine Andrews (Harvard), Laura Jewitt (Columbia), Kathryn Stoner-Weiss (Harvard), Regina Smyth (Duke), and Henry Hale (Harvard). Gavin Helf (Berkeley) was also helpful to me and to the project. Brian Sloyer (Villanova) prepared drafts of the appendices used in this book. Several people played important academic roles in the conference at Harvard and deserve recognition for it. Alexander Domrin of the Parliamentary Center of the Russian Federation and

Robert Sharlet of Union College provided trenchant commentary on the papers given at the first session, while Theodore Friedgut of the Hebrew University of Jerusalem and Darrell Slider of the University of South Florida did the same at the second. Juan Linz of Yale University gave an eloquent keynote address.

The administration of a project of this size is impossible without assistance. This was ably provided, in turn, by Janine Ludlam, Maricel Hahn, and Valerie Pellegrino. Judy Mehrman, assistant director of the Harvard Russian Research Center, was a great help, particularly in organizing the conference at Harvard. In Moscow, all the American participants were assisted at one time or another by Igor P. Romanov, the energetic head of the External Relations department of the Institute of Legislation and Comparative Law. I would also like to acknowledge the help of Patricia Kolb at M. E. Sharpe, Inc., for all she did to bring this book to fruition, and to Ana Erlic and Elizabeth Granda for their attentive editorial assistance. Finally, special recognition belongs to Tatiana Pavlovna Rumiantseva, director of the Yaroslavl Center for the Study of Public Opinion and Sociological Research. In addition to her scientific role in this project, which has been noted elsewhere, she worked harder to ensure the success of this project in the field than anyone and did so with extraordinary grace and skill.

Jeffrey W. Hahn
Villanova, Pennsylvania

Note

1. Papers from the conference were edited by Lev L. Kruglikov and Jeffrey W. Hahn and published by the Yaroslavl City Soviet and Yaroslavl Center for the Study of Public Opinion and Sociological Research under the title *Predstavitel'nye organy mestnogo samoupravleniia v sovremennom mire* (Representative Institutions of Local Self-Government in the Contemporary World), Yaroslavl, 1992.

List of Harvard Conference Participants

List of Conference Attendees, October 29–31, 1993
"Democratization in Russia: The Development of
Legislative Institutions"

Josephine Andrews, University of California–Davis
Donna Bahry, Vanderbilt University
Dmitrii Bakatin, Steptoe and Johnson International, Moscow
Donald Barry, Lehigh University
Mark Beissinger, University of Wisconsin
Harold Clarke, University of North Texas
Timothy J. Colton, Harvard University
Jane Dawson, Wellesley College
Michael Dobbs, Washington Post
Mickey Edwards, Woodrow Wilson Center, Harvard University
Frederic Fleron, State University of New York–Buffalo
Abbott Gleason, Brown University
Stuart Goldman, Congressional Research Service, Library of
    Congress
Jeffrey W. Hahn, Villanova University
Henry Hale, Harvard University
Gavin Helf, Cornell University
Joel Hellman, Harvard University
Kathryn Hendley, University of Wisconsin
Erik Hoffmann, State University of New York–Albany
Jerry F. Hough, Duke University

Eugene Huskey, Stetson University
Brendan Kiernan, Monitor Company
Allan Kornberg, Duke University
Stephen Kotkin, Princeton University
Susan Lehmann, Columbia University
Juan Linz, Yale University
Gerhard Loewenberg, University of Iowa
Michael L. Mezey, DePaul University
William Mishler, University of South Carolina
Beth Mitchneck, University of Arizona
Kevin O'Brien, Ohio State University
Lev A. Okunkov, Director, Institute of Legislation and
    Comparative Law
David Olson, University of North Carolina
Aleksandr E. Postnikov, Senior Scholar, Institute of
    Legislation and Comparative Law
Thomas F. Remington, Emory University
Bert Rockman, University of Pittsburgh
Igor D. Romanov, Institute of Legislation and Comparative Law
Blair A. Ruble, Director, Kennan Institute for Advanced
    Russian Studies
Robert Sharlet, Union College
Lilia Shevtsova, Institute of International Economic and Political
    Studies, Russian Academy of Sciences
Darrell Slider, University of South Florida
Regina Smyth, Duke University
Steven Solnick, Columbia University
Kathryn Stoner-Weiss, Princeton University
Yurii A. Tikhomirov, Associate Director, Institute of
    Legislation and Comparative Law
Michael Urban, University of California–Santa Cruz
Celeste Ann Wallander, Harvard University

DEMOCRATIZATION IN RUSSIA

1

Introduction

Analyzing Parliamentary Development in Russia

Jeffrey W. Hahn

When Boris Yeltsin abolished Russia's parliamentary system in September 1993, he not only changed the "rules" of the game of democratic consolidation as it had been played up to that time, he put an end to the game altogether. With the adoption of a new constitution on December 12, 1993, new rules were established and the first Russian republic gave way to the second one. Not surprisingly, the new rules strongly favor President Yeltsin, the man responsible for drafting them. Whether these new rules can accommodate a transition to democracy in Russia is an open question. However, analysis of the reasons why the previous rules could not do so may help us assess the chances for success in the second Russian republic. In many ways, this book attempts to conduct a political autopsy of the first Russian republic, focusing mainly on its legislative organs. Why did the period of transition from 1990 to 1993 end the way it did? What can we learn from an autopsy about the prospects for democratization in Russia? More comparatively, what can we learn about the conditions that contribute to the emergence and maintenance of democratic political institutions?

The central goal of this book is to contribute to our knowledge of the process by which stable democratic parliaments develop. We shall seek to do so by examining the experience of Russian parliamentary institutions at the national and local levels from 1990 to 1993. Arguably, the political system of the first Russian republic met the minimum criteria for democratic transitions: the old authoritarian system had broken down, a "founding election" was held, and a new parliament formed. Russia in 1990–93 seemed poised to proceed with the stage of democratic consolidation. But this did not happen.[1] The Russian experience offers an unusual opportunity to understand the processes that underlie the consolidation of democratic institutions precisely because of what it tells us about the pathology of parliamentary development: what are the reasons that explain why democratic consolidation fails? This chapter has two purposes: to develop a framework of analysis for understanding legislative institutionalization in Russia, and to set the stage for what follows by briefly describing the main phases of Russian parliamentary development from 1990 to 1993.

Parliaments and Democratization

What can we learn from the rather extensive literature on the development of legislative institutions that can help frame the issues we want to address? To begin with, we need to establish the place of parliaments in the study of democracy.[2] Legislatures perform a number of functions crucial to democratic systems. Among these are: policy making activities (agenda setting, deliberation, adoption and oversight); representational activities (communication of constituency preferences, providing constituent services); maintenance functions (political recruitment, selecting leaders, mediating elite conflict).[3] How these functions are carried out by legislatures varies considerably and legislatures can be classified accordingly. With respect to policy making, for instance, in strong legislatures (Polsby uses the word "transformative"), popularly elected representatives play a direct role in making laws, while in weak ones (which he calls "arenas") their policy-making role is more indirect; they shape laws through debate, personal persuasion, and oversight. In what Michael Mezey refers to as "marginal" legislatures, representatives play little or no policy-making role, but may communicate policy in ways that contribute to maintaining the system.[4] What distinguishes *democratic* legislatures is that of all the institutions of representative democracy, legislatures are designed to articulate citizen preferences in making decisions; legislators who fail to do so can be held accountable by those they represent. More simply, legislatures are the single most important representative institution in a democratic system. As David Olson and Michael Mezey put it: "The legislature, more than any other political institution, stands at the confluence of democratic theory and democratic practice."[5]

The importance of legislatures to democracy is not limited to countries where democracy is already established. They may also be critical to the process of *becoming* democratic. In his essay "Transitions to Democracy," Juan Linz writes, "One of the great challenges of the period between authoritarian rule and the first government based on free elections is the setting up of basic rules of the future political process meaning both the characteristics of the representative institutions to be elected and the electoral law."[6] In his view, democratic consolidation can take place only when a legal framework defining the rights and procedures by which legislative and executive institutions exercise their authority is in place. Parliaments offer an institutional framework for the mediation of social conflict. Only within such an institutional framework can contending players engage fruitfully in the politics of negotiation and compromise. Linz further argues that parliamentary regimes are preferable to presidential ones in transitional periods because they are more flexible and adaptable in times of crisis. Since they are bound to stay in office for fixed terms, presidents in such circumstances are more prone to "serious errors" of judgment. In Linz's view, "during periods of transition and consolidation, the rigidities of a presidential constitution must seem inauspicious indeed compared to the prospect of adaptability that parliamentarism offers."[7]

From the point of view of democratic theory, then, it seems clear that legislatures are a crucial element in democratic political systems insofar as they serve as the principal link between what governmental institutions do and what people want them to do. This is consistent with the view of John Stuart Mill as set forth in his treatise "On Representative Government." Modern political science, however, finds this view overly simplistic. In the first place, the popular will is at best imperfectly reflected in legislative activity.[8] More importantly, perhaps, it is clear that not all legislatures perform their tasks well. As Robert Putnam has shown, it is not enough for democratic institutions to be responsive, they must also be effective.[9] While for democracies, the questions of representativeness and performance are closely interrelated, analytically they are distinct. In his seminal analysis of how stable political institutions get built, Samuel Huntington argued that countries can have sufficiently high levels of political participation (what Dahl would term inclusiveness) without well-developed political institutions, and vice versa. According to Huntington, the problem for developing nations is that high levels of participation without institutional development produce unstable "preatorian" polities, while the reverse produces unstable "civic" polities.[10] Stable democracies need both popular participation and institutionalization.

This observation would seem directly relevant to understanding the development of legislatures in Russia and Eastern Europe. There, electoral mechanisms for broad participation were introduced before stable institutions were established, a problem sometimes referred to as "sequencing." Levels of political participation in these countries were quite high, but the capacity of legislative institutions to process participation was not. The transitional parliaments of the former communist countries have been hampered from the outset by problems that have been largely resolved in more established parliamentary systems. Among those identified by David Olson are: lack of governmental experience, fragmented parties, constitutional ambiguity, the absence of committee systems, few and untrained staff, and unrealistic public expectations. These difficulties are compounded by the fact that communist countries must remake not only their political institutions, but their economic systems at the same time, a dilemma known as the problem of "simultaneity."[11] As Olson puts it, "The new parliaments of the new democracies suffer from the paradox of too much work to do and not enough resources with which to function."[12] In short, they lack institutional capacity.

For legislatures to be effective, then, it is not enough for them to be democratic (in the sense of Dahl's polyarchy); they must also become stable or "institutionalized." Indeed, in his more recent work on democratization, Huntington goes so far as to suggest that the concept of stability (or institutionalization) be incorporated into the definition of a democratic political system, although he recognizes that there may be more or less stable democracies.[13] Larry Diamond goes even further, arguing that institutionalization is the most important factor in democratic consolidation, especially in countries seeking to introduce structural economic reform under democratic conditions. In his words:

> In fact, a stronger and broader generalization appears warranted: the single most important and urgent factor in the consolidation of democracy is not civil society but political institutionalization. *Consolidation*

is the process by which democracy becomes so broadly and profoundly legitimate among its citizens that it is very unlikely to break down. It involves behavioral and institutional changes that normalize democratic politics and narrow its uncertainty. This normalization requires expansion of citizen access, development of democratic citizenship and culture, broadening of leadership recruitment and training, and other functions that civil society performs. But most of all, and most urgently, it requires political institutionalization.[14]

But what does the term "institutionalization" mean? One of the earliest efforts at conceptualization was by Nelson Polsby in his analysis of the U.S. House of Representatives. For institutions to be "viable," he wrote, they must become "institutionalized"—that is, "organizations must be created and sustained that are specialized to political activity." For Polsby, institutionalized organizations are characterized by well-defined boundaries, organizational complexity, and "universalistic" rather than particularistic (personalized) criteria in the conduct of business.[15] Subsequent definitions tend to view institutionalization as the development of set ways of doing things, the establishment (and acceptance) of specific rules and procedures over time. Loewenberg and Patterson define legislative institutionalization as "the process by which legislatures acquire a definite way of performing their functions that sets them apart. A highly institutionalized legislature has organizational inertia: it keeps on going as it has and is hard to change."[16] This definition comes closer to the analytical framework employed by proponents of "new institutionalism," which is discussed below.

In sum, if we are to develop an analytical framework for understanding the development of democratic local and national legislative institutions in Russia, it seems clear that we need to address not one, but two central questions: Are they becoming more democratic (employing Dahl's concept of polyarchy)? Are they becoming institutionalized? Since it seems clear that both democratization and institutionalization are essential, then we need to specify criteria by which to answer each of these questions. We look at institutionalization first.

Explaining Parliamentary Institutionalization

By what criteria do we distinguish levels of parliamentary institutionalization? There have been a number of attempts in the literature on comparative politics and, more specifically, comparative legislative studies, to understand this process. Some of them offer useful insights (and a number of testable hypotheses) for understanding what happened in Russia.[17] Synthesizing this literature can be tricky since the same terms may hold somewhat different meanings depending on who is using them. However, three variables do appear to be critical in most analyses. Levels of institutionalization will vary positively with: (1) the degree of autonomy from other institutions; (2) the complexity of internal organization (including procedures); and (3) institutional continuity and routinization of norms. These variables need to be operationalized if they are to be helpful in providing direction to our understanding of the development of Russian institutions.

1. Degree of Autonomy. By degree of autonomy, we mean that definable boundaries exist between legislative bodies and other institutions in the political system external to them. In particular, we need to examine the relations of the legislature with executive, bureaucratic, and administrative structures, and with political parties and other organizations, both public and private, that are not part of the government. The greater the degree of autonomy (or, the lower the level of subordination), the higher the level of institutionalization.

2. Complexity of Internal Organization. Here we refer to the degree to which the internal functions of the legislature are differentiated and performed by identifiable subunits. Indicators of complexity include the number of committees, the size of the staff, the number of rules and procedures, the scope of the work, and difficulty of the issues with which members deal. The more complex, the more institutionalized.

3. Continuity of Norms. This refers to the acquisition by members over time of mutual expectations of legislative behavior, the development of a consensus about how to conduct legislative activity. Polsby refers to the importance of "impersonal codes" replacing personalistic bases for conducting internal business and using universalistic rather than particularistic norms for internal organization. Factors contributing to this routinization of conduct would include transfer of leadership across more than one generation, the repetition of procedures, the establishment and acceptance of precedent, and the accumulation of experience. The greater the continuity of norms, the greater the degree of institutionalization.

A more recent theoretical framework broadly referred to as "new institutionalism" offers an alternative approach to understanding the process of institutionalization. At its most basic, this approach argues that institutions develop the way they do in response to the rational choices of self-interested actors. At the same time, however, institutions also shape the strategic decisions that players adopt in pursuit of their goals. In this sense, institutions can be considered either independent or dependent variables: strategic political choices determine how political institutions evolve; how political institutions evolve constrains and molds the choices adopted.[18] "New" institutionalism is distinguished from the "old" in that the focus on institutions by an earlier generation of political scientists was largely atheoretical and descriptive, concerned with the formal-legal attributes of governmental structures. The behavioral "revolution" in political science of the postwar period went beyond formal institutional explanations of political outcomes, focusing instead on the role of individuals and groups in the political process. Behavioralism sought to develop theories of politics at ever higher levels of generalization.[19] The new institutionalism shares the concern of behavioralists with theory building, and shares their methodological and substantive focus on the behavior of individuals and groups. However, by arguing that political attitudes and behavior can only be understood in the context of institutional constraints, it returns institutions to the center of analytical concern. In this respect, it represents something of a "synthesis" of traditional institutional analysis with the behavioral approach.[20]

Just what are institutions? Most proponents of the new approach to studying institutions would probably agree with the definition offered by Douglass North: "Institutions are the rules of the game in a society or, more formally, are the humanly devised constraints that shape human interaction."[21] From a rational choice perspective, institutions are rules devised by players to get around the dilemma of collective action. But what, then, are rules? According to Elinor Ostrom, they are "linguistic entities that refer to prescriptions commonly known and used by a set of participants to order repetitive relationships. Prescriptions refer to which actions . . . are *required, prohibited,* or *permitted.*"[22] How does the new institutionalism deal with the process of institutionalization? Part of the answer lies in the notion of "path dependency." In earlier stages of development, societies adopt "initial rules," which are relatively indeterminate. Over time, rules that work well survive; those that do not are revised or dropped. Rules also become more specific; changes in them become increasingly incremental. As role expectations resulting from these rules become routinized, players become accustomed to "playing by the rules" (with sanctions for those who do not), thereby engendering greater institutional stability. The main point is that choices about rules made early on have consequences (sometimes unintended) for how decisions are made later. In North's words, "Path dependence means that history matters."[23]

The application of theories of new institutionalism to the substantive concerns of political scientists and to understanding empirical politics is still in the early stages.[24] In particular, the use of new institutionalism in understanding legislatures has been hampered by problems inherent in the ambiguity of majoritarian rule.[25] Those attempts that have been forthcoming have been largely confined to analyses of the U.S. Congress. There have, however, been two notable book-length attempts to apply the theoretical insights of neo-institutional analysis to the study of Russia. In his book *Red Sunset*, Philip Roeder explains the collapse of the Soviet system in 1991 in terms of institutional failure. Roeder's analysis begins with the rules-in-use established by what he calls the "constitution of Bolshevism." These rules created an institutional arrangement of "reciprocal accountability" between party leadership and party bureaucrats that ultimately made them unaccountable to any outsiders. Because of their vested interest in preserving the status quo, they were incapable of innovation and reform. The resulting stagnation, especially in the economy, destroyed the system. Roeder's discussion of "institutionalization" is particularly insightful. Starting with the indeterminacy of the rules in the early Soviet polity, he shows how these rules became more cohesive and consistent over time, generating a growing consensus among leaders about how the game was to be played. Roeder's analysis leads to the paradoxical conclusion that although "institutionalization promotes the stability of a constitutional structure," if that constitution is authoritarian, it may well prove fatal.[26]

The other major attempt to apply institutional analysis to understanding postcommunist political systems is a comparative study of parliaments in Russia and Eastern Europe edited by Thomas Remington. In the introductory chapter, Remington frames the discussion to follow by asking: "Under what conditions do political actors accept the rules of parliamentary competition as a given, and seek to win control for their party of coalition over parliament, and when do they attempt to change the rules and alter the system?"[27] For Remington, the terms institution-alization and consolidation are synonymous and refer essentially to ac-ceptance of the rules by the relevant actors: "The consolidation of a newly democratic parliament is the consequence of the investment of the players' resources in winning majorities under existing rules rather than in gaining enough power to overturn the rules themselves."[28] Rem-ington then focuses his attention on two sets of institutional arrange-ments he regards as central to postcommunist transitions: elections and executive-legislative relations. If Roeder's analysis directs our attention to the importance of "first rules" in the pathology of authoritarian sys-tems, then Remington's alerts us to the importance of rule acceptance in the process of democratic consolidation.

Explaining Parliamentary Democratization

This last point brings us back to the second issue that needs to be operationalized: How do we know if legislatures are becoming more democratic? Since an extended discussion of what constitutes demo-cratic legislatures appeared earlier, we need only briefly review and summarize the major directions for inquiry here. At the heart of all definitions of democracy is the expectation that the authority to make decisions for society is derived from the governed. In representative democracy, it means that those chosen to make decisions should, at some level, reflect the public will in doing so, and can be held account-able if they do not. Legislatures are central to democracy to the extent that they fulfill this representative role either directly, by making laws (as in strong legislatures), or indirectly, by communicating constituent concerns (as in weak ones). According to Dahl (see note 2), political systems are more or less democratic (polyarchic) based on the open-ness of public contestation and the degree of inclusiveness.

The literature on comparative legislatures reviewed earlier directs our attention to a number of variables that need to be addressed if we are to determine whether the Russian legislatures were becoming more democratic in the period 1990–93. Similar questions would seem ap-propriate to assessing the parliaments of the second Russian republic. Any analysis of whether legislative institutions are becoming more democratic must take into account at least three factors: (1) Who are the representatives? Specifically, what is the membership and composition of the legislature and how were its members chosen? (2) What are the linkages among the representatives and those they represent? Specifically, what are the mechanisms by which the people's preferences are communicated to those who represent them? (3) What is the role of the elected representatives in making policy? Specifically, to what degree are they involved in setting agendas, in drafting and debating legislation, and in overseeing implementation?

The theoretical framework of new institutionalism leads us to a somewhat different research agenda. From this perspective, democratic development cannot be described only in terms of the emergence of certain institutional arrangements such as elections, legislatures, and parties. Nor is it the product of crossing certain economic and social developmental thresholds. Rather, it involves the acceptance by all players of a set of rules that ensure that the outcome of conflicts among them are contingent. According to two leading proponents of this school of thought, "Political democracy depends not only on economic and social conditions, but also on the design of political institutions."[29] Democracy is not about substantive choices, but about the rules and procedures for making those choices. In democratic games, there are no permanent winners and losers. Losers who abide by the rules are guaranteed by those rules of the continued opportunity to play; winners recognize that their victories are conditional. How do countries become democratic? In the words of Adam Przeworski, "Democratization is a process of subjecting all interests to competition, of institutionalizing uncertainty. It is thus the very devolution of power over outcomes that constitutes the decisive step towards democracy."[30] What are the implications of this approach for understanding the pathology of democratic consolidation in Russia from 1990 to 1993? First, neo-institutionalism directs our attention to the nature of the political conflict between the contending players and then it asks why the existing institutional framework was unable to accommodate it. In short, why were the relevant elites unwilling to accept uncertain outcomes?

Russia's Legislatures, 1990–1993: Setting the Stage

As indicated in the preface, this book, and the conference from which it developed, came about as the result of a conscious effort to promote a dialogue between political scientists who are Russian area specialists, and those who know little about Russia but who bring to bear comparative perspectives from research in other fields, especially legislative behavior. It was hoped that such a dialogue would facilitate the integration of the study of Russia into the contemporary study of comparative politics. For area specialists, the end of communist rule provided the opportunity to employ approaches and methods widely used elsewhere in comparative political analysis. Russia need no longer be considered a "unique case." Some of the results of such research are presented in the chapters that follow. Conversely, comparativists can use the Russian case to verify or modify existing theory. For this to happen, however, some basic level of knowledge about the evolution of Russian political institutions in the period under consideration is needed. This section is written with those who are not area specialists in mind. It is intended to provide a very general overview of the major changes in Russian political institutions at the national and local level from 1990 to 1993.

The Old Soviet System[31]

If constitutions establish the formal rules by which the political game is played, at least at a macro level of analysis, then the rules in place when the first Russian republic ended in December 1993 were those inherited from the Soviet period. The constitution of Russia, although much amended, had been adopted in 1978 when it was common practice for constitutions in all the constituent republics of the USSR to replicate that of the Soviet Union itself. On paper, this constitution provided for a strong parliamentary system. At the national level, parliament was called the Supreme Soviet and was identified as "the highest institution of state power in the USSR" (article 108). Deputies to this parliament were elected to five-year terms on the basis of universal suffrage. The government, called the Council of Ministers and headed by the functional equivalent of a prime minister, was elected by (and in theory accountable to) the parliamentary body.

Despite the considerable formal powers accorded the Supreme Soviet, it was not a decision-making body. Consisting of 1,500 representatives, it met twice a year for a few days and unanimously ratified whatever legislation was placed before it. Real power to make decisions rested with the leadership of the Communist Party of the Soviet Union (CPSU), who oversaw the implementation of its policies by an elaborate state bureaucracy. The CPSU's monopoly of decision-making power was ensured not only because of its claim to be the only legitimate "directing force of Soviet society" (article 6), but because no one could be nominated to the legislature without at least the tacit approval of the party organization. Nomination was tantamount to election since there was no electoral competition.

This system of "soviet" rule extended from the national level down to the smallest village. All soviets below the national and republic level were called "local" soviets. Their structure and functional relationships paralleled those at the national level. Deputies to village, city, and provincial soviets were elected from single-member districts for two and half year terms. From among their members, they chose an executive committee, headed by a chair, whose job it was to administer local affairs. The executive, however, was subject to the principle of "dual subordination." Although formally accountable to the legislative council that elected it, members of the executive branch were also responsible for implementing policies from the central ministries. Since locally elected deputies also unanimously approved whatever legislation was put before them by their executive committee, and since nominations to the executive committee required the approval of the corresponding party secretary, real accountability lay elsewhere. In reality, the soviets were controlled by their executive committees, while those on the executive committees from bottom to top were answerable to the corresponding party secretary to whom they owed their positions. In this way an unbreakable "circular system of power" was created with ultimate power located in the hands of the CPSU general secretary.

The very stability of the old system made it resistant to change. After all, those with a vested interest in preserving the status quo have the least incentive for changing it. The result was economic stagnation. It was in order to undermine the resistance of the party–state bureaucracy to economic reform that Gorbachev proposed his momentous reforms of the Soviet political system to the nineteenth conference of the CPSU in June 1988. With respect to reshaping Soviet governmental institutions, three reforms held particular importance: competitive elections, executive branch accountability, and a rule of law based on an independent judiciary. In addition, Gorbachev insisted that the CPSU get out of the business of effectively running the government and limit itself to the partisan political work for which it was in theory intended. These reforms were implemented on the national level in

1989 and below it in 1990. How they affected national politics in the old Soviet Union is beyond the scope of this book.[32] What is of interest here is what they meant for the largest of the Soviet Union's republics—Russia.

1990: Origins

After the necessary constitutional amendments were introduced in the Russian Supreme Soviet in 1989, competitive elections were held in March 1990 for seats in a new parliamentary institution called the Russian Congress of People's Deputies (CPD). Consisting of 1,068 members elected to five-year terms, the CPD was initially conceived primarily as a college of electors who would chose from its numbers a permanently functioning parliament—still called the Supreme Soviet—consisting of two chambers, a Council of the Republic and a Council of Nationalities, each composed of 126 members. The CPD also elected a chair of that body. The chair would then nominate someone to head the government (the Council of Ministers), subject to approval by the Supreme Soviet. The popularly elected CPD, however, had additional powers, including the right to amend the constitution, to overturn decisions by the Supreme Soviet, and to appoint the chair and members of a new Constitutional Court, powers that would later prove troublesome for Boris Yeltsin. This two-tiered system was used only at the national level. Below it, competitive elections to the local soviets were held simultaneously. Those elected then chose, on the basis of competitive elections and secret ballots, the members of the local executive committee. The main point to be made here is that the dominant institution of the Russian political system set up in 1990 was the legislature as before. But the difference between it and the old Soviet system was that those elected owed their positions to their constituents and not to the party.

The "founding election" of March 1990 determined the balance of institutional power in Russia until Yeltsin abolished all legislative bodies in 1993. Of the 1,068 seats in the CPD, 900 were chosen from single-member districts and the remaining 168 from national territorial districts. Those elected had to receive more than 50 percent of the votes cast with more than 50 percent of the eligible electorate participating. There were 6,705 candidates nominated, an average of more than 6 per district; in only 33 cases was there no opposition. The large number of candidates and the absence of any formal party affiliation to distinguish them significantly weakened the cohesiveness of the legislative institutions that emerged. The fact that 86 percent of those running were members of the CPSU was not indicative of their political orientation since the party was so fragmented between reformers and conservatives by that time. What was significant was whether those running were associated with the old party organization or not. Opposition to these members of the party apparatus and to their nomenklatura allies in the state bureaucracy and in enterprises was organized by a political movement called Democratic Russia.

The results of the election in terms of the political composition of the new parliamentary bodies was mixed. In the Russian CPD, it was divided fairly evenly between deputies associated with the "conservative" wing of the CPSU and those supported by the democratic movement, with each holding about 40 percent of the seats and the balance held by independents.[33] The democratic movement had just enough cohesion, however, to obtain the votes needed to narrowly elect Boris Yeltsin as chairman of the Supreme Soviet at the first session of the Russian Congress of People's Deputies held in May–June 1990. At the local level, democratic movement candidates scored dramatic wins in the city soviets of Moscow and Leningrad (now St. Petersburg), but fared much less well elsewhere. Broadly speaking, they obtained sizable minorities or even a rare majority in provincial cities, but in the provincial legislatures, which were comprised of rural as well as urban constituencies, they found themselves badly outnumbered by candidates backed by the regional Communist Party organization. The results of this "founding" election are crucial, for they set in motion the dynamics of conflict between Yeltsin and parliament that ended in the destruction of the first Russian republic. The "conservative" political composition of Russia's new legislatures all but ensured that they would become the bastion of institutional opposition to Yeltsin's radical economic reforms.

1991: Transformation

The tension between Yeltsin and parliament became clear early on. Despite his election as chairman of the Supreme Soviet, Yeltsin was not able to gain support among the deputies for his legislative program.[34] Only on the issue of declaring Russian "sovereignty" within the Soviet Federation in June 1990 did he generate a consensus. Riding a conservative backlash that prevailed in Soviet politics in the fall of 1990, Yeltsin's opposition in parliament planned his removal, demanding that an extraordinary session of the CPD be held in spring 1991. Before that could take place, however, Gorbachev scheduled a referendum in the USSR on preserving the Union. Using his power within parliament's agenda-setting "Presidium" (which, as chairman of the Supreme Soviet, he dominated), Yeltsin was able to get an additional item added to the referendum in the Russian republic: would voters support the concept of a popularly elected president for Russia? The response was overwhelmingly favorable. Confronted by the popular mandate, the third Congress amended the Russian constitution accordingly. In June 1991, Yeltsin became the first elected president of Russia with a five-year term. He and his running mate, Aleksandr Rutskoi, won 57 percent of the vote, soundly defeating his nearest rival, Nikolai Ryzhkov (Gorbachev's former prime minister), who got 17 percent.

The creation of the office of president with Yeltsin as its incumbent transformed Russian politics. From an institutional point of view, what it did was to graft a strong presidential system of government onto an already strong parliamentary one. In retrospect, it was a prescription for disaster. Because both were directly elected to fixed terms in office, neither could remove the other from power. Under the system that existed until September 1993, the president could veto legislation, but parliament could override with 50 percent majority of the full membership of each chamber. The parliament had the right to initiate referenda, but the president did not. While the president had the right to appoint the head of the government, he could do so only with the approval of parliament. Aside from his broad authority in foreign affairs and his control over internal security, the Russian president had the power to issue decrees with the force of law. Such laws could not, however, contradict the constitution or laws adopted by parliament. Yeltsin's willingness to use this power to rule despite parliamentary objections became an important source of friction between the two branches. The result was an institutional standoff.

The potential for gridlock that these institutional arrangements created became apparent at the fifth CPD held in July 1991. Yeltsin wanted an old ally, Ruslan Khasbulatov, to succeed him as chairman of the Supreme Soviet, but was unable to secure enough votes and the

Congress adjourned. By the time it reconvened, the political landscape of Russia had been forever altered by the failed coup of August 19, 1991. The defeat of the coup attempt enormously enhanced Yeltsin's popularity and power and he pressed his advantage when the fifth Congress met again in November. As the old Soviet Union disintegrated and Russia asserted her independence, Russian deputies were willing to concede significant new powers to Yeltsin. In order to implement his economic program of "shock therapy" they gave him the right to rule by decree for one year. He banned the Communist Party in Russia and nationalized its property. Khasbulatov was elected chairman of the Supreme Soviet as Yeltsin had wished.

Of particular importance in the evolution of the struggle between the legislative and executive branches in 1992–93 was the power the CPD gave Yeltsin to reshape the institutions of local government. Realizing that most of the local legislative councils (soviets) were dominated by his opponents, Yeltsin sought to outflank them by strengthening the local executive branch and by subordinating it in order to ensure that his programs were implemented locally. He did this in two ways. First, he appointed "presidential representatives" in almost all the Russian provinces. Though they lack any popular mandate, they were be the president's "eyes and ears" and to ensure that local legislation complied with federal decrees. Second, he was able to persuade Congress to postpone scheduled elections of local executives at the provincial level (governors) and the municipal level (mayors) for one year. In the meantime, he appropriated to himself the right to appoint them, a power he used to pack the position with political allies. As a consequence of these actions, confrontation between the executive and legislative branches at the national level was projected to the local level as well.

1992: Confrontation

The fifth Congress of People's Deputies was the last one from which Yeltsin was able to obtain significant concessions. By the time that the sixth CPD opened in April 1992, Russia was reeling from the effects of "acting" prime minister Egor Gaidar's efforts to create a market economy in Russia by borrowing lessons from the Polish experiment with "shock therapy." The first step in this program was to eliminate price controls for most consumer goods. Inflation jumped 300 percent in first three weeks and would grow more than 2,500 percent by the year's end. In theory, inflation would moderate as state enterprises were privatized, became more productive, and market forces took over. In the meantime, however, the pound of meat that used to cost $1.00 now cost $10.00, and people were selling their old clothes in the street. Aside from the pain felt by average Russians, the program of financial austerity meant ending subsidies to large state-run enterprises and collective farms. Since many of the managers of these enterprises had close ties with the old party elites who held seats in parliament, that body became the natural center of resistance to the government's reforms. The sixth CPD under Khasbulatov's leadership passed a number of measures aimed at curbing the effects of the Gaidar plan, causing the prime minister to resign in protest, a resignation that was later withdrawn as part of a compromise between the president and the speaker. What the sixth Congress made clear was that Yeltsin could no longer command a majority in parliament; he and Khasbulatov were on a collision course.[35]

The collision took place in December 1992 at the seventh Congress of People's Deputies. Yeltsin's right to rule by decree for one year had expired and Khasbulatov wanted Gaidar replaced. For his part, Yeltsin wanted a popular referendum on the principles of a new constitution, which would create a stronger presidency and thus resolve his struggles with parliament in his favor. In a compromise brokered by Valery Zorkin, chairman of the Constitutional Court, the referendum Yeltsin wanted was to be held in April 1993.[36] The Supreme Soviet, however, got to approve the questions. Unable to obtain support for Gaidar as prime minister, Yeltsin accepted his resignation. Viktor Chernomyrdin, the former minister of the state gas industry and hence acceptable to the managers of state enterprises, was appointed to replace Gaidar. At the local level, although the one-year moratorium on the election of local executives had also expired, the decision on when and whether to hold them was postponed until the next year.

1993: Abolition

Predictably, perhaps, the Supreme Soviet and the president's staff were unable to agree on the wording of a referendum, and the compromise worked out by Zorkin came unglued. At the eighth CPD in March 1993, parliament wanted the referendum canceled. Yeltsin reacted by insisting on holding it and claimed "special powers" to do so by decree. This quickly produced an extraordinary ninth session of the CPD, which convened to consider impeaching the president. After the motion to impeach was narrowly defeated, Yeltsin softened his position on his right to call a referendum and submitted new questions for Congress to consider. These were eventually approved, but not before the Congress had revised them to suit their taste, requiring in the process that approval would need more than 50 percent of *all* eligible voters. Given the popular mood at the time it was a high threshold for Yeltsin to reach. However, the Constitutional Court ruled that since only the last two questions affected the constitution, the absolute majority rule would only apply to them. The questions were: (1) Do you have confidence in President Yeltsin? (2) Do you approve of the present reform program? (3) Do you want early parliamentary elections? (4) Do you want early presidential elections?

The results of the April 23, 1993, referendum were not legally binding on anyone, but nevertheless held considerable significance politically. Although the first two questions were little more than opinion polls since they required no mandatory action, the approval rating for Yeltsin was about two-thirds, while his reform program received the surprising support of more than 50 percent of those voting. A similar plurality favored early elections for parliament, but not for president. However, since neither of these last two votes exceeded the threshold, they required no action. The immediate consequence of the vote was that both sides agreed to a constitutional convention, which was convened in June 1993 and which spent the summer debating competing drafts.

The longer-term effect of the referendum, however, was to strengthen Yeltsin's conviction that he enjoyed a popular mandate and that the Russian people would back him in a confrontation with parliament. In August, he demanded that the Supreme Soviet hold early parliamentary elections in accordance with the popular vote in the referendum. Parliament refused unless such elections were held simultaneously with one for president. Shortly thereafter, a frustrated Yeltsin suspended his estranged vice president, Aleksandr Rutskoi, from office over a budget crisis. When Khasbulatov declared this act unconstitutional and again tried to have the president impeached, Yeltsin abolished parliament on September 12, 1993, promising to hold elections to a new parliamentary body called the Federal Assembly on December 12. When the speaker and his supporters refused to leave the building where parliament was located, Yeltsin bombed it on October 3. On October 9, he ordered the dissolution of the local soviets as well.[37] In this way the first Russian republic came to an end and the second one began.

Notes

1. The concept of democratic consolidation used here draws heavily on Juan J. Linz, "Transitions to Democracy," *Washington Quarterly* (Summer 1990), esp. pp. 157–160. According to his "minimilist conception," a consolidated democratic regime is one in which "no political institution or group has a claim to veto the action of democratically elected decision makers" (p. 158). In this sense, Yeltsin's abolition of parliament in 1993 represented the failure of consolidation.

2. The term democracy as used in this chapter relies heavily on the concept of polyarchy developed by Robert A. Dahl in his book, *Polyarchy: Participation and Opposition* (New Haven, CT: Yale University Press, 1971). In Dahl's view, the "key" characteristic of democracy is "the continuing responsiveness of the government to the preferences of its citizens, considered as political equals" (p. 1). The three great "milestones" of democratic development are the right to participate through voting, the right to be represented, and the right to organize opposition. These rights, he suggests, are embodied in three main institutions: elections, legislatures, and parties. See Robert A. Dahl, ed., *Political Oppositions in Western Democracies* (New Haven, CT: Yale University Press, 1966), p. xi. Polyarchies approximate democracy in countries with substantial populations. They are political systems characterized by high levels of "inclusiveness" (referring to the proportion of citizens with the right to participate politically) and "public contestation" (the extent to which political opposition is permitted).

3. This description of what legislatures do relies heavily on Michael L. Mezey, *Comparing Legislatures* (Durham, NC: Duke University Press, 1979), pp. 7–14; and Gerhard Loewenberg and Samuel C. Patterson, *Comparing Legislatures* (Boston: Little, Brown, 1979), pp. 43–65.

4. These types very loosely correspond to the parliamentary systems found in the United States, Great Britain, and the former USSR. Michael Mezey, *Comparing Legislatures*, ch. 2. For the discussion of "transformative" and "arena" legislatures, see Nelson W. Polsby, "Legislatures," in Fred I. Greenstein and Nelson W. Polsby, eds., *Handbook of Political Science*, vol. 5 (Reading, MA: Addison-Wesley, 1975), p. 277. The United States may be an exceptional case in combining a strong legislature with a presidential democracy, as pointed out by Juan J. Linz in "The Virtues of Parliamentarism," *Journal of Democracy*, 1, no. 4 (Fall 1990) p. 84.

5. David M. Olson and Michael L. Mezey, eds., *Legislatures in the Policy Process* (New York: Cambridge University Press, 1991), p. xii. See also David M. Olson, *Democratic Legislative Institutions* (Armonk, NY: M.E. Sharpe, 1994), p. 3.

6. Juan J. Linz, "Transitions to Democracy," p. 150.

7. Juan J. Linz, "The Perils of Presidentialism," *Journal of Democracy*, vol. 1, no. 1 (Winter 1990), p. 55.

8. On this point, see Loewenberg and Patterson, *Comparing Legislatures*, pp. 282–283. The *locus classicus* about public ignorance of congressional activity is found in Warren E. Miller and Donald E. Stokes, "Constituency Influence in Congress," *American Political Science Review*, vol. 57 (1963), pp. 45–56. The lack of knowledge about politics among the American electorate is well established in the literature. On its implications for democratic theory, see W. Russell Neuman, *The Paradox of Mass Politics* (Cambridge, MA: Harvard University Press, 1986).

9. Robert D. Putnam, *Making Democracy Work* (Princeton, NJ: Princeton University Press, 1993), esp. p. 63. For Putnam's criteria for measuring the effectiveness of political institutions, see his chapter 3, "Measuring Institutional Performance."

10. Samuel P. Huntington, *Political Order in Changing Societies* (New Haven, CT: Yale University Press, 1968), pp. 78–92.

11. The problem of simultaneity may be one of the distinguishing features of communist transitions. For further discussion of this, see Sarah Meiklejohn Terry, "Thinking about Post-communist Transitions: How Different Are They?" *Slavic Review*, vol. 52, no. 2 (Summer 1993), pp. 333–337; and Philippe C. Schmitter and Terry Lynn Karl, "The Conceptual Travels of Transitologists and Consolidologists," *Slavic Review*, vol. 53, no. 1 (Spring 1994), pp. 173–185.

12. Olson, *Democratic Legislative Institutions*, p. 130. Even Juan Linz concedes that "not *any* parliamentary system is ipso facto more likely to ensure democratic stability than *any* presidential system." Juan J. Linz, "The Virtues of Parliamentarism," p. 84.

13. Samuel P. Huntington, *The Third Wave: Democratization in the Twentieth Century* (Norman: University of Oklahoma Press, 1991), p. 11.

14. Larry Diamond, "Toward Democratic Consolidation," *Journal of Democracy*, vol. 5, no. 3 (July, 1994), p. 15 (Diamond's emphasis).

15. Nelson W. Polsby, "The Institutionalization of the U.S. House of Representatives," *American Political Science Review*, vol. 62 (1968), pp. 144–168.

16. Loewenberg and Patterson, *Comparing Legislatures*, p. 21.

17. The analysis offered here is taken from more traditional approaches to the study of institutions in modern political science. The insights offered by the theories of "new institutionalism" will be considered separately. In addition to the works already cited by Polsby (1968), Huntington (1968), and Loewenberg and Patterson, the theme of institutionalization has been addressed in Allan Kornberg, ed., *Legislatures in Comparative Perspective* (New York: David McKay, 1973). Particularly noteworthy in that book are the articles by Richard Sisson, "Comparative Legislative Institutionalization: A Theoretical Explanation," and Peter Gerlich, "The Institutionalization of European Parliaments." Critiques of the traditional approach on the grounds that it is more descriptive than explanatory can be found in John R. Hibbing, "Legislative Institutionalization with Illustrations from the British House of Commons," *American Journal of Political Science*, vol. 32 (1988), pp. 681–712; and Joseph Cooper and David W. Brady, "Institutional Context and Leadership Style: The House from Cannon to Rayburn," *American Political Science Review*, vol. 75 (1981), pp. 411–425.

18. These dual concerns of institutional analysis are expressed clearly in Terry M. Moe, "Political Institutions: The Neglected Side of the Story," *Journal of Law, Economics, and Organization*, vol. 6 (1990), p. 213. The symmetrical relationship between the variables is also noted in Putnam, *Making Democracy Work*, p. 8.

19. For one attempt at "grand" theory in this tradition, see David Easton, *A Framework for Political Analysis* (Englewood Cliffs, NJ: Prentice-Hall, 1965).

20. The epistemological roots of the new institutionalism are to be found in theories of political economy. The paradigm of the new institutionalism is rational choice, with its assumption that human behavior is motivated by the maximization of self-interest and is, therefore, endogenous. It makes extensive use of game theory and formal modeling. A closely related approach called historical institutionalism argues that human choices are formed not only by the calculated self-interest of each individual, but by exogenous forces as well, including such things as class position and historical development. For reviews of the intellectual history of new institutionalism, see Peter C. Ordeshook, "The Emerging Discipline of Political Economy," in James E. Alt and Kenneth A. Shepsle, eds., *Perspectives on Positive Political Economy* (New York: Cambridge University Press, 1990); Kathleen Thelen and Sven Steinmo, "Historical Institutionalism in Comparative Politics," in Sven Steinmo, Kathleen Thelen, and Frank Longstreth, eds., *Structuring Politics* (New York: Cambridge University Press, 1992).

21. Douglass C. North, *Institutions, Institutional Change and Economic Performance* (New York: Cambridge University Press, 1990), p. 3. In most conceptualizations, rules may be formal or informal. Both are sometimes referred to as "rules-in-use."

22. Elinor Ostrom, "An Agenda for the Study of Institutions," *Public Choice*, vol. 48 (1986), p. 5 (Ostrom's emphasis).

23. Douglass C. North, *Institutions, Institutional Change and Economic Performance*, p. 100. This discussion of path dependency draws heavily on chapters 11 and 12 of his book. For a critique of the evolutionary view of institutional development and a discussion of "unintended consequences," see Jack Knight, *Institutions and Social Conflict* (New York: Cambridge University Press, 1992), ch. 5. In his view, "the emergence of the rules can best be explained by referring to systematic distributions of bargaining power in a society" (p. 170). But since these rules are asymmetrical, reflecting power distributions at the time, they continue to be reflected in further institutional development.

24. Proponents of this approach are quick to acknowledge the resistance of more "mainstream" political science to theories of political economy, especially those that involve formal modeling. See Peter C. Ordeshook, "The Emerging Discipline of Political Economy," pp. 12–20. However, they also tend to see their approach as the way to "finally enable political scientists to get down to the business of building a cumulative discipline." Elinor Ostrom, "New Horizons of Institutional Analysis," *American Political Science Review*, vol. 89 (1995), p. 177.

25. According to Shepsle, "The theory of social choice has not been much informed by, nor systematically applied to, an understanding of legislatures." Kenneth A. Shepsle, "The Positive Theory of Legislative Institutions," *Public Choice*, vol. 50 (1986) p. 136. Terry Moe, on the other hand, feels too much attention of positive political theory has been devoted to legislatures and not

enough to bureaucracies. See Moe, "Political Institutions: The Neglected Side of the Story."

26. Philip G. Roeder, *The Red Sunset: The Failure of Soviet Politics* (Princeton, NJ: Princeton University Press, 1993), pp. 23–37.

27. Thomas F. Remington, ed., *Parliaments in Transition* (Boulder, CO: Westview Press, 1994), p. 10.

28. Ibid., p. 12.

29. James G. March and Johan P. Olsen, *Rediscovering Institutions: The Organizational Basis of Politics* (New York: Free Press, 1989) p. 17.

30. Adam Przeworski, "Some Problems in the Study of the Transition to Democracy," in Guillermo O'Donnell, Philippe C. Schmitter, and Laurence Whitehead, eds., *Transitions from Authoritarian Rule: Tentative Conclusions and Uncertain Democracies* (Baltimore, MD: Johns Hopkins University Press, 1986), p. 58.

31. The word "soviet" translated from Russian means advice or council. The first organizations called soviets were worker councils established in industrial factories at the time of the 1905 revolution. When the Bolsheviks took power in 1917 they did so in the name of the soviets, which by that time constituted their principal base of support. Although the word itself is commonly used to refer to the state system known as the Soviet Union, it also is the term that citizens of that country used when talking about their elected legislative institutions. Nationally and in the republics these parliaments were called "supreme soviets" while locally they were simply known as soviets. In this latter sense the term denoted a system of political institutions peculiar to Leninist communism.

32. The consequences of these changes in the "rule-in-use" were unforeseen (and almost certainly unintended). By breaking the circular system of power they deprived the CPSU of its control over the system, leading to fundamental realignment of power between the major political institutions and ultimately to the collapse of the Soviet Union. Detailed accounts of this collapse can be found in Philip G. Roeder, *The Red Sunset*, and Brendan Kiernan, *The End of Soviet Politics* (Boulder, CO: Westview Press, 1993).

33. For an excellent analysis of the political composition of the Russian parliament in this period, see Thomas F. Remington, Steven S. Smith, D. Roderick Kiewit, and Moshe Haspel, "Transitional Institutions and Parliamentary Alignments in Russia, 1990–1993," in Thomas F. Remington, ed., *Parliaments in Transition*. The term "conservative" in reference to Russian legislators is used here in the narrow sense of resisting changes introduced by the Yeltsin administration.

34. Regina A. Smyth, "Ideological vs. Regional Cleavages: Do the Radicals Control the RSFSR Parliament?" *Journal of Soviet Nationalities*, vol. 1, no. 3 (Fall 1990), pp. 112–157.

35. One of the main reasons for the diminution of Yeltsin's ability to gain a majority in parliament is the fact that many of the deputies associated with the democratic movement left parliament to join the government. This, and the fact the Yeltsin did not actively seek to mobilize his support there, left control of parliament in Khasbulatov's hands if only by default. Thomas Remington's chapter in this book examines how this happened.

36. As opposed to the Russian Supreme Court, the Constitutional Court was an institution without precedence in Soviet history. As the name suggests, it had

the right to review legislation to determine its conformity with the constitution. The Court began functioning in January 1992, deciding its first case unfavorably to the president, who nevertheless complied with the decision. The Court might have evolved into an institution capable of preserving the constitutional balance between the executive and legislative branches. Unfortunately, as the relations between the two branches became increasingly polarized, the Court under Zorkin was repeatedly asked to intervene, mostly by parliament. As a result it became increasingly politicized and its functions were suspended by Yeltsin when he abolished parliament. The Court resumed its functions in the second Russian republic only on March 16, 1995.

37. With respect to local legislatures, parliament decided not to insist at the seventh CPD in December 1992 on elections for chief executives, choosing to allow the local soviets in each region to do so if they wished. In a handful of cases, such elections were held and resulted in victories for the candidates from the old party–state elite. What these elections suggest is that Yeltsin was smart to avoid them and that parliament may have missed a chance to bolster its position by failing to encourage the election of new executives everywhere in the provinces. For more on the dissolution of the local soviets, see Elizabeth Teague, "Yeltsin Disbands the Soviets" *RFE/RL Research Reports*, vol. 2, no. 43 (29 October 1993). On gubernatorial elections, see Elizabeth Teague, "North-South Divide: Yeltsin and Russia's Provincial Leaders," *RFE/RL Research Reports*, vol. 2, no. 47 (26 November 1993).

I

Legislative Development at the National Level

2

Parliament and the Political Crisis in Russia, 1991–1993

Lilia Shevtsova

Political developments in Russia before Yeltsin dissolved parliament in September 1993 have become more obscure and difficult to understand with the passage of time. Moreover, with the support of Russian ruling circles, myths concerning the nature of the political process during this period have begun to spread, complicating even more a much-needed analysis of what happened. Without a clear understanding of the character of the power structure and of the activity of different political bodies during this, the first period of postcommunist development in Russia, it is harder to discern even the outlines of a new stage in the dramatic process of state-building in this country. The purpose of this chapter is to contribute to such an understanding by offering answers to the following questions: What was the nature of the political system in Russia during the First Republic of 1991–93? What were the roots of the political crisis during this period? And what was the role of parliament in this crisis?

The Political System of the First Russian Republic: Steps Toward Democratization

The political system of postcommunist Russia was formed during the last years of Gorbachev's rule. The all-Russian elections in 1990 produced a new Russian parliament while regional elections formed new local soviets. A year later, the office of President of Russia was created along with the Constitutional Court. In practice, the newly formed Russian political elite followed Gorbachev's example by combining the old Soviet system with a strong executive branch. This approach was not without merit. Gorbachev had succeeded in neutralizing communist power this way. Moreover, by preserving the soviets, he avoided destabilizing effects that could otherwise have been much more worse. Nevertheless, he failed to create an effective new power structure. The reasons for this and for the collapse of the Soviet Union were multiple and complicated, but certainly the grafting of a presidency onto a two-tiered parliament (itself a very clumsy structure) led to the emergence of a political system lacking a clearly defined, real separation of powers. However, it would be misleading to conclude that the failure of Gorbachev's regime was due only to an incompatibility of the soviets and the presidency, as some Russian analysts later assumed.

It is worth remembering that during 1990–91 there really were no serious conflicts between the Russian executive authority and the legislature. A peaceful relationship between the two branches of power continued for some time, despite the lack of well-defined spheres of responsibility. Indeed, the office of President of Russia was created by the Russian parliament in response to Yeltsin's initiative. The basis of their consensus lay mainly with the mutual desire of representatives of both branches to weaken Gorbachev's control and later to get rid of this control entirely. With Yeltsin's support, the Russian parliament was the first to begin the march to sovereignty, adopting the Declaration on State Sovereignty on June 12, 1990. Only after the Russian parliament's initiative did the Ukrainian, Belorussian, and other republics follow suit. The highest Russian legislative body—the Congress of People's Deputies—twice (in April 1991 and in October 1991) expanded Yeltsin's powers giving him the right to rule by decree until the end of 1992. Neither the leaders of parliament nor those of Yeltsin's group ever hinted that the two powers (the Russian legislature and the presidency) were incompatible. Their unanimity in some spheres, mainly in the struggle with Gorbachev's center, was quite astonishing. The honeymoon ended in December 1991 only after the legislature approved the liquidation of the USSR. The common enemy that had consolidated the two different political forces disappeared, stimulating a process of polarization between former allies.

To what extent was the Russian political system in 1991–93 democratic? And which political institution had the most influence on the process of democratization? Before answering these questions, it is worth emphasizing that the power structure in Russia that began to emerge after August 1991 did so at a time when the previous Soviet state was collapsing and no definite conceptions of a new Russian statehood or of a new power structure had yet been formed. This fact helps to explain the existence of unusually sharp contradictions within the system itself, especially the overlapping spheres of responsibility of different political bodies. Specifically, the creation of the Russian political system began before the political elite had reached a consensus on the main principles of the new statehood, on a model of a Russian Federation, and on relations among the main political institutions. This led to a situation where all three branches of power began to compete for the right to define the best possible model of a Russian state and even to become the very center of it.

This competition became even more evident when the legislature and the presidency became the channels of articulation for the interests of different segments of the Russian political elite that began to consolidate after August 1991. From the very beginning, Yeltsin's team began to construct a "presidential vertical" of independent political institutions with the apparent aim of squeezing out all other political bodies, especially the legislative ones.[1] The political balance of power that emerged in 1991 was based mainly on the relationship among institutions, not on the relations between power and society. This sphere of political linkage was neglected by all political actors, but especially by the presidential team.

Analyzing the political situation in Russia at this time, Anders Aslund wrote: "Until December 1993, Russia's fundamental problem was that it suffered from the Soviet constitution, which declared the predemocratic parliament sovereign."[2] In reality, the old constitution was only part of the problem. In a situation where all political actors and institutions in Russia unanimously demonstrated their lack of respect for constitutional order in general, "the constitution" itself simply cannot be considered the crucial factor. Perhaps the clearest demonstration of this is the fact that for more than a year Yeltsin was given the power to rule by decree without having to pay special attention to constitutional limitations.

Criteria of Democratization in Russia

To answer the question about the degree of democratization in Russia during 1991–93, we should avoid concentrating only on the search for prerequisites to democracy. Such an approach is inadequate to explain the true nature of political developments in Russia. It is very difficult to analyze the political processes in Russia—or those in any other formerly communist country—on the basis of one model of democracy. If, for example, we define democracy as Schumpeter does—as a polity that permits the choice between elites by voting in regular and competitive elections—then the new political structure in Russia hardly can be classified as a political democracy.[3] New elites have not really yet emerged; the replacement of the old nomenklatura is far from complete. As a result, there has been no opportunity for the development of elite competition on the basis of agreed-upon rules. Still, we must acknowledge that some important progress has been made toward democratization of the Russian polity that cannot be measured only on the basis of elite contestation.

Other democratic principles must be either reconsidered or used together with other criteria when applied to Russian reality. For instance, the principle of uncertainty may be regarded as one of the most important prerequisites of democracy. According to this principle, the emergence of democracy occurs when nobody can control the outcomes of the political process, when the results are not predetermined, and when they matter within some predictable limits.[4] By these standards, the Russian polity after August 1991 can be classified as the institutionalization of uncertainty. But this is due more to the existence of a weak, unconsolidated regime and the absence of rules of the game approved by all actors than to a victory of traditional democracy.

Postcommunist transformation demonstrates that there simply cannot be one definite precondition for the emergence of a democratic polity. The best way to avoid such a narrow approach is to use a set of criteria that could help to follow the evolution of the system while taking into account its internal contradictions as well. But what set of criteria should we use? While the list can be expanded or modified, the following approach is taken here. The character of the Russian political system can best be described on the basis of several dimensions: the development of a system of representation; the possibility for competition for office; the accountability of the ruling group to the ruled; the extent of civilian control over the military; and, finally, the institution-alization of economic and social conflicts.

Representation is of principal importance for the creation of modern democracy in Russia. The elections of 1990 formed at least an elec-toral basis for representation. However, Russia did not succeed at that time in creating other channels for effective representation such as political parties, associations, or movements that could constitute the primary expressions of civil society and make democracy stable. In part, this was because there was no legal basis for their emergence and too little experience. But it was also due to the fact that at the time, no consolidated economic and social group interests had yet emerged in Russian society; the social structure was undergoing profound changes. Even later in this period a variety of competitive channels for the expression of interests—functional, territorial, collective, and indi-vidual—continued to be present only in very embryonic form.

As for competition for office, the elections of 1990 in Russia were not merely a "pretense"—no parties or candidates were excluded from participation. For the first time, elections were relatively free. Still, they did not fully satisfy the requirements of either political contesta-tion or popular consultation.[5] These elections took place when no tra-ditions of electoral politics had been established. Old communist elites succeeded in retaining strong positions in the parliament, especially in the provinces. Nevertheless, more important than "who" got power is the fact that old elite groups were forced to play according to demo-cratic rules—to compete in free elections.

The principle of accountability of the rulers before the ruled never existed in Soviet political history. But for the first time Russian leaders went through a public evaluation of their records in the referendum of April 1993 in order to determine the attitude of society toward the main political actors. The mass media became an open and effective channel allowing criticism of all political leaders and government bod-ies. However, while these developments were important steps on the road to democratization, mechanisms of permanent institutional con-trol over government on the part of society were not created.

It should be mentioned that regarding the institutionalization of eco-nomic and social conflicts, Russia made little, if any, progress. The lack of well-defined divisions of responsibility between the branches of power and the inability of their leaders to come to some kind of a consensus exacerbated existing conflicts throughout the different levels of government, making matters worse. Paradoxically, these same problems also led to a beneficial result; the plurality of forces that was generated by the lack of institutionalization may have diffused the danger of global civic or political confrontation in the society at large.

Finally, during the confrontation between president and parliament in 1992–93 when both sides tried to secure the support of the "force structures," the military gained the capacity to act more autonomously. Consequently, over time, instead of increasing civilian control over the military, Russian leaders were moving toward becoming hostages to the "force structures." In any case, the military assumed a more active role, although it is too early to make conclusions about the possibility of a military coup in Russia.

It would also be constructive to use the "procedural minimal" conditions for modern democracy that have been offered by Robert Dahl.[6] In postcommunist Russia, practically all adults gained the right to vote and to run for elective office. Elected officials were chosen in fairly conducted elections. Citizens have a right to express themselves and to seek out alternative sources of information and to form relatively independent associations. In this sense, the essential "procedural" prerequisites for democracy were achieved.

Taken together, these different dimensions demonstrate that Russia after August 1991 had embarked on the path of democratic evolution. The political system of the first Russian republic was much more democratic than the communist one that preceded it. Moreover, there were guarantees against the restoration of the communist authoritarian regime. For the first time in Russian and Soviet history, during 1991–93 at least, elements of checks and balances were introduced into the political infrastructure and an independent Constitutional Court was created. Power itself was no longer concentrated in the center, it was decentralized. The breakdown of the party–state system of political linkages was itself a major accomplishment, even though it was not accompanied by the creation of new horizontal ties. Opposition was legally formed and had the right to organize factions in the parliament. Democratic breakthroughs were achieved in the spheres of political culture, in the mentality of political elites, and in the formation of new political concepts.

On the basis of the criteria used here we could conclude that Russia in 1991–93 became a case of an unconsolidated democracy with the potential of moving in several different directions: toward a consolidated democratic structure, toward a new authoritarianism, or toward some hybrid system of power. But, as Philippe Schmitter and Terry Karl wrote in 1991, describing unconsolidated democracy: "The inheritors of the ancien regime may agree that no regime other than democracy is capable of legitimate governance, but be incapable of agreeing on specific rules of contingent consent and bounded uncertainty that would allow themselves to compete and cooperate effectively."[7] What the Russian rulers who came to power in 1990–91 were lacking was the ability to reach a compromise; they failed to negotiate pacts with the opposition that could provide the basis for further democratic development. One can cite other important factors inhibiting the emergence of democracy in postcommunist Russia. Among them are: the unconsolidated character of economic and social interests; a democratic movement that was formed inside of the communist system and even inside of the Communist Party itself; the lack of an effective second echelon of political leaders; a limited number of competitors for public office; and an economic crisis that narrowed the possibility for negotiated politics and increased polarization. But the inability of relevant elites to agree on "specific rules of contingent consent and bounded uncertainty" is central to this failure.

Let us now turn to another question: Which political institution contributed more to the development of democracy in Russia, and which institution in the end became an obstacle to democratic evolution? According to popular perception, from the very beginning the soviets in general, and the parliament in particular, became stumbling blocks in the way of reforms, while the executive authority, with President Yeltsin at its head, was seen as a force interested in realizing democratic ideals. The source of this perception is easy to understand. Former communists and some right-wing nationalists played an active, if not dominating, role in the Russian parliament and in the majority of the local soviets. Moreover, newly elected deputies were inexperienced and unaccustomed to routine legislative work. The highest chamber of the parliament, the Congress of People's Deputies, resembled a rally rather than a political institution. However, the legislature fulfilled at least two very important functions. First, it served as a channel for the articulation of differing social interests. Second, it became a counterbalance to the activity of executive authority.

In fact, it was Russian executive power, with Yeltsin at the head, that was the body least interested in the development of democracy.

Already by the fall of 1991, Yeltsin made an attempt to replace the existing political system with his "presidential vertical," excluding other political bodies from the decision-making process. The president's ideal was a new authoritarian regime of a liberal-technocratic orientation. Only later (in 1993) did he switch to a new orientation—more statist and more populistic—and his autocratic style of rule become even more evident. Meanwhile, parliament, because it represented differing interests, was much more pluralistic and appeared ready, at least at the beginning, for "pact politics" and compromises. Despite the widely held assumption that the soviets and parliament were refuges for the old communist elite, it was the executive branch that incorporated more representatives of the old nomenklatura. Paradoxically, the soviets and parliament, though in many respects a more conservative force than executive power if we consider their approach to marketization and the definition of state interests, contributed more to the development of democracy than the executive branch through their role as a counterweight to the president and his government. The opposite conclusion about the authoritarian inclinations of the executive would have been possible if, after dismissing the soviets from power in September 1993, the president, having no opponents, had really tried to build a democratic system of governance. But what he did instead was something quite different.

We should also take into account the fact that the system of the soviets, including the parliament, helped to preserve continuity. This fact had ambiguous consequences for the Russian transformation. On the one hand, it slowed down radical economic reform. On the other hand, it prevented sharp breaks with the past that could have made the process of transformation much more painful for the society at large. Where the new "presidential vertical" was not effective enough, the soviets to some extent compensated for the lack of an institutional infrastructure. Arguably, it was the legislatures in Russia, even more than executive power, that reflected continuity and change in the political process, political culture, and ideology. They presided, on the one hand, over the breakup of the Soviet Union, the realization of Yeltsin's rule, and the beginning of "shock therapy." On the other hand, they preserved the Soviet heritage, and represented the conservative moods of the elite and parts of the society at large. Despite its ineffectiveness from a purely functional point of view, the first Russian parliament created at least some traditions of parliamentarianism that may prove useful during the term of the second parliament elected in December 1993.

Some analysts have argued that instead of actual checks and balances, a "dyarchy," or dual system of power, resulted.[8] But representatives of the Russian executive branch were the most ardent supporters of this "dual power" explanation of the political crisis in the country; it gave them an excuse for dissolving parliament. In reality, it was Yeltsin, with his power to issue decrees with the force of law and to form the cabinet of ministers without legislative approval, who enjoyed much more power than the legislature. In part, this was because the executive branch retained a preponderance of control over economic and administrative resources; in part, it was by virtue of its experience and expertise. Consequently, it would be an exaggeration to consider the political system of the first Russian republic as a "dual system of power."

The Roots of the Political Crisis in Russia

This brings us to the next questions: Why was the Russian transition to democracy interrupted, at least temporarily, in 1993? What were the causes of the political crisis that led to the dissolution of parliament in September of that year?[9] According to the official explanation, the political crisis in Russia in 1991–93 was the result of the existence of the soviets in general, and of parliament in particular. But in reality, the roots of the political crisis were much more tangled. The confrontation between the executive branch and the legislature appears to be more a reflection of the crisis, not its main cause.

One of the major roots of the Russian political crisis was the widening gap between political institutions and society itself, which had already became evident in the first half of 1992. Losing popular support, both powers chose confrontation as a means of survival and self-justification. The more distant they became from society, the more intense their struggle with each other. It should be mentioned as well that during 1992 the legislative and the executive branches served as lightning rods for each other, neutralizing the growth of social dissatisfaction with power itself. Even more, conflict between two bodies was an ideal instrument for a polarization that served the interests of leading Russian politicians, including the president.

There is yet another paradox of Russian political reality in this period. On the one hand, the preservation of the old institutions that had been formed in the communist era (mainly the legislature) contributed to stability of the situation in the postcommunist period. On the other hand, attempts to use the old structures for the implementation of new goals provoked conflicts and increased the political crisis; the demands of short-term stability contradicted the demands of long-term stability. The destruction of the Soviet state and the collapse of the state-run economy and of previous governmental and cultural institutions also had its effect on the development of crisis. Look at the contradictory challenges that Russia faced at the end of 1991: state- and nation-building, democratization, the transition to a market economy, and the search for a new geopolitical role. The fact that Russian society found itself forced to solve these problems simultaneously, of course, made the whole transformation more difficult and dramatic.

Another important constraint that contributed to the political crisis was the multinational character of the old Soviet Union, including the close linkage, especially of economies, among the former Soviet republics. John Stuart Mill wrote, "It is in general a necessary condition that the boundaries of governments should coincide in the main with those of the nationality."[10] Indeed, the majority of successful transitions to democracy have taken place in the ethnically homogeneous countries.[11] Russian leaders failed to propose institutional designs that might limit the exacerbation of regional and nationality conflicts in the process of democratization. Meanwhile, the struggle for power in Moscow has only encouraged such conflicts. In this connection, the superpower status of the USSR also plays a role. Russian leaders have attempted to achieve democratic goals while simultaneously preserving Russia's superpower status and geopolitical continuity with the Soviet Union. It is quite evident that the simultaneity of Russia's transformations became a factor stimulating political and social tension, thereby contributing to the political crisis.

Another contributing factor was certainly the failure of "shock therapy" tactics of the Burbulis–Gaidar government and of revolutionary liberalism as a policy in general. This, in turn, forced the ruling team to look for a scapegoat. Parliament became the best candidate for this role. To this must be added the deepening economic crisis and the growth of centrifugal, disintegrative processes at work within the Russian Federation.

Yet another factor must be mentioned. Given the embryonic state of political parties and the lack of effective self-government and mass organizations, social interests from below were compelled to "flow" to the top without any aggregation and previous resolution on the lower levels. As a result of the lack of an intermediate layer of governance between individuals and the state—one capable of resolving conflicts before they became the object of political struggle on the top—it was inevitable that tension between the two powers should escalate.

Under these circumstances, the two branches of power became substitute parties, thereby acquiring new adversarial functions. The struggle between them took place in the context of growing passivity on the part of society and increasing weakness of the democratic movement. In a way, the absence of mass activity helped to halt a highly unstable political process. But at the same time, this situation threatened to make politics the exclusive province of back-room deals and secret agreements. It was precisely at this juncture that the legitimate struggle for power moved away from political parties and interest-based movements toward an open confrontation between the executive and legislative branches. The constant regrouping of small parliamentary alliances and constant clashes of power among them, rather than the gradual formation of political parties with publicly recognizable platforms, became the predominant modus operandi of Russian politics.

One more source of the crisis was the uncritical borrowing on the part of Russia's governing elite and their advisers of ideas and mechanisms from the West. As Robert Sharlet has pointed out, we can clearly see that the attempt to fuse American and French political models and to hastily transplant this odd mixture into an alien Soviet reality had little chance of success.[12] Some of the elements that the architects of the new Russian political system tried to combine were incompatible and could produce only conflict.

As a result, numerous vicious circles began to emerge in Russian politics. Because political movements were so weak, political leaders began relying even more strongly on narrowly focused interest groups and on familiar "administrative" methods to ensure support for their policies. The political style of all primary political actors became more and more authoritarian. This in turn became a factor that prevented the formation of effective channels of representation. Growing authoritarianism on the part of most political leaders contributed to the ongoing escalation of conflict between the president and parliament.

In the face of such a vituperative struggle for power, all the remaining political forces in society were simply unable to maintain their neutrality and were compelled to take sides. Which side one took—the president's or parliament's—became the great demarcation line in Russian political life. Further aggravating this crisis was the projection of the power distribution conflict onto relations between the center and the provinces. As local executives became allied with the president, provincial legislatures found themselves increasingly sympathetic to the plight of parliament. In this way, the national struggle was often mirrored locally. Contradictions between branches of power led to political gridlock, and all institutions became incapable of dealing with current problems.[13]

Essentially, the elements of conflict inside the political system prevailed over the elements of cooperation. Russian leaders proved incapable of collective action and of reaching compromises on the crucial agenda of transformation. The system that began to emerge in Russia in 1991–92 could be called "adversarial," but it should be emphasized that the competition taking place in Russian politics was a contest between different groups of elites, not between autonomous groups within society. Russian development in these years became characterized above all by attempts on the part of all political actors and all political institutions to *monopolize* power, instead of sharing it.

Other dimensions important for understanding the nature of Russian political development in 1992–93 include: (1) the personal characteristics of the main political actors who had access to principal governmental positions; (2) the resources—economic, political, and administrative—that these actors could use to exercise their power; and (3) the rules that they followed. Taking these in turn, we can say first that the personalities of the most important Russian political figures were clearly authoritarian. This was especially true of Yeltsin and of Speaker of the Parliament Ruslan Khasbulatov. Their personal conflict and mutual hatred in a setting of weak political institutions and over-personalized politics became one of the most important negative factors in Russian political life.

Of the two personalities, Yeltsin's was definitely the stronger, and it was undoubtedly Yeltsin who more decisively influenced the chain of events in Russia. He never concealed the fact that his ideal was a strong presidential regime, which he interpreted as his own unchallengeable power without any counterbalances. In the spring of 1992, Yeltsin declared: "Taking into consideration our traditions, the problems of transitional period, and the ongoing reforms, we should install a presidential regime."[14] Yeltsin's views on the Russian political system were clearly expressed in his recent memoir, *Notes of the President:* "I do what I think is necessary. . . . Everything must be ruled by one rigid principle or decree. Frankly speaking, somebody must be the First in the country."[15] In another passage, Yeltsin emphasized that Russia did not need compromises, but "strength, even policy based on force."[16] A leader with such convictions, of course, could not tolerate an independent parliament or any other kind of opposition.

As for resources on which power could be based, with the passage of time, Russian leaders lost a great deal of control over them and this made Russian development more chaotic and unpredictable. Paradoxically, this fact had not only negative, but also some positive consequences. Lack of control on the part of any of the different leaders neutralized the impact of the often bizarre policies they tried to pursue. Besides, it may have helped society to overcome its traditional passivity, and form new mechanisms of self-survival and learn to live in a more free atmosphere.

It would be an oversimplification to draw the conclusion that Russian political elites after August 1991 did not follow any rules. Quite unexpectedly, different sets of rules and principles, both ideological and organizational, emerged at this time: liberal and populist; democratic and authoritarian; nationalist and cosmopolitan; paternalistic, clientalistic, and even patrimonial. The problem was that different political groups tried to follow different patterns of activity and behavior. No single pattern was accepted by most, let alone all, of the actors.

Let us add to this one more observation. During 1991–93, Russia was fortunate in some respects. The sources of confrontation in Russia lay more *within* the emerging political system than outside of it. This made political life full of tension, but a global confrontation between the state and society was avoided. Moreover, although this permanent struggle for power between two institutions constantly led to stalemates and deadlocks in Russian political life, it also prevented any single political force from monopolizing power and thus restoring the previous situation.[17]

In the last analysis, the political crisis in Russia was a result of the linkage between all the different factors and trends considered here. The dissolution of parliament in this situation could change the correlation of forces, even the shape of constitutional and political order, but it could not eliminate all the roots of the political crisis.

Developments After December 1993: New Paradoxes

By the fall of 1993, it had become apparent that Russian politics was once again deadlocked. The ratification of the draft constitution that President Yeltsin had authorized during the summer seemed increasingly doubtful. His attempts to create a new Council of the Federation composed of regional leaders who would be loyal to him (if only temporarily) had not met with success. The atmosphere of extreme confrontation was destabilizing, not only for political life, but for society at large. This destabilization threatened to undermine all structures of power. There were only two ways out of this stalemate: one by means of compromise, the other by means of force.

Finding a compromise would have required substantial concessions on the part of both parties. For parliament's leaders it would have meant avoiding confrontational rhetoric and a willingness not to respond to every presidential move with a countermove. On the part of the president and his entourage, compromise would have meant ending claims that the executive held a monopoly on political power. In fact, a way existed for both to pursue their paths: a reciprocal agreement to hold simultaneous elections for both president and parliament. But in so doing, they would concede to new political forces the responsibility for crafting a new structure for the state and adopting a new constitution. A significant portion of parliament and, more importantly, the president's staff, were not satisfied with this approach.

The second solution was simple: eliminate of one of the sides in the game. In actuality, the president had far more forces at his disposal than parliament, so there was little doubt who would win such a contest. And, indeed, it was Yeltsin's entourage that made the first moves toward an armed solution. The result was a strategic blunder that endangered a fragile and as yet unconsolidated Russian democracy. A combination of clashing political ambitions, emotions, and other subjective factors was responsible for the issuance of Decree 1400 by President Yeltsin on September 21, 1993, dissolving parliament altogether. According to the terms of the decree, new parliamentary elections were to be held on December 12, 1993, at which time the electorate would also decide the fate of the president's draft constitution.[18]

After the dissolution of parliament and the elections of December 12, 1993, Russia entered a new stage of development. The period of "great leaps forward," of revolutionary phraseology, reformist utopianism, and unseasoned expectations, had come to an end. What the new stage will entail remains to be seen. What is evident are new attempts on the part of Yeltsin's team to construct a "presidential vertical" without any checks and balances. Such an organization of political life in Russia puts the president in the role of the arbiter on the top, concentrating all political power in his hands, standing above all branches of power. It resembles a typically Bonapartist regime. According to the new constitution, drafted after Yeltsin's crackdown on the parliament and reflecting the president's vast ambitions, not only the legislature, but the Constitutional Court as well, have become mere decorations. Thus, parliament is deprived of the right to form a government, while the process for impeaching the president is so complicated that it becomes virtually impossible.

In many ways, it is as if the presidency were a contemporary version of the CPSU Secretariat. Some observers speak of a "superpresidential structure" in Russia today. After all, the boundaries among the executive, legislative, and judicial powers are obscure again, as in Soviet times. The broad range of powers granted the president enables him to interfere at will in the business of other institutions. Instead of a flexible power structure, a "top-down" vertical system has been reinstated. The absence of checks and balances not only prevents mid-course policy adjustments and narrows the possibilities for dissent within the government, but actually undermines the executive branch by making it directly responsible for every blunder on the part of its subordinates everywhere, without exception.

What is also noteworthy is the absence of effective communication links between the state and society. This has weakened the possibilities for constructive economic and political stabilization, which would aid, rather than undermine, reform. The personalization of politics, the dependence on the behavior of leaders and their entourages, has become even stronger than before. Overlapping functions, the lack of clearly defined spheres of responsibility for different political bodies, and the creation of numerous unconstitutional organs and mechanisms around the president make the new political system no more effective than the previous one.

At the same time, the roots of tension inside of the power structures remain, although they take on different forms. The absence of open conflicts during 1994 and the apparent stabilization of the political situation cannot be considered as proof of the effectiveness of the new system. The relative stability that emerged in early 1994 was based instead on rather fragile ground. In reality, this was only an appearance of stability, due to several factors, including the absence of any alternative to the existing ruling elite, the frustration of ordinary people, the weakness of the opposition, and attempts by different interest groups to make bargains behind the scenes in order to avoid open conflicts. Such "stability" cannot last for long, especially in a situation where the regime has penetrated the system and made all other political bodies ineffective. Under these circumstances, a change of leader or of the regime itself in Russia could become a powerful contributor to instability.

In June of 1994, Yeltsin demonstrated his disrespect for his own constitution by attempting to rule by decrees and by ignoring not only the new parliament, but also the government headed by his own appointee, Prime Minister Viktor Chernomyrdin. In December 1994, Yeltsin and his close advisers began a war in the breakaway republic of Chechnya, signifying their complete rejection of a liberal and democratic orientation. Under these circumstances one might predict the emergence in Russia of a new authoritarian regime with clear dictatorial elements. But paradoxically, if he adopts such a course Yeltsin is unlikely to succeed. After concentrating all power within the executive branch, Yeltsin could end up as one of the weakest political leaders in Soviet and Russian history. By distancing himself from the radical democrats who ostensibly brought him to power, the president has left himself without a single serious sociopolitical base of support. In addition, Yeltsin's popularity in society is in permanent decline. Under such conditions, he could easily become hostage to his own inner staff, and to the military and security forces.

Conclusions: Lessons From the Past for the Future

It is tempting to conclude from all of this that the generally accepted conditions for democratic evolution are simply not present in Russia and that authoritarian solutions, or worse, are inevitable. The list of shortcomings is daunting: historical traditions are inconsistent with the requirements of liberalism; a middle class is still in its nascent, formative stages; the severity of ethno-national problems detracts from the process of state-building; the extent and severity of economic crisis prevents speedy solutions; the new ruling elite has significant ties with the former regime; and so forth. Taken separately and together, these facts must surely represent obstacles in the path of the democratic transition in Russia.

At the same time, there are significant obstacles to any return to authoritarianism in Russia today, and even more to any kind of dictatorship. Among them are:

1. the inability of any side to monopolize power, at least for a substantial period, which in turn compels all sides to engage actively in the search for compromise;

2. the steady regionalization and decentralization of the country resulting in the emergence of new republican and regional elites, acting as a political and geographical balance to central authority;

3. the ongoing process of creating a genuine civil society;

4. the federal model of society, which serves as a counterbalance to the restoration of control by Moscow over the provinces;

5. the gradual weakening of paternalistic tendencies in the population, both among individuals and whole social groups, in favor of greater individualism and independence;

6. and the impossibility that in the long run any regime that tries to seal itself off from the larger global community of states, peoples, and ideas can survive in the contemporary world.

Let us add to this list the ineffectiveness of two major props of any authoritarian regime: a bureaucracy that is not only corrupt but split into different sections fighting each other; and an army that could hardly be considered as a force absolutely loyal to the president or to any other political leader.

While there obviously is no certainty about what the future will bring to Russian politics, what seems most likely is not another authoritarian regime, but a "mixed regime" with contradictory tendencies. In this seemingly chaotic transitional period in Russia, there do appear to be some features consistent with other postcommunist societies, despite particular differences. Among them are: a weakly developed multiparty system; fragile coalitions among ruling elites that break down and come together repeatedly; continuous confrontation between the executive and legislative branches of power; periodic clashes between the president and his cabinet (especially in countries where presidents try to monopolize the decision-making process through executive decrees); the pursuit of unregulated emergency powers on the part of executive branch; overall excessive reliance on charisma and personality factors in politics; and an ideological vacuum being filled up by all sorts of irrational myths and symbols.

Only after the first period of post-communist transformation and extrication from the previous communist rule is over and the institutionalization of the new system has begun will it become evident what kind of political structure a society needs. For Russia, there are many reasons why strong presidentialism may not be the best option. As Juan Linz has argued, presidential regimes are too rigid, too inflexible, and cannot accommodate competing interests.[19] In the Russian case, presidentialism is incompatible with the flexible federal model and would be difficult to implement in a society with numerous conflicts; it would inhibit the development of mechanisms for power sharing. Moreover, as Russian experience demonstrates, presidentialism can be unpredictable and unstable when it comes to the problem of rotation. In fact, there are few reasons to believe that strong presidentialism is a good choice for Russia. Recent events provide additional reasons why this may be so. The 1993 "Second October Revolution," and now the war in the North Caucasus, suggest that Yeltsin and his "inner circle" of advisers are attempting to establish a new authoritarian regime in Russia. By the beginning of 1995 the danger of police rule had become evident, though it is doubtful that such an effort could succeed.

In general, parliamentary democracy offers the adaptability that presidentialism lacks. Unfortunately, on the surface at least, few of the prerequisites for establishing a parliamentary type of democracy in Russia would appear to be met. This conclusion would seem to be supported by the dramatic end of all legislatures in Russia's history. Thus far, there are no strong parties, no adequate traditions of parliamentarianism, and no developed political elites.

At the same time, it is evident that Russia is already a pluralistic polity. And as the experience of the current Federal Assembly proves, parliament in Russian conditions can be a useful, perhaps indispensable, body for the articulation of different interests and for the consolidation of different types of elites, which is one of the most important prerequisites of democratic evolution. In such a pluralistic society as Russia, with its different cultures and regions, varied political elites, and consequently, its need for continual negotiation, the best option would appear to be a mixture of parliamentary and presidential systems. But to achieve this, Russian society must first overcome two of the myths created in recent years—namely, that Russia is doomed to be ruled by a personality who would play the role of tsar, and that this country simply cannot have an independent and effective parliament.

Notes

1. The "presidential vertical" line of power refers to a system of executive rule proposed by Yeltsin at the end of 1991 as a temporary administrative measure. Under its rules, President Yeltsin was allowed to appoint administrative heads, often called "governors," and to establish the offices of chiefs of administration. The functions of the soviets were to be limited substantially. This initiative represented a fundamental change in the preexisting institutional balance in favor of the executive branch. See Jeffrey Hahn's discussion of local government in "Two Years after the Collapse of the USSR," *Post-Soviet Affairs*, vol. 9, no. 4 (1993).

2. Anders Aslund, "Russia's Success Story," *Foreign Affairs,* September–October 1994, p. 66.

3. Schumpeter's classic definition is found in Joseph A. Schumpeter, *Capitalism, Socialism and Democracy*, 2nd ed. (New York: Harper, 1947), p. 269.

4. On the principle of uncertainty, see Adam Przeworski, "Some Problems in the Study of Transition," in Guillermo O'Donnell, Phillipe Schmitter, and Lawrence Whitehead, eds., *Transitions from Authoritarian Rule: Tentative Conclusions and Uncertain Democracies* (Baltimore, MD: Johns Hopkins University Press, 1986), pp. 47–63.

5. Robert A. Dahl, *Polyarchy* (New Haven, CT: Yale University Press, 1982), pp. 1–10.

6. Robert A. Dahl, *Dilemmas of Pluralist Democracy* (New Haven, CT: Yale University Press, 1982), p. 11.

7. Karl Terry and Philippe Schmitter, "What Democracy Is . . . and Is Not," *Journal of Democracy*, vol. 2 (Summer 1991), p. 75.

8. As Robert Sharlet has pointed out, this system was "a product of conflicting visions of the future, of political self-interest." Robert Sharlet, "Russian Constitutional Crisis: Law and Politics under Yeltsin," *Post-Soviet Affairs*, vol. 9, no. 4 (1993), p. 317.

9. The political crisis in Russia in 1991–93 had multiple characteristics. It was a crisis of statehood, of political structure, of federation, of national identity, of political authority, and a constitutional crisis as well.

10. John Stuart Mill, *Consideration on Representative Government* (New York: Liberal Arts Press, 1958), p. 230.

11. See Dankwurt Rustow, "Transitions to Democracy: Towards a Dynamic Model," *Comparative Politics*, vol. 2, no. 3 (1970), pp. 350–352.

12. See Robert Sharlet, "Russian Constitutional Crisis," p. 318.

13. At the same time, it must be recognized that this stalemate probably prevented even sharper polarization during 1992 and the beginning of 1993, again demonstrating the paradox of Russian political life in this period.

14. *Komsomol'skaia pravda*, May 27, 1992.

15. Boris Yeltsin, *Zapiski Presidenta* (Notes of the President) (Moscow: 1994), pp. 149–150. Quotation translated by L. Shevtsova.

16. Ibid., p. 152.

17. According to Philip G. Roeder, "The previous deadlock between legislature and executive, and the strategies of autocratic and oligarchic factions that were so lamented in both Russia and the West, nonetheless had created a balance that prevented any one faction from establishing its dominance and that preserved significant space for public contestation." Philip G. Roeder, "Varieties of Post-Soviet Authoritarian Regimes," *Post-Soviet Affairs*, vol. 10, no. 1 (1994), pp. 88–89.

18. Yeltsin's "revolution" evoked different assessments among Western analysts. Thus, Philip Roeder wrote: "The presidential coup of the fall of 1993, however, broke through the deadlock in ways that facilitated autocratic development." Roeder, "Varieties of Post-Soviet Authoritarian Regimes," p. 89. Gail Lapidus, on the contrary, argued, "In the short run, the new political arrangements that strengthen executive power and constrain the ability of the legislature to block reform-oriented policies altogether could help to weaken anti-democratic forces." She also noted, however, that "there remains the danger that where anti-democratic forces to come to power in Russia, the new arrangements could provide a mantle of legitimacy for a serious authoritarian alternative." Gail Lapidus, "Inventing Russia," *Post-Soviet Affairs*, vol. 9, no. 4 (1993), p. 289.

19. Juan J. Linz, "The Perils of Presidentialism," *Journal of Democracy*, vol. 1, no. 1 (Winter 1990), pp. 51–69.

3

The Constituency Nexus in the Russian and Other Post-Soviet Parliaments

Timothy J. Colton

Western research on parliaments in the transition away from Soviet communism has lurched forward around three major foci: the structures, rules, and norms of the legislative assemblies themselves; roll calls and coalitional patterns within them; and their tormented relations with the emerging executive branch of government. Pursuit of these issues, while not without its payoffs, has thus far been frustrating and unpredictable.

Investigation of the first problem was confounded by the provisional basis on which the first revamped legislatures were elected in 1989–90, by the crisis atmosphere that enveloped them from the outset, and by the resultant flux and improvisation in their operations. It remains to be seen for the future whether parliaments reelected in the mid-1990s under revised rules, and often (though not invariably) under new constitutions, will be less elusive objects of analysis. The second problem was difficult to bring into focus for some of the same reasons, as intraparliamentary alignments shifted and shimmied with every passing season and opportunistic behavior abounded. The third problem tended to crowd out the first two after the demolition of Communist Party rule in 1991, especially for scholars interested in the Russian Federation. Newsworthy though it may have been, this phenomenon was scarcely less elusive than the first two, as limited discord over the distribution of constitutional powers grew in many of the successor states into bellicose confrontation over all manner of issues. In Russia, the upshot in September–October 1993 was street violence in the capital city and a close brush with a national civil war. The Western rubric of "legislative-executive relations" seems a trifle pallid before the spectacle of army commandos shelling and storming the headquarters of Russia's duly elected parliament and marching its speaker, Ruslan Khasbulatov, away in handcuffs.

As new, post-post-Soviet legislatures take shape and, let us hope, begin to make laws in the coming years, this same triad of themes will in all likelihood continue to dominate research. For the enterprise to be as fruitful as it might be, however, I would argue that our agenda ought to be expanded from the first round to include study of the nexus between parliamentary players and society.[1]

The cardinal issue here is about *representation*. Mesmerized as we have been with transactions inside legislative boundaries, and between them and executive establishments, we have devoted insufficient attention to the frontier between the legislative system and the constituents whose enfranchisement, flawed and incomplete though it was, was surely the signal accomplishment of Mikhail Gorbachev's liberalization. Unless there is some correspondence between popular inputs and policy outputs, talk of democratization in any of the newly independent states will be so much hollow verbiage. A rounded brief on representation and its modalities and implications would aim to address overarching intellectual puzzles such as the following:

- What, if anything, do the preferences and decisions of legislators have in common with the preferences of individual and collective actors within their electoral constituencies? Do parliamentarians "speak for" no one but themselves, for other elite-level interests, or for more broadly groundly interests?
- By virtue of what mechanisms do deputies learn about what their constituents want and need and get feedback about their own actions in parliament? Vice versa, how informed are voters about what their representatives are thinking and doing?
- How exposed are MPs to citizens, groups, and organizations within their constituencies, and how much routine support and advocacy, especially with the state bureaucracy, do they provide their electors?
- Under what conditions are legislators more publicly accessible and more zealous and effective in fighting for grassroots inter-

ests? Are personal qualities, motivational systems, electoral and institutional rules, or political loyalties acting through the individual deputy responsible for the tenor of the relationship with constituents? Or do different kinds of constituencies breed different representative styles?

- Do the budding legislatures betray any capacity for "mobilizing consent" among the population for those policies actually adopted by the state?[2]

Questions as grand and beguiling as these cannot be dealt with in one fell swoop. The present chapter is a modest effort to remedy past neglect and to acquaint readers with some quantitative evidence about the constituency connection that, at the very least, will help them size the problem up. The chapter should furnish a partial baseline for assessing changes as they unfold in the parliamentary terms ahead. My paramount interest is in the first competitively elected legislature of Russia in transition—inaugurated in the spring of 1990, dissolved by fiat of President Boris Yeltsin in the autumn of 1993—but to provide background and reference points I present parallel information about three other late-Soviet or post-Soviet parliaments. One haunting question is how different the ill-starred legislature of the "first Russian republic" was from its counterparts elsewhere in the former Soviet Union.

Data

I came by the information exploited in these pages in the course of the Carnegie Corporation–funded project on political reform run collaboratively on the American side with Jeffrey Hahn, Jerry Hough, and Blair Ruble. I was the principal investigator who specialized in legislative development from the outset. Under that capacious umbrella, I, to use the methodological markers of the field in the United States, undertook a "behavioral study" of legislators rather than an "institutional study" or a "process-oriented study."[3]

Although I had recourse to a variety of research techniques, including open-ended interviews with about forty deputies, my primary tool was a survey of members, which I had the good fortune to carry out in four legislatures. The questionnaire, which I submitted via official legislative channels conjointly with local research partners, had of necessity to be self-administered by deputies. To lower the time and mental costs of participating, I phrased most questions in a closed, multiple-choice format. Ironclad guarantees of confidentiality and some compromises on question topic and wording had to be built in so as to gain the assent of the parliamentary leaderships.

I executed the survey almost simultaneously in May 1991 in the Supreme Soviet of the USSR and among members and affiliates of the Supreme Soviet of Russia, in November 1991 in the Supreme Soviet (Rada) of Ukraine, and in January 1992 in the Supreme Soviet of Kazakhstan.

Ideally, the questionnaires should have been identical, word for word, in each of the four cases. This proved unattainable, owing to bargaining relations with research collaborators, logistical and communication difficulties, the quirks of local situations and personalities, and the swift flow of events. The instruments wound up being fundamentally similar in the four legislatures, but with defects that now and then impede crisp comparisons, especially for the Russian deputies.

In the USSR legislature, with only months to go before its extinction after the putsch of August 1991, the questionnaire was distributed to 115 deputies, a one-third random sample of members of the USSR Supreme Soviet who had served in that body for twelve months or longer. One hundred and four MPs, or 90 percent, returned filled-in booklets. At the other three locations, circumstances precluded probability sampling. I settled for distribution of the questionnaire to the entire population of deputies, followed up by memorandum and telephone prods, and made do with the replies that trickled in. For the Russian parliament, about which I am the most curious, the objective was to reach the 251 members of the Supreme Soviet and a good slice of the approximately 400 deputies in the RSFSR Congress of People's Deputies who sat as members of Supreme Soviet committees and subcommittees without having floor rights. I culled 307 responses, 159 from the full members and 148 from the associate members. For Ukraine, Supreme Soviet deputies numbered 450, although 40 to 50 of these were completely inactive; 237 responded. Kazakhstan yielded the most disappointing harvest rate by far, 124 out of 360 deputies.

Altogether, therefore, I have 772 completed questionnaires to work with—an imperfect but suggestive cross-section of the roughly 1,900 parliamentarians in the target population. Let me sketch for the nonspecialist the electoral arrangements under which these deputies arrived in office and, ever so briefly, the legislative machinery at hand in Moscow, Kiev, and Almaty.

USSR

Two thousand, two hundred fifty deputies were elected in 1989 from "territorial districts" partitioned on the basis of equal votes, from "national-territorial districts" drawn to reflect the ethnic composition of the electorate and Soviet administrative boundaries, and from officially approved "public organizations" such as the Communist Party and the Academy of Sciences. The Congress of Deputies convened for only several brief sessions a year. The 450-person standing parliament it selected from its benches, the USSR Supreme Soviet, was bicameral, albeit with little differentiation between the houses. All Supreme Soviet deputies from territorial districts sat in the Council of the Union and all from national-territorial districts in the Council of Nationalities; deputies from public organizations were split equally between the two houses. My sample of 104 was spread evenly between the chambers, 52 deputies each; 32 deputies were from territorial districts, 44 from national-territorial districts, and 28 from public organizations.

Russia

As with the USSR, there was both a cumbersome Congress of Deputies and a compact Supreme Soviet, bifurcated into two chambers. The 1,068 congressional deputies were elected in 1990 from territorial and national-territorial districts, no seats being earmarked here for organizations. Of the 159 Supreme Soviet deputies in my Russian sample, 90, elected in territorial districts, belonged to the Council of the Federation, while 69, from national-territorial districts, were members of the Council of Nationalities. Of the 148 associate deputies in the sample (members of the Congress are but mere committee members in the Supreme Soviet subsystem), 140 were from territorial districts and 8 from national-territorial districts.[4]

Ukraine

Constitutionally, Ukraine presented the simplest picture. Its Supreme Soviet was unicameral and without a parental Congress. All members were directly elected in 1990 from territorial districts.

Kazakhstan

Like Ukraine, Kazakhstan had a unicameral Supreme Soviet and no Congress. It resembled the USSR, however, in that its 1990 electoral law stipulated that one-quarter of its members be designated by public organizations. Of my 124 respondents, 103 (83 percent) were from territorial districts and 21 (17 percent) from organizations.

In sociodemographic terms, the deputies interrogated were more or less representative of their legislative units. They were overwhelmingly male: 81 percent in the USSR Supreme Soviet, 96 percent in Ukraine, and 89 percent in Kazakhstan (the gender question was inadvertently omitted from the Russian survey). They were mostly middle-aged, the modal age group in all four councils being the forties. Healthy majorities had a higher education: 64 percent for the USSR parliament, 91 percent for Russia, 93 percent for Ukraine, and 75 percent for Kazakhstan. Occupational background was predominantly white-collar, with the USSR sample, as a residue of uncompetitive electoral procedures and quotas, having the greatest number of blue-collar members (42 percent workers and *kolkhoz* peasants, as opposed to 8 percent of Russian deputies, 11 percent in Ukraine, and 20 percent in Kazakhstan).

I was barred from inquiring about the USSR and Russian deputies' ethnic identification. In Ukraine, where this was allowed, 74 percent of the legislators surveyed were ethnic Ukrainians, 22 percent Russians, and 4 percent other minorities. In Kazakhstan, 51 percent were members of the titular Kazakh nationality, 33 percent were Russians, and 16 percent belonged to other groups. In the fragmented and bitterly suspicious USSR and RSFSR Supreme Soviets, I was also constrained from posing detailed questions about electoral district (or organization), out of fear of compromising anonymity. In Ukraine and Kazakhstan, I gathered more such information.

The deputies I polled were a mix of rank-and-file members and leaders. Except for full members of the Russian Supreme Soviet, the proportion of the respondents who occupied a leadership post in a legislative committee or subcommittee ranged from about 10 percent to about 30 percent. The abnormally high number of leaders among the Russian full deputies (almost 60 percent) reflects a selection bias in the survey; it also catches the Russian legislature's tendency toward proliferation of committees and subcommittees.[5] Nearly three-quarters of the USSR Supreme Soviet members and of the full members of the Russian Supreme Soviet worked full-time as deputies, whereas clear majorities of the Russian associate deputies and of the Ukraine and Kazakhstan deputies were part-timers.[6]

Deputies' Attitudes Toward Representation

A good starting point for this discussion is the politicians' global orientation toward representation. A series of questions in the survey invited deputies to rate their prime roles as MPs. In keeping with the comparative literature on representation, the questionnaire laid out these roles under five general headings:

1. *lawmaking* work at draft legislation;
2. *control* or oversight over the activity of government agencies;
3. *casework* on behalf of individual voters;
4. *advocacy* of the corporate interests of the district, sponsoring organization, or some other social group; and
5. *informational* activity, keeping in touch with voters' opinions about what the government is up to.

The third, fourth, and fifth pigeonholes all refer to one aspect or another of the constituency-representing function, loosely speaking.

Deputies were requested to peruse the checklist of roles and first of all to rank them prescriptively, in order of the place they ought to occupy in the work of a member of the given parliament. They were next asked factual questions about the places the given roles really did occupy in their day-to-day work as legislators.

Complications cropped up in drafting and administering these questions. In the USSR survey, I broke advocacy down into two subcategories, one for the interests of the district or of the electing organization and the other for "the interests of a social or occupational group," which could include an ethnic group; lawmaking was also parsed at the insistence of my Moscow colleagues into separate lines for committees and the Supreme Soviet. The Russian questionnaire made no reference under advocacy to social groups or to a sponsoring organization, since all of the RSFSR deputies were elected from territorially defined districts. In Ukraine and Kazakhstan, advocacy was a bifold category, as with the USSR survey, but the lawmaking category stayed unitary. Further complications arose from misjudgments in question wording and from the deputies' own fuzziness about what they ought to be and were doing. Not infrequently, MPs proved unwilling or unable to produce a systematic ranking of the respective roles, often assigning tie scores or dropping one or several roles from the reckoning.[7]

The confusion notwithstanding, some valuable information can be winkled out of the deputies' evaluations of roles. Table 3.1 shows how ideal and actual roles ranked in the estimation of the four country samples of deputies. The rankings were for seven roles in the USSR Supreme Soviet, five roles for Russia, and six roles for Ukraine and Kazakhstan.[8]

Lawmaking work, be it in committee or on the floor of the legislature, was universally the deputies' top choice. Nowhere did MPs not believe that making laws as disinterested agents of society writ large was their most pressing duty.

The representative roles that concern us here drew a lot less approval, although there was not perfect uniformity from one country's parliament to the next. There was, moreover, considerable heterogeneity in the normative value assigned to specific representative roles. Deputies everywhere tended to perceive both the informational function (keeping in touch with voters' opinions) and the promotion of the interests of social and occupational groups as relatively unattractive pursuits. In the USSR, Ukraine, and Kazakhstan, on the other hand, they placed standing up for the interests of the electing district or organization second in prescriptive terms only to lawmaking; in Russia, they ranked it fourth. Casework for individual electors was situated near the middle of most members' normative ranking, yet it was ranked a good deal lower (sixth out of seven) by the USSR deputies.

Variation according to deputies' mode of election and political affiliation can be detected in the evaluation of the appropriateness of representative work. Deputies delegated by "public organizations" (in the USSR and Kazakhstan parliaments) ascribed greater value to boosting their constituencies than territorially elected deputies did. By contrast, deputies affiliated with radical democratic factions—the Interregional Deputies' Group in the USSR Supreme Soviet, Democratic Russia in Russia, Narodna Rada in Ukraine, and Democratic Kazakhstan in Kazakhstan—downplayed the defense of constituent interests. Both of

Table 3.1

Ranking of Deputies' Average Evaluations of Ideal and Actual Roles

	Russia	USSR	Ukraine	Kazakhstan
Lawmaking				
Work in committees on draft laws and resolutions				
Ideal	—	1	—	—
Actual	—	1	—	—
Work in the Supreme Soviet on draft laws and resolutions				
Ideal	1	2	1	1
Actual	1	2	1	1
Control				
Control over the activity of government organs				
Ideal	2	4	4	3
Actual	5	6	4	4
Casework				
Helping voters who are encountering difficulties in dealing with government agencies				
Ideal	3	6	3	4
Actual	2	4	2	3
Advocacy				
Defense of the interests of the district (or of the organization that elected the deputy)				
Ideal	4	3	2	2
Actual	3	3	3	2
Defense of the interests of a social or occupational group				
Ideal	—	7	6	6
Actual	—	7	6	5
Informational				
Keeping in touch with voters' opinions about the activity of the government				
Ideal	5	5	5	5
Actual	4	5	5	6

Source: For all tables in chapter 3: Author's analysis of data from surveys of deputies to the Supreme Soviets of the USSR, Russia, Kazakstan, and Ukraine, 1991–92.

these patterns would seem to stand to reason. Organizational deputies would naturally feel themselves more tightly tied to their patrons than MPs chosen from areal constituencies would feel to their districts—entities more pluralistic and, one could say, more ambiguous in their blend of interests needing representation. One suspects that radical democrats, in turn, would be less enamored of casework and district defense by reason of their ideological bent, which impells them to think of societywide rather than constituency-based interests as being decisive in the political struggle.[9]

The assessment of actual roles performed falls out somewhat differently. Legislative work was in each and every instance the cardinal role. But some of the other roles gained on their idealized ranking, whereas others slipped. Deputies, in other words, found themselves doing some things with more alacrity or less than their theoretical conception of the representative's role would have led them to wish.

If one looks at the absolute scores pegged to the role types, for one of the pairings the actual and ideal scores were the same, while in the largest number (sixteen) the actual score was less than the ideal. The falloff from ideal to actual was the deputies' way of saying, "This or that role was not all I thought it would be," or "I have made less of a contribution in this sphere than I expected I would when I took office." The steepest negative displacements were recorded for lawmaking roles and, less consistently, for control activity. For seven pairings, the absolute score arrived at for the actual role was higher than that given to the role in the ideal. *All seven of those pairings were for representative roles,* including casework in all four of the country cases.

Table 3.1 demonstrates this same general motif for the rankings of roles. Looking at the four representative roles in the four parliaments, we find the actual ranking of the representative role unchanged from the idealized ranking in six pairings out of fifteen.[10] For two pairings, the actual ranking was lower than the idealized ranking. For seven pairings—including all four of the casework pairings—the actual ranking was *higher* than the ideal ranking. The most common tendency, in other words, was for representative work to take up more of the deputy's time and energy in real life than he thought it merited in the abstract. The Russian Supreme Soviet is illustrative here: casework, which ranked third among ideal roles, rose to second among actual roles; defense of district interests ranked fourth in the ideal but third in reality; and deputies put keeping in touch with voters' opinion fifth in the ideal but fourth in practice.

All of this bears testimony to a certain learning having taken place among many Russian and other post-Soviet legislators about the unanticipated and largely unwelcome importance of casework and other representative activity. At the same time, one should not exaggerate the import of the cognitive shift. The bulk of the deputies still preferred, beyond the shadow of a doubt, to immerse themselves in lawmaking. The numerous conversations I had with MPs in Moscow, Kiev, and Almaty between 1990 and 1993 consistently reinforced this impression. Again and again they winced and shrugged their shoulders when asked about their dealings with constituents. Rarely if ever did they want to lead off with constituency-related work in their debriefings. My profound impression is that few deputies derived much personal gratification from it.

Responses to queries about that hoary chestnut of legislative theory, the imperative mandate, shed some further light on the problem. In the survey, parliamentarians were asked whether they understood themselves to be instructed "delegates," bound to carry out the wishes of their electors, or more like the "trustees," following their own lights and consciences, that Edmund Burke praised in his landmark eighteenth-century treatise on representation.

When confronted with this choice on the questionnaire, the deputies in the aggregate firmly identified with the trustee's rather than the delegate's role definition (see Table 3.2). Most lawmakers believed that it was they, and not the citizens or organizations that had propelled them into office, who were best qualified to ascertain the public interest. There were, to be sure, country differences. The USSR deputies were by far the most prone to seeing themselves as trustees, with almost three times as many accepting such a conceptualization as opting for a delegate definition; in Kazakhstan, at the far end of the continuum, legislators preferred the trustee to the delegate definition by a margin of under 1 percent.[11] Country differences apart, there were other discernible differences among types of deputies. If 37 percent of all 772 deputies surveyed felt obliged to act as delegates, this proportion was slightly lower among members of deputies' factions (34 percent) and more noticeably lower among legislative leaders (30 percent), full-time deputies (29 percent), and members of radical democratic factions (19 percent). Delegate self-definitions exceeded the

Table 3.2

Deputies' Response to Question about Imperative Mandate[a]
(in percentages)

Response	Russia	USSR	Ukraine	Kazakhstan
All deputies				
Delegate response[b]	36	25	38	44
Trustee response[c]	49	70	52	44
Deputies who have had a divergence of opinion with voters on a specific question				
Delegate response	36	22	34	41
Trustee response	55	77	56	47
Deputies who have not had a divergence of opinion with voters				
Delegate response	43	44	55	54
Trustee response	40	44	37	41

Notes:
   [a] Question reads: "How do you think a deputy should act in the case of a divergence between his opinion and the opinion of his voters?"
   [b] Response reads: "The deputy should carry out the wishes of the voters."
   [c] Response reads: "The deputy should do what he considers necessary."

average for deputies elected by public organizations (45 percent) and came in below average for those elected in territorial districts (36 percent).

Like members of established parliaments,[12] post-Soviet deputies seemingly adhered to a learning curve that transported a goodly share of them away from a delegate's self-definition and toward a trustee's self-definition. As the bottom two panels of Table 3.2 show, recall of having clashed with voters on a policy question was correlated with a more hardline trustee's response. Relations with voters seem to have had some formative influence on deputies' views of their obligations: a conflictual encounter, perhaps triggering some subliminal attitude, appears to have pushed deputies toward the conviction that their own reading of the public weal ought rightly to prevail.

How Much Contact with Constituents?

Given the vacuum of information about what post-Soviet legislators' contacts with constituents have concretely amounted to, it is not out of

Table 3.3

Deputies Reporting That They Rely on Constituents for Information in Carrying Out Their Duties[a] (in percentages)

Information source	Russia	USSR	Ukraine	Kazakhstan
Individual voters	34	24	40	34
Organizations and groups	18	32	30	16
Sociological surveys of public opinion	14	19	23	14

Note:

[a] The question presented the deputies with a list of ten information sources and asked which ones they "mostly rely upon" in discharging their duties. In the USSR, Ukraine, and Kazakhstan, deputies were instructed to circle the top five sources resorted to. In the Russian Supreme Soviet, the form was somewhat different, as members were asked whether they had recourse to the given source almost always, most of the time, rarely, or never. The two top responses (almost always and most of the time) were coded as equivalent to the positive response in the other three legislatures. The total number of positive answers (slightly more than four) was almost identical in the four cases.

place to do some rudimentary bean counting. The deputies' questionnaire contained a battery of straightforward questions about the frequency of various kinds of interaction with members of the public and constituents; respondents were asked to locate their behavior in a numerical range rather than to volunteer exact numbers, which would have been subject to recall error and probably would have dissuaded many deputies from answering at all. This technique allows us to make order-of-magnitude estimates of the lawmakers' experience.

Tables 3.3 through 3.8 summarize deputies' responses to the principal questions about the frequency of representative behavior posed in the survey. In Table 3.3 we see how many deputies reported relying on constituents—individual voters, organizations and groups, and electors polled in sociological surveys—for information germane to carrying out their official duties. Approximately 25 to 40 percent of the deputies (depending on the country) said that they drew directly on individual voters' views, 14 to 23 percent claimed that they commissioned opinion surveys, and 17 to 32 percent said they relied on organizations and groups in their constituencies. These are not staggeringly high ratios, but they do signify some reasonably regular interaction.

Table 3.4 depicts the frequency ranges for deputy-reported meetings with electors in four specific formats: public meetings in their home

Table 3.4

Frequency of Deputies' Meetings with Constituents
(in percentages)

Kind of meeting	Russia	USSR	Ukraine	Kazakhstan
Public meeting in district or organization				
None or no answer	3	5	5	10
Every year	0	17	8	19
Every half-year	12	30	14	29
Every quarter	18	24	32	29
Every two months	19	12	18	7
Every month	37	13	18	7
Every week	11	0	5	0
More often	—	0	1	0
Reception hours				
None or no answer	43	6	2	25
Every year	5	42	0	0
Every half-year	4	8	1	7
Every quarter	16	16	9	15
Every two months	11	13	13	11
Every month	52	49	47	22
Every week	9	5	22	12
More often	—	2	5	7
In places of work				
None or no answer	—	11	6	23
Every year	—	6	3	8
Every half-year	—	22	10	17
Every quarter	—	29	25	27
Every two months	—	12	17	11
Every month	—	16	25	9
Every week	—	3	11	2
More often	—	2	3	2
Informal appointments with individuals				
None or no answer	—[a]	19	4	37
Every year	—	2	2	5
Every half-year	—	3	2	8
Every quarter	—	4	3	9
Every two months	—	5	4	9
Every month	—	9	9	10
Every week	—	19	23	7
More often	—	39	53	15

Note:

[a] The Russian deputies were asked a slightly different question: How many meetings with individuals did you hold in the average month (with ranges indicated), over and above office hours?

districts or organizations, scheduled office or reception hours (*chasy priyema*), encounters in places of work, and informal meetings with individual constituents. Table 3.5 charts contacts with officers of official and unofficial "public organizations." Deputy intercessions (*obrashcheniya*) with administrative officials on constituents' behalf—commonly dubbed "casework" in the literature on Western legislatures—are tabulated in Table 3.6. Table 3.7 ranges further afield to tally appearances by legislators in the print and electronic media, a mode of indirect interaction with the populace. And Table 3.8 deals with one conventional avenue of constituent-initiated contact—letters and telegrams from voters.

The first thing that comes to mind about these data is that they do portray post-Soviet legislators as carrying out actions familiar from world democratic practice. Behind the statistics lie flesh-and-blood Russian, USSR, Ukrainian, and Kazakhstan MPs getting together with their individual constituents in their parliamentary and constituency offices, in factories and farms, and in public forums; maintaining contact with top-down and bottom-up organizations at the grassroots; lifting their pens and voices to help individuals, groups, and organizations from their home base cope with recalcitrant government ministers and bureaucrats; projecting an image in the press and on radio and television; and regularly opening mail from scores of concerned and angry voters.

This block of tables constitutes a snapshot of aspects of legislator–constituent interaction in the early 1990s. Because it lacks a comparable benchmark earlier in time, it does not pin down with dead certitude the magnitude or, for that matter, the very existence of change away from Soviet-era practice, although common sense and anecdotal information gleaned from interviews hint compellingly that for most deputies there was appreciably more contact with the citizenry than there had been for deputies in the rubber-stamp legislatures that preceded Gorbachev's electoral and legislative perestroika.

This having been said, my visceral reaction to the data—reinforced by watching deputies at work—is that constituency contact, although far from negligible, was not particularly intense. Although Table 3.3 assures us that some legislators did after all consult individual voters, nonstate organizations and groups, and sociological surveys of public opinion on the questions facing them in the parliamentary chamber, it also warrants that majorities of the MPs in all four parliaments—sometimes crushing majorities—did not do so. Citizens, public opinion

Table 3.5

Number of Working Contacts with Representatives of "Public Organizations" in Average Month (in percentages)

Organization	Russia	USSR	Ukraine	Kazakhstan
Official organizations				
None or no answer	26	45	15	36
1	12	19	30	24
2–5	35	22	35	32
6–10	10	10	11	4
More than 10	16	4	9	5
Unofficial organizations				
None or no answer	16	54	11	40
1	13	13	20	19
2–5	35	28	39	35
6–10	13	5	13	5
More than 10	24	1	13	5

Table 3.6

Number of Intercessions by Deputies with Government Officials in Average Month (in percentages)

	Russia	USSR	Ukraine	Kazakhstan
On own initiative				
None or no answer	—	7	6	18
1–5	—	66	52	61
6–10	—	14	28	11
More than 10	—	13	14	10
At request of individuals				
None or no answer	2	5	3	19
1–5	39	45	41	56
6–10	27	30	32	16
More than 10	31	20	25	10
At request of groups				
None or no answer	6	11	8	36
1–5	64	60	66	49
6–10	21	22	19	10
More than 10	9	8	8	6
At request of organs and organizations on territory of district (or of organization that elected deputy)				
None or no answer	10	8	1	27
1–5	65	49	59	52
6–10	18	30	25	14
More than 10	8	14	15	8

Table 3.7

Number of Appearances of Deputies in Mass Media over Preceding Year
(in percentages)

Press articles and interviews	Russia	USSR	Ukraine	Kazakhstan
Central (USSR and RSFSR) press				
None or no answer	62	39	90	86
1	19	22	6	9
2–5	10	27	3	3
6–10	7	4	1	0
More than 10	2	9	0	2
Republic and local press				
None or no answer	—	17	—	—
1	—	6	—	—
2–5	—	49	—	—
6–10	—	18	—	—
More than 10	—	10	—	—
Republic press				
None or no answer	—	—	32	36
1	—	—	21	27
2–5	—	—	33	28
6–10	—	—	10	3
More than 10	—	—	3	5
Local press				
None or no answer	6	—	3	23
1	2	—	5	18
2–5	29	—	42	44
6–10	29	—	32	10
More than 10	35	—	19	5
Interviews on radio and TV				
USSR and RSFSR channels				
None or no answer	—	33	90	88
1	—	23	9	7
2–5	—	36	4	5
6–10	—	6	0	1
More than 10	—	3	0	0
Republic and local channels				
None or no answer	—	17	32	32
1	—	10	22	27
2–5	—	52	34	31
6–10	—	14	9	10
More than 10	—	8	3	2

polls, and organizations stood far behind a plethora of other sources as pools of information for the deputies. In the Russian Supreme Soviet, for example, individual voters (consulted routinely by 34 percent of the deputies) ranked sixth among ten information sources, behind the

Table 3.8

Letters and Telegrams Received by Deputies in Average Month
(in percentages)

	Russia	USSR	Ukraine	Kazakhstan
None or no answer	2	1	0	6
1–10	37	39	35	57
11–50	45	46	50	36
51–100	10	12	11	0
101–250	3	0	4	0
More than 250	4	2	1	0

legislators' friends (at 84 percent), the mass communications media (78 percent), fellow deputies (58 percent), scientific literature and specialists (49 percent), and deputies' personal assistants (36 percent); organizations stood still lower, in ninth place, and opinion surveys brought up the rear of the ten sources.[13]

No less troubling from the standpoint of democratization and the prospects for decent representation, in every species of contact making we discover deputies who undertook precious little of the substantive activity or even none of it whatsoever. At the slothful pole, 37 percent of the members surveyed in the Supreme Soviet of Kazakhstan did not meet with constituents on an impromptu basis, 25 percent did not hold regular office hours, 23 percent did not see constituents at places of work, and 10 percent sat in on no public meetings in their home district or organization (see Table 3.4). In the Russian Supreme Soviet, where the median MP interacted much more with constituents than in Kazakhstan, a paltry 9 percent of the deputies scheduled office hours more than once a month, and only 11 percent participated in open meetings with electors in their districts more than once a month. Few deputies in any of the four assemblies had more than five working contacts per month, or about one a week, with official and unofficial organizations (see Table 3.5). The modal response for casework intercessions with administrative officials was one to five per month, or up to about one per week (see Table 3.6). Deputies had seldom conspired in more than ten press articles or media interviews over the preceding year—approximately one such appearance in the average month (see Table 3.7). And, so far as constituent input is concerned, the modal number of letters and telegrams received by deputies in the average month was eleven to fifty in Russia, the USSR Supreme Soviet, and Ukraine, and one to ten in Kazakhstan (see Table 3.8).

Comparative evidence bears out the impression of fitful and lackadaisical interaction with constituents. To mention only several empirical meters:

- Members of the U.S. House of Representatives studied by Richard Fenno averaged thirty-five trips back to their districts each year; these trips were occasions for copious consultation with political contacts and endeavors at mending fences and building bridges to voters and interest groups.[14] The archetypal post-Soviet deputy in the early 1990s paid a visit to his district or base organization about once a month, or approximately one-third as often.

- The mail bag brought more than twenty-five letters per week to 88 percent of British MPs in the 1960s, and more than fifty letters per week to 50 percent of MPs. Forty-eight percent of members of the West German Bundestag received more than twenty-five.[15] In contrast, 17 percent of Russian deputies, fewer than 15 percent of USSR and Ukraine deputies, and no Kazakhstan deputies at all got as many as fifty letters and telegrams *per month.*

- One survey found U.S. congressmen and their staffs to be providing seventy-one instances of constituency service per week; the number in Britain was thirty-six. Most American and British legislators proudly advertise their casework assistance to voters and publicize the regular "surgeries," as they are termed in Britain, where lawmakers and staffers make themselves available to lend a hand.[16] The modal number of errands run for individuals by Russian deputies, and by their counterparts in the USSR, Ukraine, and Kazakhstan parliaments, was one to five *per month.*

Explaining Representative Behavior

If post-Soviet deputies' engagement with constituents and provision of services to them is as desultory as it has been, then the question inevitably arises, why is this so? How can this low-performance syndrome be accounted for?

One avenue of attack would be to attempt holistic comparisons with other countries (mature democracies included) that evince different magnitudes of involvement, trying to highlight causal elements that might give rise to the discrepancies. Political culture and the dead weight of the Soviet past would loom large in almost any such macro-level analysis. It is beyond controversy, for one thing, that deputies' role expectations, as mirrored in Table 3.1 and other evidence, were often inimical to vigorous representative activity. The roots of these preconceptions were complex; they joined pieces of the historic Soviet mindset (the distaste for grassroots political participation) to new attitudes bred in reaction to Communist authoritarianism and its decay (especially the eager embrace of the right to debate and make laws, unfettered by Communist Party controls). National tradition and social-ization would incline a democratically elected legislator in the United States, France, or India to treat voters differently and to afford public and constituent relations a higher priority in his workweek.

A macro explanation could not fail to acknowledge the distinctive institutional environment of early postcommunism. The Gorbachevian reforms had depressingly little positive impact on the capacity of legis-lators to act in concert with their constituents after election day. While there was vague rhetoric aplenty about legislative "professionalism," very few deputies acquired, or feasibly could have acquired, the out-look of the professional lawmaker, imbued in parliamentary folkways and committed to elective service as a vocation. The motivational tie that studies of Western legislatures have stressed as infusing the urge to be attentive to constituents—the desire to build name recognition and popularity among the electorate, and thereby to maximize chances of reelection—was frayed from the very beginning. When it came to mundane support systems to assist deputies in reaching out to voters—offices in the legislative building and the constituency, secretarial help, money for travel, and the like—provision was either nonexistent or exiguous.[17] Political parties, which might have opened up another channel to social interests, were tiny, disorganized, and fractious.[18]

Mass attitudes should also figure in any comprehensive theory. One would not take a large risk in hazarding that a basic reason legislators were as a class so deaf to voices from below is that their constituents let them get away with it. On most Soviet and ex-Soviet territory in the late 1980s and early 1990s, there were at best the first tender shoots of an associational, participation-minded "civil society." Absent the ex-ternal pressure to be more forthcoming, lawmakers as often as not could afford to busy themselves with what caught their fancy, without worry about political penalty for not opening the door to constituents. The prevalent popular stance toward government and all its works was one of alienation and mistrust. Many citizens resented even minor improvements in parliamentarians' conditions of work (such as giving them more and better-paid assistants) that, among other things, would have enhanced their ability to keep in touch with voters.[19]

Two reservations must be lodged about this holistic line of reasoning. First, it glosses over the fact that not all members of post-Soviet parliaments behaved alike. Granted, the median deputy kept a low profile in the representative arena; but the tables presented above do testify to not a few legislators breaking the mold, being either more active or more passive than the average. Second, it is readily apparent that the constituency nexus assumed different shapes for different categories of deputies, and not just for different individuals. The easiest discontinuity to sniff out from the tables is among country groups. In terms of timing of meetings with citizens, for example, Russian Supreme Soviet deputies were more active than the others, Kazakhstan deputies were the least assertive, and Ukraine and USSR lawmakers fell in between (see Table 3.4).

It is here that the micro-level survey data can profitably be brought back into play. They enlighten us not only about average or typical behavior but about the extent and distribution of the variation among individual legislators. They describe, furthermore, not only constituent relations as such but traits, attitudes, and actions of the legislators that may furnish cogent explanations of constituency-regarding behavior. Having at our fingertips systematic information about possible causes as well as observed effects for so large a number of deputies, we have the opportunity to test causal hypotheses using statistical methods.

In order to do so, it is necessary first to hammer out a summary quantitative indicator or indicators for the dependent variable. The constituent-related behaviors treated in this essay are quite specialized and diverse, and of limited inherent interest. We would like to have indexes of representative performance that bracket together more picayune measures or tap some shared or overriding dimension or dimensions.

To accomplish this, I recoded the answers to the relevant survey questions to register the midpoints in the response ranges, not the ranges themselves.[20] I subsequently subjected these data to factor analysis, a procedure that extracts dimensions of variance that may be posited to underlie a multiplicity of directly observable variables. The

Table 3.9

Factor Loadings for Deputies' Accessibility to Constituents and Casework on Constituents' Behalf

Variable	Accessibility	Casework
Public meetings in district or organization	.748	−.007
Informal appointments with individual voters	.658	.100
Office hours	.518	.023
Intercessions at request of groups	−.003	.854
Intercessions at request of organizations	−.047	.798
Intercessions at request of individuals	.237	.779

Note: Loadings derived from a principal components factor analysis with varimax rotation.

factor analysis was performed on the entire pooled data set. Experimental runs with all questions touching on relations with the public disclosed that a pair of strong factors could be isolated in the responses: one tracing deputies' physical accessibility to constituents, and the other describing the undertaking of casework on constituents' behalf. Table 3.9 gives the factor loadings from an analysis performed with the six survey-defined variables that consistently bore most heavily on the two factors ascertained.[21]

I could confidently proceed at this juncture to compute summary dependent variables capturing the variance on the two dimensions: (1) an Accessibility Score, formed by adding the recoded values for the three variables to load high on the first factor (attendance at public gatherings, informal meetings with individual voters, and periodicity of office hours); and (2) a Casework Score, summing the three variables highly intercorrelated with the second factor (intercessions with officials at the behest of groups, organizations, and individuals). The mean values for these two measures, for the four country subsets and for all 772 deputies, are set down in Table 3.10. Notice that the means fluctuated from parliament to parliament, but that there was a much wider spectrum across countries for the Accessibility Score (where the top-ranking parliament, Russia's, scored on average 4.2 times the lowest-ranking parliament, Kazakhstan's) than for the Casework Score (where the ratio of top-ranked Ukraine to bottom-ranked Kazakhstan was only 1.7:1).

Table 3.10

Deputies' Mean Accessibility Scores and Casework Scores

Parliament	Accessibility Score	Casework Score
Russia	14.73	22.63
USSR	6.06	20.82
Ukraine	8.74	23.42
Kazakhstan	3.52	13.54
Combined	9.92	21.17

Comparison of country averages, although of some utility, is no substitute for a deeper analysis. Table 3.10 adduces but one independent variable, the national unit, without any control for the potential effect of other explanatory variables. Who is to say that the ostensibly large intercountry differences manifested on the Accessibility Score are not spurious and that some other variable or variables do not lie behind them? We ought to consider what such conditions might be and systematically screen for their influence.

I conducted such a test by running separate ordinary-least-squares regressions against the two constructed dependent variables. Sixteen independent variables, sorted into a half-dozen conceptual categories, were selected to represent plausible causes of interdeputy variation in constituent relations.

Personal Attributes

One possibility to be considered is that deputies with certain personal traits—youth (and perforce energy) and high social status are the ones on which we have information—would be disposed to take their representative responsibilities more seriously than others. The indicators used for these attributes were age group (coded on a five-point scale) and possession of a higher education (coded as a categorical or dummy variable).[22]

Electoral and Institutional Rules and Structures

Could it be that the formal rules and structures in which legislators were enmeshed, which were by no means consistent from parliament to parliament and even within parliaments, affected deputy–constituent relations? Some rules and norms were mandatory; others were permissive, giving deputies bounded opportunities to define an organizational niche for themselves. The survey threw up data on six structural features of theoretical interest: mode of election of the deputy (territorial district versus designation by a public organization, as occurred in the USSR and Kazakhstan parliaments); full or partial membership in the legislature (an issue only for our Russian deputies); full-time or part-time participation in the legislature's work; occupancy of a leadership position in the legislature; number of personal assistants retained by the deputy; and concurrent membership in a legislative assembly at another level of administration. Aside from personal assistants, each of these indicators was coded as a dummy variable.

Self-Definition of Role

All respondents were asked whether they took a delegate's or a trustee's approach to the issue of imperative mandate. Perhaps deputies who espoused the delegate's point of view, which makes it incumbent to follow their electors' wishes rather than their own in making policy decisions, would be more constituency-minded than their colleagues. To ascertain whether this was true, delegate orientation was introduced into the regression as a dummy variable.

Political Affiliations and Ambition

Did affiliation with a deputy's faction within the legislature, and the greater density of interaction with fellow-minded legislators that it would entail, attune a politician more to constituency relations (or, obversely, attune him less)? An a priori case can be built for either thesis. What about membership in a faction of radical democrats? It was mentioned above that Westernizing democrats leaned toward a trustee's role definition, which would imply a relatively aloof relationship with constituents, but one could imagine them being more constituency-friendly if they interpreted democratic values differently. Faction membership and membership specifically in a radical democratic caucus were both coded as dummy independent variables for purposes of the analysis.[23]

Political ambition is a related variable of interest. One might suppose that those relatively few legislators (19 percent of our total sample) who planned to seek reelection would, all things considered, cultivate warmer relations with their voters than would one-term deputies. Intent to stand for reelection was entered as a dummy variable.[24]

Constituency Pressure

The analyst could put the shoe on the other foot by placing the emphasis on constituents themselves, not the characteristics or motivation of the deputy. Could it not be that encouragement and pressure from voters to be responsive would induce deputies to behave accordingly? The more the input flowing spontaneously from the constituency, it could be postulated, the more the deputy would comply in word and deed. I have employed as an independent variable the one hard measure I have for constituency stimulus: quantity of letters and telegrams received monthly by the deputy (recoded as an absolute figure instead of a range).

Country Context

A final inviting explanation is also contextual, but works on the plane of the nation rather than the localized electoral constituency. It holds that some characteristic or alloy of characteristics of the whole country and its political system will make themselves felt on the constituent nexus whatever the effect of personal, structural, and other variables. Such a theory might conceivably forecast national differences to be so decisive as to make other factors immaterial. To enable this argument to be verified, each of the four country units whose parliaments are under the microscope was coded as a dummy variable. The reference category in the regression analysis (omitted as required to preserve degrees of freedom) is the USSR.

These, then, are the explanatory variables we are in a position to probe. The coefficients generated by regressing them against the deputies' Accessibility Scores are set forth in Table 3.11, and against the Casework Score in Table 3.12. They tell a fascinating and in some respects counterintuitive story.

For deputies' accessibility, six independent variables (not counting the constant intercept) yielded regression coefficients statistically sig-

Table 3.11

Regression Coefficients for Accessibility Score

Independent variable	B	Beta
Personal attributes		
Age group	.013	.002
Higher education	.836	.041
Electoral and institutional rules and structures		
Election by a public organization	.252	.009
Full member of legislature	−.465	−.026
Works exclusively in legislature	−1.112*	−.078
Leadership position	−.445	−.028
Number of personal assistants	.861*	.107
Concurrent member of another legislature	.267	.018
Self-definition of role		
Defines self as delegate	−.346	−.023
Political affiliations and ambition		
Member of a deputies' faction	.147	.009
Member of a radical democratic faction	.886	.053
Intends to seek reelection	.746	.041
Constituency pressure		
Letters and telegrams received	.013*	.059
Country context		
Russia	7.770*	.530
Ukraine	1.599*	.103
Kazakhstan	−3.195*	−.164
Intercept	5.073*	—

Notes:
   * Significant at the .05 level.
   Mean of dependent variable = 9.92. R^2 = .381.

nificant at the .05 level. The regression went no small way toward predicting the dependent variable, explaining 38 percent of the variance in it.

Not one of the indicators signifying personal attributes, role definition, or political affiliations and ambition was reliably predictive of an accessible style. Of the two structural variables correlated with high exposure to voters, one (number of personal aides) had a positive sign, yet the second (a full-time commitment to service in the legislature) had a negative sign. The former result is not hard to grasp, inasmuch as staff assistants gave overburdened deputies a pragmatic hook for cooperating with constituents. The latter result, surprising at first blush, makes sense if we remind ourselves of deputies' predominantly nega-

Table 3.12

Regression Coefficients for Casework Score

Independent variable	B	Beta
Personal attributes		
Age group	1.756	.067
Higher education	−5.000*	−.076
Electoral and institutional rules and structures		
Election by a public organization	2.342	.024
Full member of legislature	−1.258	−.021
Works exclusively in legislature	1.133	.024
Leadership position	6.213*	.120
Number of personal assistants	−.943	−.036
Concurrent member of another legislature	.769	.015
Self-definition of role		
Defines self as delegate	1.025	.021
Political affiliations and ambition		
Member of a deputies' faction	4.988*	.097
Member of a radical democratic faction	−2.607	−.048
Intends to seek reelection	1.384	.023
Constituency pressure		
Letters and telegrams received	.158*	.224
Country context		
Russia	1.879	.039
Ukraine	5.425	.107
Kazakhstan	−.394	−.006
Intercept	9.018	—

Notes:
 * Significant at the .05 level.
 Mean of dependent variable = 21.17. R^2 = .098.

tive view of constituent relations. Paradoxically, the more hours they had at their disposal to carry out parliamentary tasks, the more miserly they were with visitations with their electors. Note that some of the deductively more attractive hypotheses about constituency relations—above all, the notion of a link with reelection intentions—are disproved by the quantitative evidence. The first crop of post-Soviet lawmakers were not subject to the "electoral connection" so visible among their cousins in the United States Congress.[25]

It is intriguing that four of the six independent variables associated in nonrandom fashion with greater approachability to constituents were about political context—local and systemic. Clearly, pressure from the deputy's constituency, quantified here by letters and telegrams received, did matter. The more the advice and exhortation from below, the harder legislators tried in return to keep lines of communication open.

Equally clearly, country context mattered, and it mattered a great deal. The country effect was the most potent of any that the regression analysis uncovered.[26] All other things being equal, Russian deputies scored substantially higher on accessibility to constituents than the reference group (the USSR deputies), and Ukrainian deputies somewhat higher. Kazakhstan deputies deviated in the opposite direction, scoring much lower than their USSR counterparts and lower still than the Russians and Ukrainians. The ultimate reasons for these cross-country contrasts, though not susceptible to direct analysis from the survey data, were imbedded in the changing institutional and cultural environments within which legislators operated. At the turn of the 1990s, the overall political situation in the Russian Federation—the heady optimism about democratization, Yeltsin's populism at its apex,[27] mass mobilization (in the big cities, at least) for the revolt against the Soviet center—*evoked* a more populist style than elsewhere. In Kazakhstan, at the opposite extreme, almost everything, from palace leadership to mass mood, seemed to conspire against accessibility. For our second dependent variable, the Casework Score, the tale is markedly different and more obscure. The explanatory power of our independent variables was only 10 percent, about one-quarter of the leverage gained upon the Accessibility Score. By inference, much more of this behavior resulted from extraneous factors or from idiosyncratic variation from deputy to deputy.

Three of the four independent variables for which the regression rendered statistically significant coefficients had no predictive horsepower for deputy accessibility. For willingness to intercede in individual, group, and organizational petitions to officials, one of the two personal attributes, higher education, was correlated with a high score, but negatively. Better educated and, by extension, more sophisticated legislators shied away from casework.[28]

The single structural variable to be robustly correlated with diligent casework was occupancy of a leadership role in the legislature. This association was presumably spawned by two mutually reinforcing factors: the greater objective influence that parliamentary leaders wielded with the bureaucracy, and the subjective perception among constituents that leaders had greater authority and thus would be forceful brokers with the bureaucracy. In the area of political affiliations and ambition, one explanatory variable pans out: membership in a parliamentary faction. The causal connection here is not self-evident, but one may speculate that participation in a legislative caucus deepened deputies' knowledge of governmental affairs, inspired them to link casework with broader issues, and augmented their personal connections.

Contextual variables were heartily predictive of deputies' Accessibility Scores. For Casework Scores, one contextual indicator only—constituency pressure, as measured by the inflow of letters and telegrams—significantly colored the dependent variable. Constituency input was the only predictor to attain statistical significance for *both* of our dependent variables. The second dependent variable, by the usual methodological yardsticks, outstripped all other independent variables in causal weight.[29] At the same time, the country effect was in this instance nil. The very same Russian, Ukrainian, and Kazakhstan parliaments that differed so dramatically in one realm of constituent relations—deputy accessibility—were peas in a pod in the other dimension—service to the public through casework.[30]

Conclusions

Generalizations about the constituency nexus in legislative politics during the Soviet transition must be mounted with caution, as our evidentiary base is woefully thin and the scene we behold highly volatile. Survey data from four parliaments in 1991–92 do permit us, however, to try out several tentative conclusions.

Representation was indisputably a low priority for the parliamentarians we observed, although it loomed rather larger in reality than deputies wanted it to be in the ideal. Constituency relations existed nonetheless, and took a miscellany of concrete forms, for which we have been able to articulate empirical indicators. By these measuring rods, post-Soviet legislators fell demonstrably short of the performance standards set by established democracies: they had far less contact with voters and transacted far less business with them and on their behalf.

Synoptic accounts of the behavior of all or most post-Soviet legislators vis-à-vis their electors are more impressionistic, and necessarily less grounded in checkable facts, than explanations that take as their unit of analysis the individual deputy. I undertook such an analysis by segregating two dimensions of representative activity and using multiple regression to estimate the causal impact of a cluster of independent variables. Simple accessibility to citizens proved easier to explain than the second dimension, constituency service through casework, but in both cases some regularities and orderly relationships emerged.

What do the causal relationships uncovered portend for the future? While some, perhaps many, of the attitudes and structural arrangements described here will resist change, it would be a mistake to think of them as engraved in stone. The obliviousness to the effect of constituency service on reelection chances, for example, may fade if and when the rewards and perquisites of a legislative career increase in value and if political entrepreneurs demonstrate the electoral payoffs of patronage, the pork barrel, and doing and being seen as doing petty favors for voters.

Our data point unambiguously to the importance of social and political context. The exceptionally large country effect noted for deputies' accessibility to constituents is unlikely to vanish any time soon, although most of the post-Soviet states—Russia prominently among them—have such unstable and underinstitutionalized political systems that precise country trajectories cannot be projected with any confidence. The consistently strong effect on both dependent variables of local constituency input suggests the need to take a systemic approach to political representation and indeed to postcommunist institutional development as a whole. If the survey data quarried here are any guide, no change will do more for the quality of political representation than the evolution of a civil society and of the norms of "civil engagement" that Robert Putnam has dissected in his recent study of Italy.[31] Russians, Ukrainians, and others will, to a considerable extent, get the representation and the respect from political elites that they demand and deserve.

Notes

1. The same point about relations with society applies to executive institutions, but that is not the subject of the present chapter or volume.

2. See the pioneering essay by Samuel H. Beer, "The British Legislature and the Problem of Mobilizing Consent," originally published in 1966 and reprinted in Philip Norton, ed., *Legislatures* (Oxford: Oxford University Press, 1990), pp. 62–80.

3. Behavioral research on legislatures is ultimately concerned with explaining how decisions are made, but, according to John Wahlke, "focuses more on the

individual choice-making behavior, the decisional premises of legislators and others, tending to view external pressures and influences through the perceptions of the legislative actors subjected to them." In the 1960s and 1970s, studies in this area broadened to take in legislators' understandings of their roles and their relationships with parliamentary colleagues and other participants in the political process. "The term 'legislative behavior' thus comes to cover perceptions, attitudes, beliefs, habit patterns, and actions of a variety far greater than was originally suggested by the term. Increasingly, 'legislative behavior' is used to refer not just to intracameral activities of legislators and the ideas and attitudes relating thereto, but to extracameral behavioral phenomena—being recruited and campaigning for legislative office, errand running for constituents, and many others." John C. Wahlke, "Contemporary Perspectives on Legislatures," in Heinz Eulau and John C. Wahlke, eds., *The Politics of Representation: Continuities in Theory and Research* (Beverly Hills and London: Sage Publications, 1978), pp. 242–243.

4. Deputies from national-territorial districts tended disproportionately to belong to the Supreme Soviet, since there were only 168 of them, and 125 Supreme Soviet seats to fill. There were 900 members from territorial districts, eligible for the same number of Supreme Soviet seats, 125.

5. If 58 percent of the Russian full members polled held leadership positions (such as chairman, deputy chairman, or secretary of a committee or subcommittee), only 23 percent of the Russian deputies not on the Supreme Soviet, 30 percent of the USSR deputies, 20 percent of the Ukraine deputies, and 13 percent of the Kazakhstan deputies held such positions.

6. The exact percentages working full-time were 73 percent for the USSR, 74 percent for the full members of the Russian Supreme Soviet, 46 percent for the Russian associate members, 35 percent in Ukraine, and 23 percent in Kazakhstan.

7. The difficulties with the format were evident before the Ukraine and Kazakhstan surveys were done, but the costs of altering the form of the questions outweighed any benefits. Among other things, retention of the flawed original form maximized comparability of the Ukraine and Kazakhstan answers with the USSR and Russia.

8. For ranking purposes, I amalgamated the fifth and lower-ranking category or categories into a single set when there were more than five options.

9. USSR deputies from public organizations gave defense of constituents an average score of 1.57 (with 1.00 being the highest score), versus an average for all USSR deputies of 2.12. Kazakhstan deputies elected by organizations rated constituent defense at 2.14 (average 2.50). Radical deputies from the Interregional Group in the USSR Supreme Soviet gave this same role an average score of 3.00; Democratic Kazakhstan deputies also scored it at 3.00.

10. There are fifteen pairings, not sixteen, because the question about defense of the interests of a social or occupational group was not asked in Russia.

11. Both figures round to 44 percent but, reckoned more precisely, they were 44.4 percent for the trustee response and 43.5 percent for the delegate response.

12. See Gerhard Loewenberg and Samuel C. Patterson, *Comparing Legislatures* (Lanham, MD: University Press of America, 1979), pp. 180–181.

13. In the USSR Supreme Soviet, organizations and groups ranked eighth, individual voters ninth, and sociological surveys tenth. In Ukraine, voters were in

fifth place, organizations in seventh, and sociological surveys in tenth place. In Kazakhstan, voters stood seventh, organizations ninth, and surveys tenth. The mass media were the most frequently utilized source of information in the USSR, Ukraine, and Kazakhstan parliaments.

14. Richard F. Fenno, Jr., *Home Style: House Members in Their Districts* (Boston: Little, Brown, 1978), p. 35.

15. Consult Loewenberg and Patterson, *Comparing Legislatures,* pp. 174–175; also Ivor Crewe, "MPs and their Constituents in Britain: How Strong Are the Links?" in Vernon Bogdanor, ed., *Representatives of the People? Parliamentarians and Constituents in Western Democracies* (Aldershot: Gower Publishing, 1985), pp. 52–54.

16. Bruce Cain, John Ferejohn, and Morris Fiorina, *The Personal Vote: Constituency Service and Electoral Independence* (Cambridge, MA: Harvard University Press, 1987), pp. 63, 70–71.

17. In all four of the legislatures studied, the ordinary deputy would have one or two personal assistants (*pomoshchniki*) paid out of the state budget. But the salaries authorized were so abysmally low that most assistants held down another job. Even in the USSR Supreme Soviet, rank-and-file MPs shared offices and telephones with colleagues. Stenographic services were niggardly: a common sight on the floor of all four parliaments was of deputies handwriting correspondence, including letters to constituents.

18. Strictly speaking, there were no organized party caucuses in the four legislatures when I carried out my interviews. Groups such as Communists of Russia in the RSFSR Supreme Soviet banded together only some members of an existent party (in this case the Communist Party); some other intraparliamentary fractions were the kernels of what would later be political parties.

19. Interviews showed this to be an issue in all four of the parliaments studied. The legislative leaderships often made cynically self-serving use of public resistance to expenditures on benefits for MPs, employing popular disaffection as an argument against improvements that, among other things, would have made ordinary deputies less dependent on committee chairmen and the presidium for information and routine support.

20. I made one adjustment during the recoding, to the subscores for informal meetings with individuals. The question put to the USSR, Ukraine, and Kazakhstan deputies paralleled the questions about other kinds of access, asking whether they had such meetings once a year, once a half-year, once a quarter, once every two months, once a month, once a week, or more often. RSFSR legislators checked off how many meetings they held in the average month, and had no option to signal less frequent meetings. I was loath to throw away so promising an indicator of openness to voters. Thirty-nine percent of the USSR deputies and 53 percent in Ukraine (15 percent in Kazakhstan) reported having impromptu meetings more than once a week. For other contact types, I recoded this response as constituting six acts per month. Interviews with deputies convinced me that for personal meetings, ten would be a better estimate; I recoded the variable thus for the USSR, Ukraine, and Kazakhstan. For Russia, interviews suggested that the question form had inflated the responses. I therefore recoded the most frequent response category (described as over twenty on the questionnaire) as twenty. Even after the change, Russian deputies still show an unusual

number of meetings with individual electors—but they come out ahead on most other indexes of constituency contact in any event.

21. The variables omitted here have to do primarily with appearances in the mass media, contacts with official and unofficial organizations, and letters and telegrams from voters. Both media appearances and contacts with organizations are public relations but not necessarily constituent relations, inasmuch as such behavior is not aimed narrowly at the district or organization that sent the deputy to parliament. Letters and telegrams are voter-initiated, not legislator-initiated, and the variable summarizing them is treated in the ensuing analysis as an independent variable, not part of the dependent variable.

22. The age question had to be framed in age ranges, owing to fears that a query about exact year of birth might compromise respondents' anonymity. The age ranges employed had values for age under thirty, in the thirties, in the forties, in the fifties, and in the sixties and seventies.

23. Seventy-one percent of all deputies interviewed belonged to one or more deputies' fraction, and 25 percent were members of a radical democratic faction. The proportion of deputies affiliated with a faction ranged from 84 percent for the Russian Supreme Soviet to 82 percent for the USSR, 76 percent for Ukraine, and 19 percent for Kazakhstan. Membership in a radical democratic faction was 29 percent in Russia, 28 percent in Ukraine, 19 percent in Kazakhstan, and 12 percent in the USSR Supreme Soviet.

24. The proportion of deputies indicating intent to run again was highest for the Russian deputies (25 percent of the sample), followed by Kazakhstan (24 percent), Ukraine (16 percent), and the USSR (a lowly 4 percent).

25. The classic argument relating "the single-minded interest in re-election" to legislative behavior is David R. Mayhew, *Congress: The Electoral Connection* (New Haven, CT: Yale University Press, 1974). But Mayhew was writing specifically about the U.S. Congress and did not claim universal validity for his theory, pointing out that there are countries in which legislators are content to serve short terms. Only time will tell whether the Russian and other post-Soviet parliaments will tend toward the model Mayhew found in the United States.

26. Gauging the relative importance of explanatory variables in regression analysis is fraught with difficulty. But one criterion often used is to compare the magnitude of the Beta coefficients, which are computed with all variables expressed in standardized (Z score) form. The highest Beta scores recorded in Table 3.11 are for the Russia and Kazakhstan country variables, with the Ukraine country indicator ranking a close fourth behind the third-ranked personal assistants variable. Another sometimes helpful technique is to introduce the independent variables stepwise, seeing the effect of the addition of variables at the margin on the proportion of variance explained. When the three country variables are entered as a group subsequent to the entry of all the other variables, the variance explained increases sharply, from 22 percent to 38 percent.

27. Boris Yeltsin, it should not be overlooked, was himself chairman of the Russian Supreme Soviet from May 1990 until his election as president of the republic on June 12, 1991. My survey of Russian deputies was done in the final few weeks of his tenure as parliamentary chairman.

28. The second personal attribute, age group, was also positively associated with the Casework Score, but not quite at the desired significance level ($p = .07$).

29. The most serviceable gauge is again the size of the Beta scores, where constituency pressure far exceeds all other explanatory variables.

30. The positive coefficient for Ukraine is sizable and does come close to clearing the conventional significance threshold ($p = .08$). Stepwise entry of the noncountry and country variables results in an increase to explanatory power of merely seven-tenths of one percent.

31. Robert D. Putnam, *Making Democracy Work: Civic Traditions in Modern Italy* (Princeton, NJ: Princeton University Press, 1993).

4

The Structure of the Russian Legislature and Its Impact on Party Development

Jerry F. Hough

Russian democracy has had many defects, but one of the most important has been the lack of meaningful parties to structure choices for the electorate. Even when the 1993 election law forced the creation of parties by having half the Duma deputies elected by party list and giving the parties having strong incentives to run candidates in the districts, the fourteen parties that appeared on the ballot still did not give the electorate a meaningful choice. None was the equivalent of a U.S. Democratic, British Labour, or German Social-Democratic Party. The closest approximation to a conservative party in the Western sense—Russia's Choice—opposed big business and the pro-tariff policy that conservative parties always adopt in the early and middle stages of capitalist development!

Moreover, whatever the defects of the choice given the voter in the 1993 party list election, they paled in comparison to the problems in the district elections for the Duma and the Council of the Federation. Less than half of the candidates in the Duma election had party affiliations, and many of the affiliations candidates did have were relatively meaningless. Party identification was virtually absent in the case of the major candidates in the Soviet of the Federation elections. When local elections were held in 1994 and 1995, party participation was sporadic, and in March 1995 there was little evidence in the regions of serious preparation for the scheduled December 1995 Duma elections.[1]

The consequences of the ill-formed party system have been those predicted by party theory. Voter interest and turnout was heavy in the enthusiasm of the first elections in 1989 and 1990, but it has declined seriously since that time. Moreover, the real participation in the Duma district elections and the local elections of 1993 was much lower than that in the party list voting. Voters were given the option of voting for "none of the above," and this option received 15 to 20 percent of the vote in the Duma elections in large cities. The complete results in Moscow and St. Petersburg were never even reported, surely out of embarrassment over this fact.

The situation was even worse in the major local election held simultaneously with the national election in December 1993—that to the Moscow City Duma. "None of the above" received more votes than the winner in 31 of the 35 districts—e.g, 37,681 vs. 29,180 for the winner in District 1, 30,379 vs. 18,017 for the winner in District 2.[2] Since "none of above" received much less support in the party list vote, it was not a sign of general alienation, but a protest against a list of candidates about whom the voters knew virtually nothing. That informational function is one of the chief ones to be filled by parties, and it was not being filled in Russia.

There are many reasons that meaningful parties have been slow to form in Russia. Competing parties were prohibited at the time of the 1989 election, and the clause about the leading role of the Communist Party was not removed in 1990 until after the nomination of candidates to the Russian legislature was completed. Hence factions and parties had to develop in the legislature after the election. Yet the development of a party system from within a legislature system is not a negative phenomenon. Such parties tend to arise around real legislative issues, and they tend to be populated with politicians whose legislative activity has led them to develop the skills of compromise and accommodation. The unfortunate fact about the Russian experience was that the factions in the legislature did not develop into meaningful parties.

This chapter will explore the reasons for the failure of the legislative factions to become the basis for meaningful political parties. Many of these reasons are either inherent to the early stages of democratization or to be found outside the legislature. To an extent that has not been fully appreciated in either the Russian case or the general theory of party development, however, some of the reasons lie in the way the work of the Russian legislature itself was organized. If the evolution of the political system in the early years of Russian independence is to be understood and a comprehensive theory of democratization to be developed, analysts must understand the logic of these subtle factors and the manner in which they worked themselves out.

The Development of Factions in the Russian Legislature

Political life in Russia has changed so much in the last five years that it is hard to remember the old system. A Westerner could see activity corresponding to Western definitions of interest groups and factions in that political system,[3] but this activity could not be acknowledged in the Soviet Union. Lenin thought political organizations and parties that "represented other classes" had no right to exist. He believed the "trade union consciousness" of workers also served the interests of the capitalists and had no more right to be represented in the political process than did capitalist interests. Lenin was utterly contemptuous of the "parliamentarianism" that permitted the representation of diverse class, party, and intraparty interests, and he forbade factions within the Communist Party that might perform the same function.

Even the USSR Congress of People's Deputies and Supreme Soviet elected in 1989 were slow to recognize the legitimacy of organized group activity. The Russian legislature elected in 1990, however, was quite different from the USSR Congress even in its presession organizational activities, not to mention its first session. A *Komsomol'skaia pravda* correspondent caught this point in the first days of the first Congress of People's Deputies:

> Strains have appeared in the political melody of the Russian Congress that were never heard previously. Take this example. A deputy gets up and introduces a suggestion from the deputy group "Smena." Another makes a proposal from Democratic Russia. And listen carefully. No one fell into a swoon or began to wail about schism, about opposition, about the danger of factional division. Compare this with the USSR Congress. They only hinted at an inter-regional deputy group, and noise erupted. They tried to talk about a multi-party system. Uproar.[4]

The recognition of the legitimacy of group activity based on political ideas rather than institutional base came even before the Congress opened. On March 31 and April 1, a group of deputies met at the invitation of Mikhail Bocharov, a close associate of Boris Yeltsin's, to form "an association of deputies" called Democratic Russia in preparation for the forthcoming Congress. In reality, Democratic Russia was an embryonic party whose primary purpose was to elect Yeltsin as chairman of the Supreme Soviet and to enact the radical program. Two hundred deputies attended, but Bocharov claimed that 370 deputies supported the association.[5] When the first organizational meeting of deputies was held on April 30, again only 215 deputies appeared,[6] but Bocharov proved to be right about the size of Democratic Russia's consistent voting support at the first Congress. The difference between 215 and 370 reflected a division between hardcore radicals and more moderate reformers, who formed an uneasy alliance inside Democratic Russia.

Instead of denouncing Democratic Russia as an unacceptable faction, the conservatives formed another large group, Communists of Russia, which was said to embrace 355 deputies. In a sense, Communists of Russia was misnamed, for nearly 90 percent of all deputies were members of the Communist Party at the time of the election, including three-quarters of the 400 most radical deputies supporting Democratic Russia.[7] In practice, Communists of Russia included the more conservative deputies, but the group was as divided as Democratic Russia, for it included both the relative conservatives who still supported Gorbachev in 1990 and the hard-core conservatives who opposed Gorbachev. The one issue that united Communists of Russia was support for the continuation of the Soviet Union as a federal system. Hence they were generally united in opposing Yeltsin and his attempts to create a loose confederation or to break up the Soviet Union, but some thought a reconciliation between him and Gorbachev might be the solution to the country's problems.

Even in the most repressive years of the Soviet system, the Communist leaders normally observed democratic forms in governing the country. The old Supreme Soviet had its agenda determined in the party apparatus and approved all legislation unanimously, but it always had organizational meetings prior to its sessions to approve the agenda. These had consisted of one representative from each of the regions—normally the top party official in the delegation.

The first sign that noninstitutional organizations were going to be important in the Congress itself came when representatives to the preparatory commission were elected at the regional deputy meetings. Seventeen of the members of the commission have been identified, and none was the top official from the region. The representative from Bashkiria was a party first secretary from a small city, while the Primorsk and Tula regions elected managers of medium-sized plants. The other representatives were either jurists or scholars. Regions were recognizing that the preparatory commission was really going to prepare the session rather than confirm the plans of others and that they needed representatives who could represent their viewpoint in complex negotiations.

An even more important development occurred at the end of April when the preparatory commission could not reach agreement on the .agenda. A second preparatory commission—a "conference of representatives"—was created to resolve the differences. It included ideological and occupational groups as well as regional ones and was the first dramatic and official acknowledgement that ideology-based and policy-based groups would not only be tolerated, but would have to be key players in the legislative process if acceptable compromises were to be found.[8]

The Congress rules that were drafted in the preparatory committee permitted any fifty deputies not only to form an organized group or faction (*fraktsii*), but to register it officially. Each deputy could join up to five different factions. At the beginning of the first Congress of People's Deputies, there were slightly more than twenty deputy groups that had officially registered, but the number had risen to thirty-two weeks later.[9] Members could and often did belong to more than one.

Three types of registered groups were formed. One type had a territorial base. Although all the regional delegations met for a number of purposes (e.g., the election of Supreme Soviet deputies), only the large Moscow group with 64 deputies seems to have registered officially. Nearly all the registered territorial groups had a supraregional basis. They included (1) the North (Sever)—83 deputies, (2) the Urals—65 deputies, (3) the Non–Black Earth Regions— (unknown), (4) Central Russia—126 deputies, (5) the Far East and Zabaikal—62 deputies, (6) Siberia—65 deputies; (7) the autonomous republics and territorial units—83 deputies, and (8) Democratic Autonomy—26 deputies. Most of the territorial groups were relatively inactive, but those representing the North and, above all, the autonomous republics and territorial units play quite important roles. (The Democratic Autonomy group soon disappeared.[10])

A second type of registered group was based on common occupation: (1) the *Agrarniki* from the rural sector (officially "Food and

Health")—120 deputies before the Congress and 183 by the opening of the Congress,[11] (2) Military and KGB officers—55 deputies, (3) the Journalists of the "Glasnost' "—51 deputies,[12] (4) the Worker–Peasant Union—72 deputies,[13] (5) the Educators, Scientific, and Cultural Workers—71 deputies, (6) Transportation, Communications, and Computers (in practice, only Transportation and Communications)—51 deputies, (7) Medical Workers—97 deputies, (8) Legal System Workers—65 deputies, (9) Economics and Management—61 deputies, (10) Communal Economy Workers—number not listed, (11) Industry (really Industrial Managers)—53 deputies, and (12) Soviets and Local Self-Administration—59 deputies.

The real character of the occupational groups varied. Some functioned as traditional occupational interest groups. For example, the day before the Congress, the deputies listed as "railroaders" were invited to the Ministry of Railroads, and the ministerial leaders "called upon them decisively to defend the interests of the employees of the branch."[14] The immediate stimulus for the creation of the group was the decision of the preparatory commission to propose a single standing committee of the Congress for industry and transportation. The railroad deputies thought it crucial to have a separate standing committee for transportation and communications,[15] and this central goal of the group was achieved by the end of the Congress.[16] In practice, the standing committee became the major legislative interest group of the industry, and the deputies group faded from view.

In most cases, however, the occupational groups played a broader role in promoting a general policy thought to be in the group's interest. For example, the military group, the agrarniki, and the industrialists became long-lasting, powerful groups that served as spokesmen for broad policy positions on the conservative and center-right segment of the political spectrum.

The third type of registered group was strikingly new: a group that was openly political and was not based on a defined institutional interest. Both Democratic Russia and Communists of Russia were also registered groups, but the number of deputies officially enrolled in them was much lower than the number who considered themselves as loose members of the umbrella organizations. Others were quite serious participants in legislative life. These were (1) Etika—54 deputies, (2) Non-Party—61 deputies, (3) Independent Deputies—52, (4) Independent Trade Unions—89 deputies, and (5) Smena—51 deputies.

Some of the other deputy groups seemed rather frivolous, and were never heard from again—for example, the 53-deputy Group for the Return of Russian Citizenship to Solzhenitsyn, the 69-deputy Chernobyl, the 51-deputy Refugees and Russians Abroad, and the 83-deputy Ecology.

Smena (Change) in particular was a prodemocratic, proreform group that played quite an important role in the Congress of People's Deputies. It developed its own agenda and rules before the first Congress, and presented its drafts to the preparatory committee and then the Congress. Its members caucused in intermissions and administered the first defeat on the conservatives by getting the conservative editor of *Sovetskaia Rossiia* excluded from the editorial committee.[17] It was to be the shift of Smena to the anti-Yeltsin side because of the latter's undemocratic actions that produced the first fundamental transformation of the balance of power in the Congress of People's Deputies.

The Failure of Strong Parties to Develop

The voting in the first four Congresses suggested that a two-party system might be forming within the legislature. Although the organizers of Democratic Russia and the Communists of Russia both proclaimed that their groups were not parties, they essentially functioned as such at the first Congress. They nominated candidates, they mobilized deputies into common voting behavior, and they took the lead in organizing the agenda.

In the early Congresses, Democratic Russia normally could mobilize 350 to 400 deputies on virtually any issue and Communists of Russia 300 to 350 deputies. In early 1991, a co-chairman of the Communists of Russia could still talk about thirty different groups in parliament, but two barricades.[18] It was easy to believe that Democratic Russia and the Communists of Russia would evolve into two large umbrella parties.

The deputies in the middle were contemptuously called the "bog" by those on either side, but their roll-call voting on a series of issues gives the impression of a group of Congress moderates who wanted Yeltsin as republican leader, even as an elected president, but who wanted him and especially the Congress radicals reasonably constrained. It was also easy to imagine these deputies forming a third centrist party. Indeed, many were later enlisted in a broad centrist coalition known as Civic Union.

In retrospect, however, the basic two-party character of the first Congress flowed from the fact that it was dominated by several major issues that had a yes-or-no character to them—especially the election of the chairman of the Supreme Soviet and the passage of the Law on Sovereignty. Given the unorganized nature of the elections and the corps of deputies who emerged from them, it was natural that two major political groupings should arise at the Congress to try to organize the struggle on these issues.

Once the political struggle became more complex, neither Democratic Russia nor the Communists of Russia developed into meaningful parties. Despite claims from the Yeltsin camp that a two-party system did develop in the Congress (the dwindling democrats and the united red–brown coalition, with no one in between), the Russian Congress came to feature more than a dozen factions or semiparties. The occupational and territorial factions largely disappeared, and the remaining factions generally represented ideological points of view.

The failure of a two-party system to develop in the Russian legislature is obviously not in itself a reason for grave reproach. Most legislatures have multiparty systems rather than two-party ones. However, the party-faction system of the Russian legislature had a series of peculiarities that seriously interfered with the development of a strong democracy in Russia.

First, the number of factions in the Congress of People's Deputies was peculiarly high, especially for a country in which deputies were elected in single-member districts. Moreover, as will be seen in Table 4.1, the distribution of roll-call voting scores of the factions suggests that the number of factions was artificially high.

Everyone wanted a new constitution in which the two-tier Congress and Supreme Soviet would be combined into one bilateral legislature. There would be a new election law, whose features were still unknown. However, the most probable variants were either a system based on single-member districts or, more likely, a German-like system that combined proportional representation with single-member districts. The latter was being defended as particularly likely to create pressures for large, strong parties as found in Germany, with perhaps a few smaller ones. Clearly the factional leaders in the Congress were not positioning themselves for the next election.

Second, while the factions were the dominant institution in the Congress of People's Deputies, they were quite weak in the Supreme So-

Table 4.1

Size of Membership and Average Ideological Rating of Factors, Russian Congress of People's Deputies, June 1993

Name of faction	Number of Members	Rating Score
1. Agreement for Progress	54	1.33
2. Democratic Russia	47	1.36
3. Radical Democrats	47	1.36
4. Left Center	61	2.72
5. Motherland	52	3.10
6. Workers' Union	49	3.10
7. Change	52	3.12
8. Free Russia	53	3.19
9. Industrial Union	54	5.17
10. Russia	53	5.26
11. Sovereignty and Equality	46	5.70
12. Agrarian Union	128	5.84
13. Fatherland	49	6.82
14. Communists of Russia	66	7.17

Source: Membership in the factions was calculated from the computerized Supreme Soviet directory of Congress deputies. The rating score was computed from the roll-call rating calculated by Alexander Sobianin for deputies at the first Congress (1 was extreme radical, 2 radical, 3 moderate radical, 4 left-center, 5 right-center, 6 moderate conservative, 7 conservative, and 8 extreme conservative).

viet, which served as the real legislative body in the country and even drafted the measures on constitutional change that were the major focus of activity at the Congresses. A leader of the Rossiia faction (Baburin) declared, "It seems to me that there are no factions in the Supreme Soviet in the full meaning of this word because there is no factional unity."[19]

Third, the factions had no connection with analogous party-like bodies at other territorial levels. The only nationwide political group independent of the Communist Party in 1989 was the Interregional Group of USSR Deputies, but it did not make a coordinated effort to nominate candidates for the Russian Congress. One of its leaders, Boris Yeltsin, who found the USSR Supreme Soviet a frustrating arena because of Gorbachev's control of a majority in that body, did decide to turn to Russia as his major base of operation. A close political associate, Mikhail Bocharov, made the same decision (and was to be Yeltsin's candidate for chairman of the Council of Ministers at the first Congress), but the two were exceptions.

The more surprising development—or lack of development—was the failure of the Communist Party to create ties that expanded beyond the legislature. One would have thought that the Communists were in a good position to adopt a fairly moderate, even populist, position, asserting that they alone had the ability to take coordinated actions in both the USSR and RSFSR legislatures (and in the local soviets) to solve the problems of the country. Neither the central nor the republican Communist Party leadership knew how to do this in a convincing manner.

Thus, the founding Congress of the Russian Communist Party began just as the first Congress of People's Deputies ended, but the leaders of Communists of Russia were not elected to the party Central Committee. There seemed to be little interaction between, say, the Central Committee secretary for agrarian policy and the relatively conservative agrarniki faction in the Congress. There was little contact between the conservative Soiuz faction in the USSR Congress and the Communists of Russia in the Russian Congress.

Fourth, the factions did not develop into parties with branches in the regions, and they had little visibility beyond the politically active in Moscow. The names of the factions of 1993 found in Table 4.1, not to mention those of the factions of 1990, have little overlap with the list of parties that competed in the December 1993 election, found in Table 4.2. Even if Civic Union—a coalition of centrist factions—is considered a faction, only four out of fourteen 1993 factions formed the base of a 1993 party. Democratic Russia's leaders were largely drawn into Russia's Choice, but the latter was dominated by members of the executive under Yeltsin, not his allies in the Congress.

Similarly, Communists of Russia had little representation in the Communist Party that appeared on the ballot in December 1993. Relatively few of persons on the Communist list had been deputies in the Russian Congress. One leader of the Communists of Russia faction, Ivan P. Rybkin, switched to the Agrarian Party. It was originally charged that the Communists and the Agrarian Party were really two faces of the same party, but while the two cooperated on many policy questions in the Duma, they were quite separate and became increasingly so as the 1995 election approached.

The most striking evidence of the failure of the factions to develop mass support or even recognition was provided by a massive study of public opinion in the three weeks prior to the December 1993 election.

Table 4.2

Familiarity with Political Parties on the First and Last Days of the 1993 Russian Election

	November 18–20		December 7–11	
Name of party	Percentage that knows	Percentage with opinion	Percentage that knows	Percentage with opinion
Kedr—Ekologiia	27.0	16.2	42.7	27.8
Future of Russia	29.4	17.6	46.3	27.4
Dostoinstvo	32.6	21.8	42.3	26.2
Women of Russia	46.5	34.6	64.5	50.3
Civic Union	43.4	28.1	57.3	37.4
Agrarian	46.7	32.1	58.0	41.0
Yavlinsky–Boldyrev– Lukin	56.6	41.0	68.5	50.4
RDDR—Sobchak	59.4	46.1	70.3	52.0
Communists	61.2	47.2	70.3	55.0
PRES—Shakhrai	62.1	43.6	72.0	53.2
Democratic Party— Travkin	62.6	44.3	73.3	54.4
Liberal Democrats— Zhirinovsky	73.2	60.3	81.8	68.4
Vybor Rossii—Gaidar	74.4	60.5	83.2	68.8

Note: The November 18–20 figures are based on the 1,959 respondents interviewed on those days and the December 7–11 figures on the 5,259 respondents interviewed on those days.

One thousand respondents were interviewed in each of thirty-five oblasts of Russia,[20] with the interviewers instructed to do one-third of the interviewing each week and to keep the mixture of urban and rural respondents more or less even. This provided an average of 1,700 respondents for each day of the campaign, although in practice the number per day was below average at the very beginning and very end of the campaign time. Table 4.2 shows how many respondents claimed to know of the various parties at both the beginning and the end of the campaign.

Table 4.2 makes clear that the mass of the Russian population was often quite unfamiliar with the parties and their programs at the beginning of the campaign unless these were identified with a well-known charismatic leader. The heart of the moderately conservative opposition in the Congress were Civic Union and the agrarian faction, but less than half the respondents claimed to have heard of them at the beginning of the election and less than one-third claimed to have an opinion of them. Everyone, of course, knew about the old Communist Party, but it had split into several different groups and parties. Large numbers of people answered honestly that they were unsure of the nature of the Communist Party that was on the ballot. Moreover, these figures on voter familiarity surely err on the high side, both because of respondent desire not to show ignorance and because the most apolitical citizens in the country likely refused to be interviewed in a survey called a preelection study.

The Reasons for Ill-Formed Parties:
Extra-Legislature Factors

There are, of course, many reasons why a well-functioning party system did not develop in Russia in the first five years after the elections of 1990. First, the formation of meaningful parties is almost always difficult in new democracies. In the United States, parties formed for presidential elections only eight years after the Constitution was ratified, and modern parties with real connections to the population did not form until 1828. The groups that called themselves parties in eighteenth-century England are described in terms that seem identical with the amorphous and personalistic factions of the Russian Congress.[21] And, of course, the formation of a meaningful party system has also been quite difficult in the new East European democracies.

This problem was particularly great in the Soviet Union because of the lack of even quasi-free elections and legislatures in the preceding decades and the lack of experience on the part of a great majority of the deputies. The radicals usually had almost no prior political or administrative experience. Even the conservatives, despite the frequent charge to the contrary, included too few deputies who were truly from the nomenklatura, not too many. Too few had experience above the county and small-town level. This led to unprofessional legislative behavior on both sides of the political spectrum, but perhaps more importantly it contributed to Boris Yeltsin's contempt for the Congress of People's Deputies. Yeltsin had been the governor of a large state and then a top Moscow politician for nearly fifteen years; he had been elected president of Russia, and then had defeated Mikhail Gorbachev after playing a heroic role at the time of the August 1991 coup attempt. He found it difficult to take seriously professors without political experience (such as Ruslan Khasbulatov and Sergei Baburin) or forty-five-year-old former air force colonels (such as Aleksandr Rutskoi)—let alone deputies who were even less experienced and distinguished.

Second, the Soviet experience with political parties—or rather with a single political party—has made it very difficult for Russians to accept that disciplined parties are compatible with democracy. This problem was particularly difficult for the Communist Party. If the Communist Party had begun to function as a normal parliamentary party with the kind of discipline found in, say, Great Britain, it would have seemed like a continuation of the old party dictatorship. In the 1993 election, many of its strongest candidates ran as independents in the district elections because they surely thought the party label would detract from their vote total, not add to it. The association of strong parties with dictatorship clearly was an inhibiting factor for other political forces, too.

Nevertheless, the problems of Communists of Russia went much deeper. As noted above, the Russian Communist leaders did not include the legislative leaders of Communists of Russia in the Central Committee, and they seemed unable or unwilling to function as a normal parliamentary party. There seemed to be little contact between the conservative Soiuz faction in the USSR Congress and the Communists of Russia in the Russian Congress. It was as if everyone were ashamed of being Communists: they seemed to be suffering the kind of loss of self-confidence that Crane Brinton argued is the one sure sign of an impending revolution.[22]

Third, Boris Yeltsin was quite determined to avoid the establishment of democratic institutions that would limit his power. From the beginning, his policy of economic reform featured large-scale subsidies that were deliberately kept off budget in order to ensure that the budgetary power of the Congress and Supreme Soviet would have little meaning. The key decisions, including those on subsidies, were made within the executive, and the legislature and the Central Bank were simply used as scapegoats for the resulting economic difficulties. The power of the executive attracted politicians to it, and the executive's control of the privatization process created a powerful patronage tool that Yeltsin used quite effectively with a range of people both inside and outside the executive.

This fear of competing power centers extended to political parties as well. Yeltsin's closest political adviser in the first years, Gennadii

Burbulis, repeatedly suggested the creation of a presidential party. Yeltsin always resisted, and Burbulis confirmed the obvious reason in a private interview: Yeltsin was afraid that any party would tie him down to some particular program. He wanted the freedom to be a thoroughgoing populist.[23]

Fourth, the candidates in the first USSR and Russian competitive elections were often not the kind of people suitable for or interested in working in political parties of the Western type. One group was composed of the type of person often elected in the one-candidate elections of the past: state governors, mayors, factory directors, collective farm chairmen, and the like, who easily could serve in a national legislature for four to six days a year, but who could not and did not want to serve in a legislature for weeks or months at a time.

Another large group of deputies were really more revolutionaries than legislators in the normal sense of the term. They entered politics in order to destroy or transform the old system, not in order to draft detailed legislation, let alone provide assistance to constituents on the proverbial problem of potholes. In their parliamentary activity, they gave little attention to constituency service and little effort to supervising the executive in a detailed manner, and much of the legislation they drafted tended to be of a declarative character rather than a juridically sophisticated one. It is not surprising that a very large percentage both of USSR and RSFSR deputies chose to abandon a legislative career after their first term in office.[24]

The Reasons for Ill-Formed Parties: Intra-Legislature Factors

Whatever the desires of Boris Yeltsin and the general obstacles to the formation of effective parties and personnel in the earliest stages of democratization, factions were, after all, created within the legislature in response to rules established within the legislature. These rules had a powerful impact on the characteristics of the groups that were formed—and to a large extent in directions that were not ideal.

In particular, there were two aspects of the structure of the legislature and its rules that had a serious negative impact on the formation of solid political parties: (1) the two-tier structure of the legislature, with the factions of the Congress of People's Deputies being much weaker than that in the Supreme Soviet; and (2) the adoption of the rules that a faction need have no more than 5 percent of the deputies to be registered and that factions had equal power and representation regardless of the number of their members.

Separation of the Organizational Structure of the Congress and Supreme Soviet

The first major structural fact about the Russian legislature was determined by top officials within the Communist Party—to replicate the two-tier structure of the USSR legislature, with a part-time Congress of People's Deputies and a Supreme Soviet that concentrated more full-time on legislative work. The reasons for this decision at the USSR level were apparent on the face of things: the Congress, with one-third of its deputies elected in national-territorial districts and one-third by "public organizations," was almost certain to be relatively responsive to the party leadership and would serve as a check on a Supreme Soviet that tried to become too independent.

The Russian Congress of People's Deputies could not, however, have been seen as a conservative check on the Russian Supreme Soviet, for it had little of the inherent conservative bias of the Russian Congress. It had no deputies from the public organizations, and only 15.8 percent of its deputies were elected in national-territorial districts. In practice, these districts did give disproportionate representation to remote rural—and, in practice, conservative—areas, but the extent of the conservative bias was reduced by the relatively small number of the districts and by the fact that half the latter were awarded to Russian oblasts as well as the cities of Moscow and St. Petersburg, with the more populous units receiving more than one seat.

The legislative body that seemed likely to be conservative—and that was actually expected to be more conservative—was the Supreme Soviet. Half its 256 deputies were selected from national-territorial districts and constituted one of the houses of the Supreme Soviet, the Soviet of Nationalities. Since there were only 168 deputies elected in national-territorial districts, a very high percentage of the deputies elected within them had to be elected to the Supreme Soviet.[25] Any conservative bias introduced into the Congress by the national-territorial districts was certain to be magnified in the Supreme Soviet, all the more so since the concurrence of a majority of the deputies of both houses was required for the passage of legislation.

Whatever the reasons for the creation of a two-tier legislature,[26] it created an intra-legislature organizational problem not found in normal legislatures. To be specific, there were two legislative organs to organize, not one. The earlier discussion of the formation of umbrella groups like Democratic Russia and the Communists of Russia, as well as smaller factions, referred to the Congress, not the Supreme Soviet.

The factions came to perform quite important roles within the Congress. The leaders had not seriously thought about the question of access to the floor in the Congress debates—or, if any of them had, they had not taken decisions to rationalize the procedure—and the right to speak was determined by the order in which deputies requested the floor. This was an impossible solution in a Congress that only met for a few weeks a year and that had over 1,050 deputies, and the radicals realized at once how to exploit the situation. In large numbers they signed up before the debate had really started, thereby monopolizing the debate. Almost immediately this produced the necessary response of giving the factions the right to nominate a substantial number of the speakers so that all sides could be represented in the debate. This rule came to be observed very strictly.[27]

A second major role for the factions was to provide the members for "reconciliation commissions" (*soglasovitel'nye komissii*), which were formed to solve contentious issues at the Congress. Such commissions—simply meetings of group leaders—regularly convened at the beginnings of sessions to agree on the agenda and the membership of the secretariat, the editorial committee, and so forth. More important, however, a reconciliation commission was regularly formed whenever the Congress became deadlocked.[28]

Sometimes the decision of a reconciliation commission was not accepted (for example, in 1991 to resolve a deadlock on whether to elect Khasbulatov or Sergei Baburin Supreme Soviet chairman, by electing the former chairman and the latter first deputy chairman), but this was a rare occurrence. The leader of a conservative faction, Baburin wrote the following in March 1991—a time of confrontation between Yeltsin and Gorbachev—but he could have made the same point at virtually any time from 1990 to April 1993:

> When deputies fight out their battles at the microphones in an atmo-
> sphere of emotional fervor, it seems that they are irreconcilable. When,
> however, they begin to converse in the smoking room, it turns out that

the differences are considerably fewer and that they are entirely surmountable. The deputies themselves are then astonished: Look, we can negotiate.[29]

While Yeltsin and his supporters often came to speak of an irreconcilable opposition in the Congress, this author has the opposite impression—namely, the opposition frequently found some compromise with the Yeltsin forces in the reconciliation commissions. The bitterness arose as Yeltsin and his forces repeatedly reneged on compromise agreements once the Congress was over.

But if the factions and their leaders played a crucial role in the work of the Congresses, they were far less important in the legislative work of the Supreme Soviet. The executive committee of the Supreme Soviet—its Presidium—was composed of the seven leaders of the Supreme Soviet and its two houses and the chairmen of the twenty-four committees. The leadership of the Supreme Soviet was deliberately spread over the ideological spectrum, but the leaders do not seem to have been the representatives of factions in any real sense of the term. The chairmen seem to have had almost no connection with the factions other than by chance.

There were several reasons that the Supreme Soviet and its Presidium were organized on a different principle than the Congress, and that the factions of the latter did not have a key role in the former. First, of course, when the rules on the organization of the Supreme Soviet were adopted, the factions were only being created, and a Presidium formed of faction leaders would have been unnatural.

As the factions became more institutionalized, however, the rules were not changed. Basically, the leaders of the Supreme Soviet—first Boris Yeltsin and then Ruslan Khasbulatov—felt that factions might limit their freedom of action. They were much less threatened by a Presidium that was dominated by committee chairman who themselves were not selected by parties or factions and did not have an independent base of power.

Ruslan Khasbulatov was to be grossly misrepresented as a hardliner in the post-1991 bitter conflict between Boris Yeltsin and the Congress. In fact, he was a radical economic reformer who was selected first deputy chairman of the Supreme Soviet as the nominee of Democratic Russia and a close ally of Yeltsin. As a representative of the non-Russian republics (he was a Chechen elected in the Chechen-

Ingush republic), Khasbulatov was deeply committed to a democratic legislature and a diffusion of power from Moscow into the provinces. When Yeltsin was president, Khasbulatov was elected to replace him as chairman.

Yeltsin and Khasbulatov were able to ensure that the Supreme Soviet was not as conservative as was universally expected. In general, those on the radical-liberal side of the spectrum were often more interested in a legislative political career than the conservatives, and Yeltsin and Khasbulatov were to facilitate their entry into the Supreme Soviet and the body of non–Supreme Soviet deputies working full-time in Moscow, usually in the committees. At the first Congress, the deputies elected to the Supreme Soviet in June 1990 had an average score of 4.36 on a scale of voting in which extreme radical was 1 and extreme conservative was 9, compared with 4.21 for the other deputies.

By June 1992, the situation had changed radically. There had been a considerable turnover in Supreme Soviet membership, and another 124 Congress deputies had become full-time legislators, usually concentrating their work in the committees. If we use the same scale from the first Congress roll-calls to ensure comparability, then we find that the 244 Supreme Soviet deputies in June 1992 had an average score of 3.83. A total of 368 deputies were working in the legislature on a full-time basis. They had an average score of 3.26 in their first Congress voting, while the committee chairman averaged 3.39.

It might be argued that the 1990 scores do not reflect the deputy views of June 1992, and such an argument is made by Yeltsin analysts who define reform solely in terms of support for Yeltsin. However, relations between Yeltsin and the legislature in June 1992 had not yet deteriorated to the extent they did a year later, and everyone recognized that the Supreme Soviet remained supportive of the Yeltsin position for a considerable period after the Congress moved toward opposition. Indeed, Yeltsin himself implicitly acknowledged this by focusing his attack on the Congress and speaking of the Supreme Soviet in quite different terms.

Whatever the reason, the organizational structure of the Supreme Soviet was not based on factions, and this fact seriously retarded the transformation of the factions into more meaningful parties. The Congress of People's Deputies focused on issues that required constitutional amendments, for it was the body in the system with the power to pass such amendments. Inevitably in the political conditions of 1991 to

1993, these were issues involving the relative power of Yeltsin and the legislature, issues of great importance but not of day-to-day concern for the broad population. The failure to integrate the congressional factions into the work of the Supreme Soviet reduced the factions' incentives to become deeply involved in the kind of nonconstitutional legislative activity that was the central concern of the Supreme Soviet and that is crucial in developing a comprehensive party program.

The weak role of the factions in the Russian Supreme Soviet also made it very difficult to develop parties that existed in the USSR and the regional legislatures as well as at the Russian level. The constitutional issues that were handled in the Russian Congress were generally quite specific to that level of government. If the factions had been more concerned with developing a general legislative program, it would have been more natural for them to ally with like-minded deputies at other territorial levels in parties that had coherent programs.

Congressional Procedure and the Number of Factions

As indicated above, the first Congress was dominated by two large party-like organizations, Democratic Russia and the Communists of Russia, and an amorphous moderate group in the middle. Both Democratic Russia and Communists of Russia contained major cleavages, and it was not a surprise that each proved subject to disintegration. Nevertheless, it was more surprising that the "party system" that emerged consistently contained thirteen to fourteen factions over the last two years of the Congress and that these factions were so ephemeral that only four of them survived to run as parties in the December 1993 election.

Moreover, the number of factions seems even stranger if their membership is examined. With the exception of the Agrarian Union, the number of deputies in each faction was suspiciously close to fifty. In addition, the average ideological rating scores of the factions did not spread evenly over the spectrum, but were bunched into five, or probably four, groups that seemed like natural parties. Using a scale in which 1 was an extreme radical and 8 an extreme conservative, we find that three radical factions had an almost identical average score of around 1.35, five were grouped around 3 (moderate radical), two around 5.2 (center-right), two stood at 5.8 (moderate conservative), and two were quite conservative. Indeed, the right-central and moderate conservative should probably be combined.

Why had this unusual pattern emerged? It is difficult to avoid the conclusion that the organizational rules of the Congress were decisive. As has been noted, the Congress leadership had turned to the factions as the solution to two problems that arose during the first Congress: first, how to regulate the flow of speakers into the debate to get all points of view represented, and, second, how to form an ad hoc committee to reach a compromise on crucial points.

The problem, however, was that the factions were not fixed groups, and deputies, it may be remembered, might belong to as many as five of them. If each faction were given the right to nominate a speaker and to be represented in the reconciliation commissions, and if each deputy could join up to five factions, then clearly there was an incentive for the number of factions to multiply.

At the fourth Congress in May 1991, one of the deputies, Gennadii V. Saenko, charged that this is precisely what had happened. He accused both Communists of Russia and Democratic Russia of spinning off satellite groups in order to multiply their membership on the reconciliation commissions. The number of group members, he reported, exceeded the number of deputies. Saenko proposed that the Congress distinguish between deputy groups and factions, that only the latter be allowed on the reconciliation committees, and that each deputy be permitted to join only one faction.[30] This proposal was, in effect, adopted, and the occupational and territorial factions essentially disappeared.

The question still remained—how was representation to be given to the factions? Were they to be awarded seats on the commissions and the right to nominate speakers in proportion to their membership, or was each to be given equal access? Perhaps because the reconciliation commissions functioned by compromise and consensus rather than by vote, no attempt was made to give the factions representation in proportion to their membership.

The logical outcome of this set of rules was that which is observed in Table 4.1. Relatively like-minded deputies were clearly dividing themselves into factions that numbered as close to the fifty-deputy minimum as possible. In a number of cases the chief motivation for the formation of a faction was undoubtedly the desire of an ambitious deputy or deputies to have a leading role in a faction, but a different set of rules that either set higher minimum standards for the size of a recognized faction or that established incentives for the formation of larger factions would have ensured that ambitious deputies would not have had the opportunity to form their own factions. Indeed, the one single-issue, nonideological faction—the Agrarian Union—that needed only a single representative to defend the economic interests of the farm lobby did not split into two, as it easily could have done.

Conclusion

Yeltsin's dissolution of the Congress and his establishment of a new legislature, the State Duma, gave the political elite a chance to correct the problems with party formation that existed in the old constitution.

To some extent, this occurred. The electoral law was deliberately patterned after German law, with half the seats awarded on the basis of party-list voting and half awarded in districts. The parties were given an incentive to run candidates from their list in the districts, for if such a candidate won, he or she was not counted against the seats won in the party-list race. Moreover, there was no runoff in the district races, giving parties the incentive to form alliances beforehand so that they would have a better chance to win a plurality of the vote.

Any party that won 5 percent of the vote was permitted to form a faction. New factions, however, had to be have forty members—nearly 20 percent of the deputies not elected by party list—to be officially recognized, and this reduced the number of factions. In the State Duma, the executive committee was then formed primarily of the party and faction leaders, while the committee chairmen attended as nonvoting members.

The factions and parties in the Duma also played a key role in nominating the legislative leaders: they were given one point per member and then could "spend" the points for different leadership posts, down to and including one point for a committee chairman and one-half point for a committee deputy chairman.

In 1994, the Duma factions negotiated among themselves for the committees they would get to control, but in practice, when several factions wanted the same committee, new overlapping ones were created so that each faction could have won. Thus, three economic policy committees were formed, each headed by a deputy representing a different faction. A special Geopolitical Committee was formed and given to Vladimir Zhirinovsky's Liberal Democratic Party in lieu of the Foreign Affairs or Defense Committee that he wanted. Hence, in a real sense the committees truly became creatures of the factions.

The degree to which strong parties will, in fact, form out of the legislature is something that only the future will tell. As indicated above, Yeltsin opposed the creation of a presidential party, and he has naturally been even more afraid that other powerful parties would arise that would serve as an effective focus of opposition to himself. Those who drafted the electoral law in 1993 included provisions for fairly long campaigns, and the logic of the German-like electoral system required some time for political blocs to form.[31] Instead, when Yeltsin dissolved the Congress in September 1993, he called an election for ten weeks hence. By the time the ensuing struggle for power was resolved, only two months remained until the election, and by the time the Ministry of Justice certified the parties for the ballot, only one month.

Moreover, the radical, pro-Yeltsin forces did not unite into a single party, but formed three separate parties, two of which claimed to be centrist. State-controlled television gave special coverage to Vladimir Zhirinovsky and his Liberal Democratic Party, and other conservative and centrist parties had little opportunity and few finances to compete effectively.

Yeltsin's behavior provides the best testimony about the importance of political parties in a well-functioning democracy. He clearly fears that such parties will provide a mechanism to formulate an alternate political program and to organize opposition to himself. His determination to destroy embryonic party systems illustrates yet another of the obstacles to the creation of a solid party system. Surely such a system will eventually develop, but the formation of well-functioning democratic systems has been a long process in both the West and the Third World. It will not be easy in Russia, either.

Notes

1. Information on all the candidates for the 1993 Federal Assembly election and on the 1994 and 1995 local elections was gathered for the author from the regional Russian press by Violetta P. Rumiantseva.

2. *Pravda*, January 4, 1994, p. 2.

3. See the discussion in Jerry F. Hough and Merle Fainsod, *How the Soviet Union Is Governed* (Cambridge, MA: Harvard University Press, 1979), pp. 522–543.

4. *Komsomol'skaia pravda*, May 17, 1990, p. 1.

5. TASS, April 1, 1990.

6. *Sovetskaia Rossiia*, May 10, 1990, p. 2.

7. In the early summer, thirty-nine deputies left the Communist Party, reduc-

ing the percentage of Communists among all deputies to 86 percent, and among the 400 most radical to 66 percent.

8. First Congress, vol. 1, p. 54.

9. *Trud,* May 19, 1990, p. 1.

10. The names and numbers of the registered groups were announced on the floor of the Congress. The following list is drawn from this source. First Congress, vol. 2, pp. 266–267, 407, 460; and vol. 3, p. 263. No. 28 cannot be found, but presumably is the Non–Black Earth Group, which is mentioned elsewhere.

11. *Sovetskaia Rossiia,* April 22, 1990, p. 2.

12. See *Argumenty i fakty,* no. 23 (June 9–15, 1990), p. 2.

13. The stenographic report of the first Congress repeatedly referred to a "worker-deputies" group, and it is likely that this union, in practice, took on that character.

14. *Gudok,* May 20, 1990, p. 1; and May 17, 1990, p. 1.

15. *Gudok,* May 27, 1990, p. 1.

16. *Gudok,* June 20, 1990, p. 1.

17. First Congress, vol. 1, pp. 37 and 52.

18. Second Congress, vol. 1, p. 212.

19. *Pravda,* March 19, 1991.

20. Another 16,000 respondents were interviewed in the sixteen former autonomous republics, but they are not included in this analysis.

21. See Lewis Namier, *The Structure of Politics at the Accession of George III* (London: Macmillan, 1959).

22. Crane Brinton, *The Anatomy of Revolution*, rev. and exp. ed. (New York: Viking Press, 1965), pp. 51–52.

23. Interview with Burbulis, March 12, 1995.

24. See Timothy J. Colton's chapter in this book.

25. In practice, the Supreme Soviet had more seats reserved for national-territorial deputies than those who wanted to serve full-time in it. To get enough representatives from each region, the Congress had to change the rules and permit deputies elected from territorial districts within a region to be selected for a Supreme Soviet national-territorial seat if a national-territorial deputy could not be found.

26. It most likely resulted from the desire to give the ethnic units a Soviet of Nationalities in the legislative process, but to prevent them from having a veto on the most important issues. A Congress with supreme powers and a low percentage of national-territorial districts solved this problem.

27. See, for example, Fifth Congress, vol. 1, p. 145.

28. Third Congress, vol. 1, pp. 48–49.

29. *Pravda,* March 19, 1991, p. 3.

30. Fourth Congress, vol. 1, pp. 200–201.

31. Jerry F. Hough, "Institutional Change and the 1993 Election Results," in Timothy J. Colton and Jerry F. Hough, eds., *Quasi-Democracy in Russia: The 1993 Election* (submitted to the Brookings Institution but not yet accepted).

5

Ménage à Trois: The End of
Soviet Parliamentarism

Thomas F. Remington

Crisis and Confrontation

Between its inception in spring 1990 and its catastrophic demise in the fall of 1993, the Russian legislature underwent an extraordinary transformation. Having elected Boris Yeltsin chairman of the Supreme Soviet by a slim margin at the first Congress in May–June 1990, the Russian deputy corps gave nearly a two-thirds majority at the ninth Congress in March 1993 to a motion to remove him from the presidency. By summer 1993 the leadership of the Supreme Soviet had been taken over by its most conservative elements. Virtually no liberal committee chairs remained in office. The confrontation between parliament and president over the president's powers brought about a protracted constitutional crisis, which Yeltsin persistently sought to resolve by extraconstitutional means, such as forcing a national referendum on a new constitution and assuming extraordinary powers himself. Yet although the parliamentary leadership opposed Yeltsin's constitutional and policy plans, its confrontational stance made the deputies neither popular nor powerful. The culmination of the crisis occurred in September 1993, when Yeltsin decreed the dissolution of parliament, stripped all one thousand deputies of their powers, and called for new parliamentary elections. A better understanding of the radical shift in the political balance within the deputy corps can shed light on the evolution of Russian democratic institutions in the immedi-

ate postcommunist period. The case may also illustrate the dynamics of
the development of young representative institutions in a highly turbulent environment.

Three explanations are commonly offered for the deputies' turn
from support to opposition toward Yeltsin and reform. Many deputies,
and especially their chairman, Ruslan Khasbulatov, claimed that in
resisting Yeltsin, they were defending a society suffering from the
effects of misguided, radical economic experiments and a gathering
presidential dictatorship. Shock therapy had led to severe recession and
a breakdown of the social order, so the deputies were faithfully defending the interests of the voters in fighting Yeltsin.

A second theory argues that the legislative system was flawed from
the start by the use of the peculiar two-tiered structure that Gorbachev
devised for the union legislature, and more generally by the continuity
of old soviet forms into the postcommunist period. As Yeltsin put it in
his opening address to the Constitutional Assembly in June, "Soviets
are incompatible with democracy." Therefore the problem was structural, and the solution was a new and internally consistent constitution.

Finally, a third view attributes the confrontation to the makeup of
the deputy corps elected in 1990. The deputies were said to be dominated by members of the old communist nomenklatura, who had succeeded in winning a far larger presence in the Congress than their
actual popular support would justify, and who had used it ever since to
fight reform.

In this essay, I will assess these arguments, and then advance an
alternative explanation for the sharply conservative trend in the
parliament's balance after its fifth Congress.

Faithful Delegates

The parliamentary leadership frequently depicted itself as the real
democrats, in contrast to the corrupt, power-seeking, and misguided
officials around Yeltsin. The latter were using dictatorial methods because their policies were profoundly antipopular. As Khasbulatov put
it in a speech on June 1, 1993:

> Having realized the utter bankruptcy of shock therapy, its authors, natu-
> rally, are trying to escape real responsibility, escape discussion of these
> problems. . . . The hasty railroading through of a new Constitution has

as its goal, first of all, to dump the entire blame for the present break-down on the Soviets above all, on the representative branch, on the Supreme Soviet, on the Congress, declaring them, of course, yet another enemy of the people; and second, to free itself from a genuinely indepen-dent representative organ of power, which, in accord with its constitu-tional principles and status, can demand a stern accounting from the reformers. And how could it be any other way? How can they escape oversight, escape accountability? And third, to untie the hands of corrupt officals and bribe-takers in the executive branch, to solve heightened economic and social problems with ordinary command-administrative methods, by means of willful pressure, another revolutionary leap, to make good on promises given to their foreign protectors about support-ing reform.[1]

In September 1993, of course, Yeltsin did use unconstitutional methods in dissolving parliament. The shelling of the parliament build-ing in October 1993 confirmed the impression many observers had of Yeltsin as a leader willing to use any means to achieve his aims and display his power. Yet it does not follow from this that the deputies were representing the will of the voters when they opposed Yeltsin. Through 1992 Yeltsin sought to put the constitutional question to the voters in a referendum; the deputies balked. A referendum was finally held in April 1993, and it is difficult to interpret the results other than as a victory for Yeltsin over his parliamentary opponents. The referen-dum posed four questions to the voters dealing with confidence in Yeltsin, approval of the president's and the government's social policy, and support for early presidential and early parliamentary elections. The results are probably the best nationwide test we have on the country's attitudes at the time toward the dispute between president and parliament. Whatever the public's more elaborated policy views, on these simple up-or-down questions the voters were consistent in backing Yeltsin (58.7 percent) and his government's economic policy (53 percent), and in demanding new parliamentary elections (67.2 per-cent). In addition, 49.5 percent favored new presidential elections. Turnout, at 64.5 percent, was higher than many expected, although lower by 10 percent than the presidential election of 1991.

Broken down by region, popular support for Yeltsin on the first question corresponds closely to his support in the presidential elections two years before.[2] The only regions in which a swing of more than 20 percent of the voting margin occurred (with the sole exceptions of

Magadan and Kaliningrad) were ten ethnic national enclaves where the vote clearly responded to local considerations.

Moreover, examined by type of district, the results parallel Yeltsin's 1991 showing.[3] In cities of at least 100,000 voters, Yeltsin received, on average, 70 percent of the vote in both 1991 and 1993, although turnout fell from 71 percent to 59 percent. In medium-sized and small cities, Yeltsin received 60 percent in both 1991 and 1993, although turnout fell almost 10 percent. In rural areas, turnout hardly fell at all and Yeltsin's support was again in the 40–45 percent range. However, in a number of rural districts as well as small cities, certain areas reported substantially higher than average turnout under circumstances where virtually all the "excess" votes were unanimous "no, no, yes, no" ballots—that is, the straight communist ticket. In a certain number of cases, the unexpected appearance of election observers in a polling station led to a considerably lower reported turnout (and a correspondingly lower anti-Yeltsin vote) than that reported by neighboring polling stations, even in the same village. This fact lends credence to the assertion that as many as eight million "excess" anti-Yeltsin ballots were recorded either through fraud or manipulation.[4] It is therefore reasonable to suppose that if the elections had been free of such effects, overall turnout would have been only 57 percent and Yeltsin's support on the first question would have been higher by as much as 12 percent.

The deputies' resistance to holding either a referendum or early parliamentary elections seems to reflect their awareness that, between themselves and the president, the president and his policies enjoyed much more support among the voting public. Electoral considerations do not, therefore, appear very helpful in explaining the confrontational stance taken by the congresses from the sixth Congress forward since the voters show no inclination to reward the deputies for opposing Yeltsin. Indeed, a survey taken at the end of 1992 found that only 7 percent of the population had a favorable opinion of the Supreme Soviet (Yeltsin's approval rating at that time was 28 percent).[5] Public reaction to Yeltsin's announcement of March 20, 1993, that he was declaring a "special regime," as well as to the events of September–October, illustrated again how weak the parliament's base of support was in society.

Finally, the results of the December 1993 parliamentary elections provide little support for the "faithful delegate" argument. In elections to the new State Duma, proreform parties received one-third of the party list vote. Antireform parties (Communists, Agrarians, and Zhirinovsky's Liberal-Democrats) received about 43 percent of the party list vote. Zhirinovsky, of course, positioned himself as an opponent of both the old communist system and the new reform course. Removing his 23 percent from the opposition vote leaves the communists and agrarians with only 20 percent of the party list vote. In the district races, around one-third of the seats went to deputies in proreform factions, and about the same number went to deputies in opposition factions. Of those winning candidates who were not nominated by a party, about half joined the nonpartisan New Regional Policy faction while about a quarter each joined one of the democratic factions or one of the opposition factions. Thus, overall, opposition and democratic forces were about equally successful in the parliamentary elections. And the president's constitution was approved by the national referendum. The results of the elections are, however, again clouded by suspicions of large-scale falsification.[6]

We should also bear in mind that the parliamentary elections of December 1993 differed in an important respect from the April 1993 referendum and the presidential election of June 1991. Unlike the two previous campaigns, the December election did not pit Yeltsin directly against his opponents. Yeltsin had done extremely well in his popular elections in 1989, 1990, and 1991, winning three major electoral victories in three successive years. His skill in mobilizing popular support against his opponents served him well again in the April 1993 referendum. But in December Yeltsin remained outside partisan politics, neither forming a presidential party nor lending much support to Gaidar's Russia's Choice movement. Instead he pushed for ratification of the constitution. He chose not to allow the parliamentary elections to pose a test of his own political strength.

Design Flaws

The second line of argument emphasizes the effects of the peculiar organization of the legislative system. Derived from the Leninist theory of soviets, as modified when Gorbachev proposed a new parliamentary system for the union, the Russian legislative structure was widely faulted for its internal inconsistency. A representative opinion was voiced by the legal scholar Avgust Mishin:

The congress system headed by a chairman was flawed from the very start. This was demonstrated by the sad experience of the analogous system in the former Soviet Union. We need parliamentarism, where a system of checks and balances works effectively. The current three-headed parliament—Congress, Supreme Soviet, Presidium of the Supreme Soviet—is incapable of working constructively and it is impossible to reform or improve it. It is necessary to liquidate the Congress, Presidium of the Supreme Soviet and, of course, the ridiculous and dangerous job of quasi-president—the Chairman of the Supreme Soviet.[7]

In its hierarchical form as well as the internal dominance of its full-time executives over the elected representatives, the system was also directly analogous to the CPSU and many other organizations of the communist period. The argument is made, for instance, that the adoption of a nesting-dolls hierarchy of Congress, Supreme Soviet, and Presidium was intended to give the leadership of the Presidium ample opportunity to sway the Congress and manipulate the Supreme Soviet much as the Politburo usurped the decision-making prerogatives of the Central Committee of the CPSU and party secretaries at every level replaced party committees and bureaus as the actual policy makers.[8] Moreover, by the rotation rule and diffusion of lawmaking authority, the system hampered professionalization among the deputy corps and impeded effective deliberation and decision making.

It is now accepted that the original design, featuring Congress, Supreme Soviet, and Presidium, was a model developed by a group of legal specialists and officials during 1988 as part of the package of constitutional reforms that Gorbachev presented to the nineteenth Party Conference.[9] Quite clearly it was a compromise between radical and conservative positions that met the party leadership's objective of balancing representation with executive dominance of the legislative branch. It restored certain traditional elements of the Soviet state framework, such as the separation between outer and inner parliaments (Congress and Central Executive Committee) from the 1918 constitution; and preserved the elements of the Presidium and bicameralism first introduced in the 1924 constitution and retained through the Gorbachev period. Any tendency for the Supreme Soviet to acquire political independence was checked by the constitutionally superior Congress and the politically dominant "inmost parliament" of the Presidium. In 1989 the same structure was adopted by the Russian Supreme Soviet as the basis for its new legislature, elected in 1990. The only modifications were that the Russian Congress would be formed by two rather than three streams of representation (there would be no reserved seats for public organizations) and that there were to be fewer seats overall, with equally sized popular districts vastly outnumbering those from national-territorial areas.

The new legislative structure injected parliamentary elements into an older Leninist model of soviet power. The soviet model possessed other properties that proved problematic when representative institutions were actually called upon to exercise lawmaking power. First, it held that soviets fused all state power at a given administrative level in a single organ; second, it presumed that the soviets formed a territorial hierarchy under the guidance of the Supreme Soviet. Both of these premises continued to be reflected in the text of the constitution. The practice of soviet power differed both from parliamentarism, in that it did not operate with competing "government" and "opposition" parties seeking to gain control of the executive by acquiring a majority of seats, and from separation of powers, where government is formed independently of parliament. Yet elements of all three models were reflected in the 1990–93 constitutional system, facilitating conflict and crisis in relations between president and legislature as the parliamentary leadership used its dominance of the Presidium to manipulate the agenda and proceedings of the Supreme Soviet and Congresses and to defend the corporate interests of the deputies.[10] A particularly acute point of contention was the constitutional status of the chairman of the Supreme Soviet.

As Professor Mishin indicates, the chairman of the parliament was the chief executive official of the state until the presidency was created. Yet when establishing a presidency to oversee the executive branch, neither the union nor Russian deputies modified the constitutional status and powers of the Presidium or the chairmanship of the Supreme Soviet. The chairman of the parliament retained certain vestigial powers befitting a head of state, while the deputies' defense of the traditional rights of the soviets to exercise both lawmaking and dispositive (*rasporiaditel'nye*) powers brought them into constant conflict with the executive branch over the allocation of state resources and the determination of economic policy. And while the deputies agreed to amend the Russian constitution to add language about the separation of legislative from executive power in articles 1 and 3, they left in place the traditional soviet principle that gave the highest organ of soviet power competence to decide all questions, both executive and legislative, affecting the state (articles 2 and 104). Moreover, as Russia proceeded with the privatization of state land and productive assets, the stakes of the fight became serious. The question of ownership rights and hence profits from privatization of state assets became an acute point of contention between soviets and executive bodies at the center and at lower levels throughout the country. One result, as Andranik Migranyan has written, is that in the absence of other partisan links, the deputies mobilized around a defense of their corporate prerogatives and formed a "soviet party," while the president's supporters rallied to the defense of the executive branch and formed the equivalent of a "presidential party."[11] In several ways, therefore, both the structure and inherited powers of the Russian parliament did indeed work to promote confrontation between executive and legislative branches.

Yet although this line of explanation is helpful, it is incomplete. It fails to account for the Congress's inconsistent voting record on both constitutional and policy issues. The constitution has been repeatedly amended, after all, and majorities were found for some radical political and economic changes. Even after the presidency was created in 1991, the deputies were willing to delegate sweeping policy-making powers to Yeltsin, which they then sought to retract. At the first Congress, Yeltsin was elected chairman of the Supreme Soviet and thus the highest state official in the country, and the Declaration on Sovereignty was adopted, stricking a lethal blow at the union itself. At the third Congress (which the communists called in an attempt to remove Yeltsin), the deputies ended by approving Yeltsin's proposals for direct popular election of a state president. At the fourth Congress, two-thirds majorities were won for a series of constitutional amendments on the presidency, and at the fifth Congress simple majorities were found to give President Yeltsin broad decree power and to postpone the holding of subnational elections. The sixth Congress also approved the basic outlines of the Rumyantsev constitutional draft, which would have eliminated the Presidium and the Congress and breathed life into bicameralism. But it failed to adopt the new constitution, thus leaving the old one in place with its motley patchwork of amendments and powerful central chairman and Presidium. The seventh Congress voted for a national referendum on confidence in president and parliament which the eighth Congress canceled, while the ninth approved it again but only after coming within seventy-two votes of a two-thirds majority to remove Yeltsin from office. Why so contradictory a record? Clearly we must appeal to contextual factors to supplement structure if we are to explain the hairpin turns in deputy voting behavior over time.

Conservative Deputies

A third explanation, focusing on the composition of the Congress, is also often cited. According to this view, the deputies were political dinosaurs left over from the communist era, intent on preserving their privileges and status as deputies, and wresting control over the economy from Yeltsin. They used their traditional influence in the localities to get elected despite the anti-nomenklatura mood of the electorate. The power elite's tactics can be understood, perhaps, in light of the frequently cited fact that 86 percent of the elected RSFSR deputies were Communist Party members. But since most of the democrats were also Communist Party members at the time of election, this factor in and of itself is of little significance. More relevant is the point, cited by Alexander Sobianin, that just one week before the CPSU itself was dissolved—that is, *after* the coup—675 deputies still registered themselves at the fifth Congress as Communists.[12]

A variant on this view has been advanced by Jerry Hough and Regina Smyth. It holds that the voters were not cowed or defrauded in the elections but simply did not support radicals except in several large cities. Rather, they mostly elected people comfortable with power who would defend society against radical change. Hence the elections were fair but the country was conservative, especially its rural, small-town and middle-sized city populations.[13]

However one explains the results, all who have looked closely at the 1990 elections would agree with Gavin Helf and Jeffrey Hahn's general observation: "The democratic movement did well in the cities; the conservatives did well in the regions."[14]

How to classify deputies sociologically, however, depends on one's theory of the distribution of status in the old regime. For instance, a simple, dichotomous scheme featuring "intelligentsia" on the one hand and "officials" on the other has been advanced by Gregory Embree. Embree calculated that 56 percent of the deputies elected as RSFSR deputies in 1990 (and virtually the same percentage of deputies elected in 1989 from the RSFSR to the USSR legislature) were members of

the intelligentsia. (Among them he includes the sizable group of industrial and agricultural managers.) He also finds that 30 percent of the
deputies were party and government officials.[15] Tabulating three roll-
call votes in the Russian Congress and one in the union Congress by
the social backgrounds of the deputies, he finds that social category is
closely related to political stance.

An alternative method for assessing the effect of social background
on deputies' voting is that proposed by the Information-Analytic
Group headed by Alexander Sobianin. Sobianin's group found a close
association between administrative status and support for reform when
analyzing roll-call voting for ten crucial issues at the first Congress.[16]
Sobianin's breakdown of the deputy corps by social group emphasizes
the level of responsibility in the hierarchy over sector of occupation.[17]
After further refining the method, Sobianin divided the deputy corps
into five basic social groups based on occupation and rank at the time
of election:[18]

1. highest echelon of administration (231 deputies, or 21.7 percent);
2. middle echelon of administration (386, or 36.3 percent);
3. lowest echelon of administration (216, or 20.3 percent);
4. workers and peasants (51, or 4.8 percent);
5. employees of mental labor and other social groups (179, or 16.8
   percent).

He found a close linear relationship between membership in these
categories and voting at the early Congresses.

Sobianin's group also monitored the voting behavior of these groups
at later Congresses, estimating mean pro- and antireform ratings for
each (see Table 5.1). These figures reveal a conservative evolution for
four of the five groups, reflected in the broadly downward shift in the
mean for all deputies. The sociological view is good at explaining the
relative political positions of the five groups at any given Congress,
but weak in explaining the trends of change in deputies' positions
across time.

(Note that the clustering to be observed at the second half of the
fifth Congress reflects the dynamics immediately following the coup:
many conservative deputies were eager to assert Russian state power
vis-à-vis the union by such measures as giving President Yeltsin broad
economic and political powers, while many democratic deputies feared

Table 5.1

Mean Political Ratings of Russian Deputies by Status at Time of Election

	Congress					
	First	Third	Fifth	Sixth	Seventh	Eighth
Social group:						
Top echelon	−75	−72	−15	−51	−54	−73
Middle echelon	−9	−14	+8	−26	−34	−50
Lowest echelon	+54	+52	+24	+17	+2	−17
Worker/peasant	+45	+40	+17	−3	−20	−37
Intelligentsia	+77	+70	+20	+35	+24	+12
Mean for all deputies	+7	+4	+9	−11	−20	−37

Source: A. Sobianin and E. Gel'man, "Spisok narodnykh deputatov RF po ikh dolzhnosti na ianvar' 1990 g.," appendix to report, "VII S"ezd narodnykh deputatov Rossii v zerkale poimennykh golosovanii" (Moscow: Informatsionno-analiticheskaia gruppa, 1992).

Yeltsin's power and his reliance on strong local power elites. The result of these new cleavages was a convergence toward a narrow range of political scores in the center.)

How might we sum up the discussion so far? We examined three commonly cited explanations for the course taken by the deputies toward radical and self-destructive confrontation between the legislative branch and the president and his reform policies. First, the notion that the deputies were representing the will of the nation in opposing Yeltsin and Gaidar—which the deputies themselves frequently claimed—was put to the test in the April 25 referendum and found faulty. The high continuity in levels of voter support for Yeltsin from 1991 to 1993 by region and type of district, and the clear popular preference for Yeltsin over his opponents in that period, make it difficult to explain the rise of sharp deputy opposition to Yeltsin by any desire to reflect faithfully the voters' will. Even the December elections, so often considered a repudiation of Yeltsin and his policies, gave about equal shares of seats to proponents and opponents of his policies and did not directly test Yeltsin's popularity.

Second, we considered the argument that the entire legislative system suffered from innate flaws that were a product of the original Gorbachev design for the union legislature, which grafted quasi-parliamentary features onto a model of soviet power inherited from the early communist era. We noted that the new structure was internally inconsistent and was conducive to confrontation between executive and legislative powers. Yet design flaws alone cannot explain the deputies' initial willingness to modify the Russian constitution by creating a powerful presidency and to invest that presidency with the power to carry out a radical program of economic reform, but later to attempt to withdraw that grant of power.

The third argument had to do with the makeup of the deputy corps itself in terms of social background. At the time of the impeachment vote, much was made of the fact that 86 percent of the deputies were Communist Party members when elected, that the constitution itself was a product of the Brezhnev era, that the deputies were predominantly products of the nomenklatura, and so on. Certainly the resistance to radical reform by that significant part of the deputy corps with positions of high responsibility in the party, state, and economy is expected. But we are still left with two puzzles: first, how to explain majority support for measures such as the Declaration on Sovereignty adopted at the first Congress, the Yeltsin presidency created in 1991, and the delegation of power to Yeltsin to carry out his radical shock therapy program; and second, how to explain the post–fifth Congress conservative trend among the deputies from lower administrative ranks and from among the free professions. Presumably these anomalies can be accounted for only when we consider changes in the structure of power in the legislative and executive branches that took place after the 1990 elections, including the breakup of the union, as well as the effects of the policies pursued by Yeltsin and the government. In particular, we need to consider the effect of the creation of the Supreme Soviet and the presidency on the deputies. Like the argument about flawed structural arrangements, the sociological explanation is too static to explain the remarkable change we have witnessed in the past three years.

Ménage à Trois

The alternative account offered here emphasizes the importance of institutional changes that resulted in substantial alteration of the strength and composition of the coalition commanding a majority in the Congress. The term "ménage a trois" is used to call attention to the effects of the change from a condition of equilibrium resulting from a stable balance between two players—"democrats" and "conservatives," both sets of deputies, in a two-player game—to the unstable triangle that formed when a new player appeared on the scene in the form of the president. The cycling of majorities characteristic of an unstructured three-person game meant that no lasting majority could be found either for policy choices or for institutional arrangements.[19] I will argue that the creation of the presidency had several significant consequences. The position of the democratic forces within the parliament weakened as many deputies concentrated their energies on the presidential administration. The political base and influence of the conservative, communist wing of the parliament expanded. Conflict between president and parliament over constitutional supremacy intensified. In turn, these processes led finally to the violent denouement in which the president and his democratic allies among the deputies destroyed the peculiar system of soviet parliamentarism.

I make several assumptions about the deputies. I do not assume that all Russian deputies were actuated by a desire for reelection. Many deputies seemed to fear that they were so unpopular they would probably be defeated if they did try to run again.[20] On the other hand, 20 percent of them did choose to run for the new Federal Assembly and over half of these gained reelection. The electoral motive was surely not absent.[21] More important, it appears, is the value the deputies placed upon power and status, and the benefits and privileges that came with them. Second, I make the assumption that deputies were politically insecure but unconstrained. They lacked the harnesses and safety nets that might otherwise be provided by organized interest groups and competitive parties to hold them accountable and give them guidance, cues, information, resources, and support. Their party ties were extremely weak and their links to their home districts only slightly stronger. But while they had few organizational means to mobilize voter support, by the same token they were not constrained ideologically. There were few external barriers to drifting and bandwagoning. Since there were no local political machines or national parties to reward or penalize deputies for their positions, deputies seeking political careers needed to find other ways to hold on to power, privilege, status, and security. In such circumstances we would expect to see pronounced follow-the-leader effects since their support came from the leadership of the institution itself, and not from groups or parties outside it.

Table 5.2

**Mean Political Ratings of Deputies by Employment Category
as of April 1993**

				Congress			
Group	Absolute number	Third	Sixth	Seventh	Eighth	Ninth	Shift, 3rd–9th
Legislative	427	22	–3	–16	–35	–26	–48
Executive/ Judicial	203	3	612	10	–5	–3	–6
Managers	279	–36	–45	–52	–67	–64	–28
Other	124	28	–2	–18	–30	–24	–52
All	1,033	3	–11	–21	–37	–32	–35

Source: A. Sobianin and E. Gel'man, "Spisok deputatov po sotsial'no-professional'nomu sostavu (v nastoiashchee vremia) s reitingami v poriadke ubyvaniia R9" (Moscow: Informatsionno-analiticheskaia gruppa, 1993).

Finally, I assume that the deputies were materially insecure. Over the three years of the system's existence, at least half the deputies changed jobs. This is, in part, tied to the breakdown of the nomenklatura system itself and the loss of security for those deputies whose careers were tied to it. In particular, the dissolution of the CPSU meant that the over one hundred deputies who were employed by the party apparat at the time of election had no job to return to. Many of these became employees of the Supreme Soviet. In all, nearly 40 percent of the deputies came to work for the legislature itself and over 40 percent were employees of soviets at some level.[22] By summer 1993, over 200 deputies worked in some part of the executive branch, over half of them as presidential appointees (55 as chiefs of administration of regions and cities; 25 as local representatives of the president; 25 in various staff or ambassadorial posts under the president).[23] Several, indeed, gave up their deputy mandates entirely; among them, besides Yeltsin himself, Sergei Shakhrai, Vladimir Shumeiko, Aleksandr Rutskoi, Yuri Yarov, and Efim Basin, all relinquished their deputy status upon assuming an executive branch job. (Others, such as Yuri Afanas'ev and Nikolai Travkin, resigned as deputies for political reasons.)

Change of jobs is politically significant because, as Tables 5.2 and 5.3 indicate, current occupation was correlated with political position: where one stood depended upon where one sat. (Tables 5.2 and 5.3,

like Table 5.1 and subsequent tables and figures, employ Alexander
Sobianin's ratings to measure the political positions of individual deputies and various categories of deputies. The method used to construct
these scores is explained in note 16; it is comparable to the method
used by American interest groups to compare the voting records of
members of Congress on sets of issues considered important by the
organization. Sobianin's scores are useful summaries of the alignments
of Russian deputies in a unidimensional policy space where support for
Yeltsin and radical democratization and market reform defines one end
of a continuum and opposition to these defines the other. Sobianin's
ratings are widely used in both Russia and the West as guides to the
ideological stance of parliamentarians. I have drawn the data from the
periodic reports issued by the Sobianin group, which has kindly
granted permission for their use here.)

Table 5.2 breaks the deputy corps of April 1993 into four groups:
those employed by the Supreme Soviet or lower soviets; those employed by the executive branch or the judicial branch; those who were
enterprise managers; and those in working-class, intellectual, or other
occupations. The figures show that those working for the Supreme
Soviet had shifted very strongly from a proreform to an antireform
stance, while those working in the executive and judicial branches had
hardly shifted at all. Managers had shifted, although not as much as
those working for the Supreme Soviet. The small category comprising
all the rest had moved a total of 52 points, on average, slightly more
than the first category.[24]

Table 5.3 examines some of the deputies in the first two categories
more closely, comparing Supreme Soviet employees with presidential
appointees, breaking each of these down into smaller subcategories,
and comparing each group across the sixth and ninth Congresses.

Quite clearly, both selection and self-selection were at work here.
Both Yeltsin and Khasbulatov were acutely aware of the power of
patronage. After September 21, for instance, in order to help persuade
the deputies not to resist his decree dissolving parliament, Yeltsin
promised each a year's salary as severance pay and the right, if they
had worked in the Supreme Soviet for three years, to keep their Moscow apartments. Similarly, the broad patronage powers enjoyed by the
chairman of the Supreme Soviet over the distribution of committee
chairmanships and other paying jobs in the Supreme Soviet, a recruitment process in which Khasbulatov's friends were rewarded for their

Table 5.3

**Political Ratings of Supreme Soviet Employees
and Presidential Appointees**

Current position	Sixth Congress			Ninth Congress		
	Absolute number	Percentage of deputies	Score	Absolute number	Percentage of deputies	Score
Top leaders of Supreme Soviet	9	0.9	−25	8	0.8	−57
Committee chairpersons	28	2.7	−13	23	2.2	−31
Department committee chairpersons, subcommittee chairpersons, secretaries	168	16.0	−10	169	16.4	−20
Full-time committee members, staff	144	13.7	−16	175	16.9	−31
Total Supreme Soviet employees	349	33.3	−13	375	36.3	−27
Presidential advisers; government ministers	26	2.5	44	17	1.6	36
Presidential representatives in regions	31	3.0	68	29	2.8	82
Ambassadors, trade representatives, presidential staff	16	1.5	−16	16	1.5	−29
Chiefs of administration, regions, centers	47	4.5	4	41	4.0	9
Total presidential appointees	120	11.4	27	103	10.0	28

Source: A. Sobianin and E. Gel'man, "Spisok deputatov po sotsial'no-professional'nomu sostavu (v nastoiashchee vremia) s reitingami v poriadke ubyvaniia R9" (Moscow: Informatsionno-analiticheskaia gruppa, 1993).

support with jobs and privileges, may help account for the shift in deputy political positions. While only 250 deputies were able serve in the Supreme Soviet as members (and in fact, there were always fewer members), close to 400 found paying jobs in it and 200 *held office* in it as committee or subcommittee chairs and the like.[25] The scarcity and high prices of amenities such as cars and apartments in Moscow made deputies dependent on powerful patrons who could supply these; and in fact, the chairman of the Supreme Soviet could arrange to sell cars to deputies at well below market prices and provide housing for those seeking to live in Moscow. For example, to be assigned an apartment in a particularly desirable neighborhood—in one of the apartment buildings on Rublev Highway—required Khasbulatov's personal approval. Moreover, the chairman controlled access to such perquisites as the use of official dachas and chauffeur-driven cars and inclusion on overseas parliamentary delegations. The chairman also had extensive rights over parliamentary proceedings, such as right of recognition on the floor, wide discretion to decide which bills would come up and when, influence over the appointment of chairs and members to committees, and full control over several critical staff departments of the Supreme Soviet. Among these, for instance, was the Information Department, which maintained full electronic files on all deputies, including their voting records. Indeed, it was the only source in Russia for the records of *all* electronically tabulated votes—not just roll-call votes, but even those votes that were considered closed but were recorded and stored electronically. And, in fact, these votes were analyzed.[26] The chairman was thus in a unique position to monitor deputies' behavior. (Indeed, there is evidence that Khasbulatov maintained an intelligence service that tapped phones and followed certain deputies.) In addition, by taking over the network of closed telephone lines that formerly linked the RSFSR Council of Ministers with regional and local offices, the chairman gained a secure communications link with regional and local soviets. This network was regularly used for large-scale telephone conferences between Khasbulatov and soviets in deputies' home districts when Khasbulatov was attempting to develop a base of support outside Moscow.

The chairman therefore had enormous opportunity to reward loyalty and punish dissent, and Khasbulatov was not reluctant to take advantage of it. This was made evident in the summer of 1992, when Khasbulatov reorganized the responsibilities of the deputy chairs, depriving his first deputy chairman, Sergei Filatov, of all power over staff and budget decisions, and ultimately forcing him out of the Supreme Soviet leadership. (An effort by the democratic forces on the Presidium and in the Supreme Soviet to counter Khasbulatov's move by removing him fizzled.) If we are correct in assuming that deputies were vulnerable to the levers in the hands of the Supreme Soviet lead-

Table 5.4

Political Ratings of Supreme Soviet Employees by Position

	Congress				
Category	Third	Sixth	Seventh	Eighth	Ninth
Leadership ($N = 8$)[1]	−20	−29	−54	−77	−57
Committee chairs ($N = 23$)[2]	+30	+3	−5	−31	−31
Subcommittee chairpersons ($N = 169$)[3]	+39	+7	−6	−28	−20
Committee members ($N = 175$)[4]	+23	−2	−18	−35	−31

Source: See Table 5.3.

Notes:

[1] The leadership category comprises the chairman and deputy chairmen of the Supreme Soviet and the chairs of the two chambers.

[2] Includes chairs of the commissions of the two chambers.

[3] Includes deputy chairs of committees and commissions and committee secretaries.

[4] Includes members of commissions of the chambers, and equivalent bodies such as the Constitutional Commission and Supreme Economic Council.

ership because of the weakness of alternative sources of support, we would expect to see a substantial number of deputies tending to trim their own voting positions to that of the dominant power within the institution. This, indeed, is precisely what the data show. For those deputies holding paid jobs in the system of the Supreme Soviet as of the end of March 1993, Table 5.4 shows their average political ratings, by category, between March 1991 and March 1993.[27]

The recruitment of deputies to paying jobs in the Supreme Soviet therefore depended on both self-selection by deputies and the choices made by the chairman and leadership of the Supreme Soviet, who had considerable influence over the voting positions of the deputies. Over time, change of parliamentary chair and deputy chairs affected the selection of committee chairs and other paid offices, and the political temper of the deputy corps more generally. In turn, the election of new chairs and deputy chairs of the Supreme Soviet depended on a change in the voting majority of the deputy corps. A small change in the voting balance in the Congress, therefore, was magnified through the patronage powers of the leadership into a larger advantage for the ruling coalition. We must therefore seek to explain how the shift from a roughly equal balance of power between conservatives and reformers to a preponderance for the conservatives came about.

All analysts agree that the elections of 1990 produced a highly polarized distribution of political positions in the Russian deputy corps. Around 40 percent of the deputies voted a strongly reformist line, and an equal proportion took a strongly antireformist position (see Figure 5.1). The bipolar distribution of positions and the rough equality of strength between left and right held steady through the first four Congresses: on a wide range of issues, the same alignments held. (See chart below for dates of the Congresses.)

First: May 16–June 22, 1990
Second: November 27–December 15, 1990
Third: March 28–April 5, 1991
Fourth: May 21–25, 1991
Fifth: July 10–17, 1991; October 28–November 4, 1991
Sixth: April 6–21, 1992
Seventh: December 1–14, 1992
Eighth: March 10–13, 1993
Ninth: March 26–29, 1993

At both the first and second Congresses, only 15–20 percent of the deputies did not vote consistently with one side or the other.[28] In the third and fourth Congresses, the middle ground shrank further, to around 10 percent of the deputies. At these Congresses, the democrats succeeded in capturing a sufficient number of deputies from the center to win victories on certain key issues, including the decree on power and the decree on sovereignty, Yeltsin's election as chairman of the Supreme Soviet, and subsequently the constitutional amendments on the presidency and the law granting Yeltsin wide decree power to implement reform and block the union government. They did not win on all issues, of course. At the first Congress they failed to elect a strongly reformist Supreme Soviet. They failed to enact the new constitution worked out by the Constitutional Commission between the first and second Congresses. Politics at the first four Congresses centered around the efforts by the reformist and antireform flanks to win over allies from the center and gain a majority. Neither had a firm majority, but the democrats had a slight advantage. Although I have no direct evidence on the point, Yeltsin presumably used the patronage powers of the chairmanship to influence voting positions of deputies. Moreover, and perhaps more importantly, Yeltsin's parliamentary al-

Figure 5.1. **Polarization of Russian Deputies, Congresses 1–3**

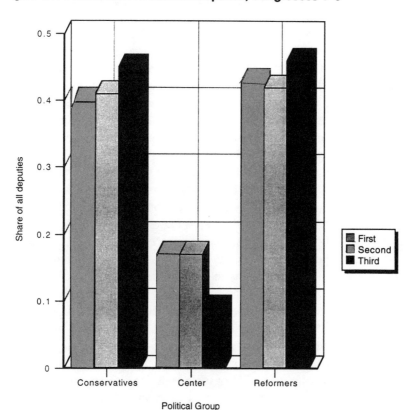

Source: Author's analysis of role-call voting in the Russian Congress of People's Deputies, Congresses 1–3 (1991).
Notes:
Conservatives = deputies with political ratings from –34 to –100
Center = deputies with political ratings from –33 to +33
Reformers = deputies with political ratings from +34 to +100

lies had an incentive to build majorities on important issues and therefore sought to increase their influence in parliament.

The hard-line right counterattacked in early 1991 (simultaneously with the assault on other fronts, such as the violent attempted takeovers in the Baltic states, the shows of force on the streets of large cities, Shevardnadze's resignation, and so on). Conservative Russian deputies demanded that Yeltsin present a report to the third Congress, evidently as part of a strategy aimed at removing him. In the meantime, however, on March 17 the Russian referendum returned a strong majority for a Russian presidency. Gorbachev's heavy-handed pressure tactics (he surrounded the Kremlin with tanks and APCs on the opening day of the Russian Congress) backfired, further polarizing the deputy corps and strengthening Yeltsin's hand. More than 90 percent of the deputies were consistently allied with one camp or the other and the democrats won important victories on the presidency and on Russia's power to block decisions of the union government. The fourth Congress likewise gave a slim majority to Yeltsin's supporters on key issues, notably on holding presidential elections in June.

The creation of the presidency ultimately weakened the democrats, however, because it divided their loyalties. Some became suspicious of strong executive power, others supported a powerful presidency as the only institution capable of bringing about a decisive break with the past. Yeltsin and his closest associates left the parliament for the executive branch. For example, Sergei Shakhrai, the forceful chairman of the legislation committee, resigned in October. Yeltsin's political adviser Gennadii Burbulis left the apparatus of the Supreme Soviet and became a presidential counselor. Burbulis had run the strategic analysis unit for Yeltsin in the parliament that helped Yeltsin bargain and ally with deputies. The departure of his brain trust and of key legislative supporters seriously weakened Yeltsin's ability to construct majorities for measures he wanted to pass. Indeed, Yeltsin tended to neglect his base of support among the deputies, seeking to free executive decision making from legislative oversight rather than to build a consistent majority within the Congress. At the same time, between late 1991 and early 1993 a number of deputies formerly identified with the democratic wing split off and began voting with the communist camp. Very few of the conservatives, however, shifted to the other side. Some of Yeltsin's aides, such as Burbulis, subsequently admitted that they had erred in not cultivating better relations with the deputies. Some of Yeltsin's advisers, however, evidently concluded sometime in 1992 that the parliament was a hopeless cause and that sooner or later Yeltsin would abolish it.

The democratic forces had united against the communists during and after the elections, again during the conservative counterassault of the winter 1990–91, and again during the putsch, but began to divide over issues that appeared after Yeltsin left the Supreme Soviet. These included the candidacy of Khasbulatov for chairman of the Supreme

Soviet, and the power of the president to appoint local heads of administration. On both issues, the democratic wing split, allowing the conservatives to form a majority with a number of former democrats and centrists. In turn, the conservatives began to consolidate their control within the Congress, Supreme Soviet, and Presidium by rewarding a number of middle-of-the-roaders and reformers who made spectacular flips from the democratic to conservative positions.

At the sixth Congress, the old left–right cleavage had eroded. Different majorities formed over different issues; the left–right dimension was now supplemented by a new one over presidential power.[29] The new structural adjustment program of the Gaidar government provoked strong resistance among many deputies, and a so-called centrist position (broadly sympathetic to the pleas of state enterprise directors suffering from sharp government spending and credit cuts) appeared ascendant. The deputies' inability to control the makeup and course of the government provoked substantial frustration and the passage of an antireform resolution demanding relaxation of the shock therapy program; Gaidar and the government responded by submitting their resignations. The confrontation was then eased by a compromise resolution endorsing the government's program but demanding modifications. Around one hundred deputies who formerly backed the Yeltsin position now voted most of the time with the conservatives.

But no "centrist" bloc emerged with a stable majority. Rather, through 1992, the communist conservatives consolidated their power in the institution. By the end of 1992 the number of deputies who had been identified with the democratic wing and now voted consistently with the conservatives was 188. Gaidar was defeated when Yeltsin proposed him as prime minister (rather than acting prime minister, as he had been). Yeltsin demanded a referendum on the principles of presidential power. A last-minute compromise arranged by Valery Zorkin, chairman of the Constitutional Court, produced an agreement accepted by the Congress that a referendum would be held in April provided that Khasbulatov and Yeltsin could agree on the formulation of the issues to be put to the public; Khasbulatov, however, balked and refused to allow the referendum. The tense eighth Congress in early March 1993, which canceled the referendum, marked the crest of the conservative trend. Some 676 deputies had a political rating of −34 and lower and only 242 had ratings of +34 and higher. Around 250 deputies had changed their scores by at least 50 points in the conservative direction since the first Congress. The ninth Congress was held six days after Yeltsin appeared in the famous televised broadcast of March 20, when he threatened to suspend the Congress and introduce presidential rule. Six hundred seventeen deputies voted to remove Yeltsin, falling only 72 votes shortly of the required two-thirds of all deputies needed for passage. Since 109 deputies did not take part in the voting, the motion could conceivably have succeeded.[30]

Who were the roughly 250 deputies who had shifted so sharply from the democratic to the conservative side? Sobianin provides the following breakdown of their current occupations:[31]

- Supreme Soviet of Russia, 140;
- soviets of other levels, 6;
- executive branch, 21;
- enterprise directors, 43;
- lower administrative echelon, 32;
- workers and peasants, 8.

Over half belonged to the category that we identified as being particularly vulnerable to the carrots and sticks wielded by the leadership of the institution itself. The shift of a small number was enough to produce a bandwagon effect as the leadership took an increasingly conservative line. As more deputies defected to vote more often with the conservatives, the mean ratings of every category of deputies shifted rightward and the communist/nationalist wing enjoyed ever larger majorities. (See Figure 5.2.)

Ruslan Imranovich Khasbulatov himself illustrates the point. Voting consistently with the democratic camp at the first three Congresses, Khasbulatov commenced a radical change after Yeltsin left the legislature. His Sobianin score at the third Congress was a perfect +100. By the seventh congress it had fallen to –60. First deputy chairman of the Supreme Soviet under Yeltsin, Khasbulatov found himself unable to get elected chairman at the fifth Congress—many democrats as well as communists mistrusted him. At the second part of the Congress, Khasbulatov allied himself with the hard-line communist opposition, winning their conditional support for the chairmanship and thereafter voting consistently against Yeltsin.[32] In the increasingly conservative climate of the Supreme Soviet and Presidium over 1992 and 1993, it became necessary for committee chairs and other full-time legislators

Figure 5.2. **Political Alignments of the Russian Congresses**

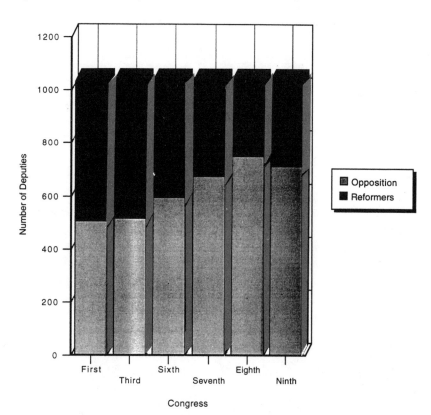

Source: Author's analysis of role-call voting in the Russian Congress of People's Deputies, Congresses 1, 3, 6, 7, 8, 9 (1990–93).
Notes:
Reformers = deputies with political ratings from +1 to +100
Opposition = deputies with political ratings from 0 to –100

to trim their sails or risk being pushed out of their jobs, as happened to several ranking officeholders (such as Sergei Filatov, who had been first deputy chairman under Khasbulatov, Viacheslav Bragin of the media committee, Sergei Krasavchenko of the economic reform committee, and Mikhail Mitiukov of the legislation committee). Note that Khasbulatov himself was probably being pushed at least as much by his anti-Yeltsin partners as he was pulling on the Congress: the degree to which Khasbulatov himself was responsible for the disastrous confrontation that resulted remains an interesting but somewhat indetermi-

Table 5.5

Political Ratings of Two Committee Chairs Contrasted

	Congress					
	First	Third	Sixth	Seventh	Eighth	Ninth
N.P. Medvedev	+86	+90	+91	+64	−40	−100
V.N. Podoprigora	+100	+98	+63	+84	+100	+92

Source: Interview with staff of the Information Department.

nate question. Perhaps Khasbulatov became the ally and servant of a strongly antireform coalition, the political position of which was more extreme than he preferred, in order to attain and hold on to personal power within the institution.

Let us illustrate the point by comparing two committee chairs, Vladimir N. Podoprigora and Nikolai P. Medvedev.[33] Podoprigora chaired the Joint Committee on Interrepublican Relations, Regional Policy and Cooperation, while Medvedev chaired the Council of Nationalities Commission on National-State Structure and Interethnic Relations. Both were born in the early 1950s, and both were low-level Communist Party staff officials in their regions before being elected deputies. Both campaigned on the democratic platform and started out voting consistently for reform positions. But while Podoprigora's scores remained firmly on the democratic side, Medvedev tilted sharply toward the conservative camp in the last two Congresses (see Table 5.5). Although both men are fairly typical of Sobianin's third social group—the lowest echelon of administration—in their initial political liberalism, the difference in their political evolution is not well explained by background factors.

Both Podoprigora and Medvedev found themselves coming under intense pressure from the parliamentary leadership. Podoprigora continued to vote consistently with the democrats while Medvedev shifted away from their camp, although he insisted that he remained a moderate with good relations with both sides. About two weeks before Yeltsin abolished parliament, however, Medvedev was invited by Yeltsin to head the presidential administration for liaison with regional representatives and accepted the offer (Khasbulatov called him a "traitor" for doing so). Podoprigora remained in office in the parliament until the dissolution decree, when he immediately sided with the president. Yeltsin appointed him head of the group that reorganized the staff structures of the new Federal Assembly. He then ran for the Council of the Federation and won.

The point of this comparison is to illustrate the play of push and pull factors as influences on democratically minded deputies: Khasbulatov pushed, Yeltsin pulled. The result was to leave the powers of the leadership of a very centralized legislative institution in the hands of figures closely allied with the most extreme elements of Russia's communist and nationalist opposition. The physical departure and political defection of the democrats became a self-reinforcing process.

The comparison also reveals a fairly typical pattern of political evolution for deputies serving in parliamentary offices. Consider Table 5.3 again. For individuals serving as committee chairs at the time of the ninth Congress,[34] their average political score fell from +30 at the third Congress to –31 at the eighth and ninth Congresses; among subcommittee chairs it fell from +39 to –28 and –20. Note that these swings of 60 and 70 points are far wider than those for the deputy corps as a whole, where the average deputy shifted from a score of +3 at the third Congress to –37 and –36 at the eighth and ninth. In other words, the committee chairs were far more liberal as a group than the median deputy in the early Congresses but little different by early 1993—less because of turnover in the chairmanships than because *many of the same individuals changed their own political positions sharply.* Thus, because of the powerful mechanism of selection and self-selection in the recruitment of deputies to jobs in the Supreme Soviet and on the president's staff, members of the anti-Yeltsin opposition assumed nearly all the leadership positions in the parliament by the summer of 1993.

As confirmation we might cite the flap over whether the Supreme Soviet was to participate in the work of Yeltsin's constitutional assembly in June 1993. Ten members of the presidium—including First Deputy Chairman Nikolai Ryabov and a number of committee chairs, among them several centrists not formerly known for their pro-Yeltsin leanings—broke with Khasbulatov and urged that the Supreme Soviet take part. For their disloyalty they were punished; Ryabov was stripped of his duties and the committee chairs were forced to give "accounts" of themselves to the Supreme Soviet, which in several cases led to their being removed from their posts. Some said it reminded them of the way Communist Party meetings in the past had examined individual members' personal behavior. Mikhail Mitiukov, formerly chairman of the legislation committee, which was split (one of the successor committees being given to Vladimir Isakov, a leader of the hard-line communists), was accused by Khasbulatov of leading the fight against the Supreme Soviet "from within."[35]

Summary and Conclusions

The three explanations presented above for the radical change in the political temper of the Russian deputy corps over 1990–93 are wanting, but each illuminates an aspect of the problem. The deputies miscalculated if they expected opposition to Yeltsin to bring them political support. Yet voters clearly did punish the democrats for the economic hardships they had experienced over 1992 and 1993, and gave a larger vote share to Zhirinovsky's party than to any other. Certainly the old constitution was an inconsistent mélange of disparate elements. Instead of separation of powers, the Russian system started out using a model that gave all allocative power in the state to the soviets. The creation of a presidency did not clarify the respective spheres of power over ownership of property, control of the cabinet, powers over local government, foreign policy, and other issues. By itself the flawed constitutional structure could not explain the shifting balance of political forces within the Congress, yet surely it encouraged each side to cite constitutional backing for its political aims. Similarly, although the deputy corps itself comprised many representatives of the old power elite, the conservative tide drew in many who initially sympathized with the Democratic Russia electoral movement.

None of these explanations by itself suffices to explain what happened, but each serves to complement an account focusing on the self-reinforcing effects of the change in institutional arrangements that occurred with the creation of the state presidency in Russia. An equilibrium between democrats and their opponents in which neither had complete control over policy was upset when Yeltsin left the legislature for the Kremlin. Democrats had fewer and fewer incentives to fight for their legislative aims and more and more reason to rely on presidential power to achieve their political objectives. The opposition acquired an expanding share of the votes in the Congresses, which it used to oppose Yeltsin and his government. The chairmanship then passed to a figure who allied himself with the anti-Yeltsin opposition—Khasbulatov. He could use the strategic powers of the chairmanship to reward those who supported him and force aside his opponents. He was able to exercise and aggrandize power so long as he served the interests of the majority coalition in the deputy corps, which sought to remove Yeltsin from the presidency and end the radical reform course of his government.

It should not surprise us that the deputies as a whole were less consistent in their policy outlooks than are legislators in societies where political parties and other organized interests link them to voters, guide and constrain their voting behavior, and provide them with alternative paths to political careers and the benefits associated with power. The chairman of the Russian Supreme Soviet was able to satisfy the desires of many deputies for power, privilege, status, and material well-being by giving them paid jobs in the system of the Supreme Soviet. This was particularly important to those who found themselves cut off from their careers and basic material benefits when the CPSU and its nomenklatura system were abolished. Just as a stable two-player game gives way to unstable triangular relations and cycling majorities when a third player enters the game, or a stable marriage unravels when a third party appears, Yeltsin's election to a new presidency altered the balance of power between democrats and communists. His departure from the legislature for the executive branch left a vacuum in the chairmanship and certain key positions in the committees and apparatus of the Supreme Soviet. Yeltsin and his associates no longer expended much effort on building majorities on key issues for a democratic-centrist coalition. Khasbulatov's election to the chairmanship filled the vacuum with a new majority coalition of conservatives and former democrats. As this coalition grew, the initial small advantage for the communists gave way to ever more lopsided margins and majorities for ever more radically conservative positions, since the conservatives needed to make fewer and fewer concessions to their democratic opponents, and since more deputies were pushed or pulled from their legislative offices into presidential appointments. Executive-legislative confrontation became self-reinforcing, resulting in Decree 1400 of September 21, 1993, and its bloody aftermath.

Since 1991 the Russian constitutional system has broken down twice. Following the August 1991 coup attempt, all the governing structures of the Soviet Union, including its parliamentary institutions, collapsed. The weak, manipulated Congress and Supreme Soviet of the USSR could not contain the demands of the republics for sovereign power; its leader allied himself with the opposition to President Gorbachev's efforts to form a new but much looser union. Similarly, the chairman of the Russian Congress and Supreme Soviet allied himself with a coalition strenuously opposed to President Yeltsin's power and policies. The collision brought about the demise of that constitutional system. What are the odds that the new constitutional arrangements that came into being through the December 1993 referendum and elections will prove any more lasting than their predecessors? An answer to this question is premature. Nevertheless, three observations may be in order.

First, the arrangements that came into effect in 1994 began with a presidency already established. In both the prior cases, that of the USSR parliament of 1989–91 and the Russian parliament of 1990–93, the presidency was created midstream. The constitution was altered piecemeal to accommodate the new institution but was neither replaced nor thoroughly amended: inconsistent provisions continued to plague the polity thereafter. To the extent that the "design flaw" theory is valid, the new constitution will benefit from the elimination of the overlap between legislative and executive spheres of power that characterized the USSR and Russian transitional constitutions. It remains the case, all the same, that the president's powers to pass laws by decree still must be clarified by the Constitutional Court. Similarly, the new Federal Assembly operates under new rules of procedure. Of particular interest in this respect is the structure of the lower chamber, the State Duma. Here the Presidium has been replaced by a council made up of the leaders of all the registered factions in the chamber. Collectively they decide agenda and sometimes hammer out substantive bargains necessary to pass divisive bills. The chairman's power derives from his ability to negotiate consent among these political leaders (his patronage powers have been largely removed). This seems to provide a more stable environment for the exercise of leadership within parliament.

Second, we pointed out that the absence of party ties in the 1990–93 parliament left deputies vulnerable to the pressures wielded by a powerful and politically interested leader. A functioning competitive party system, where parties structure majorities, would be expected to have a stabilizing effect on the operation of the legislature and its relations with the executive. It would help tie deputies to voters, giving them incentives for party loyalty and hope for reelection, and thus keeping them from straying too far from the political temper of the electorate. It would stabilize political conflict within the legislature by rewarding deputies for ideological consistency, and would diminish tendencies for bandwagoning, thus moderating policy decision. Finally, it would stabilize relations between the legislative and executive branches by clarifying the rules determining political control of the government. Preliminary observation of the operation of the new Federal Assembly suggests that these predictions have been borne out in fact.[36] Following the elections, when half the seats in the lower chamber were filled through proportional representation, deputies do in fact vote with their party factions most of the time, and party leaders are able to structure deals that can command majorities. Indeed, most of the major agreements enabling parliament to act and to reach compromises with President Yeltsin have been brokered by party faction leaders.

Finally, the political aims and strategic premises of the leader matter. In contrast to Ruslan Khasbulatov, Ivan Rybkin enjoys a very favorable reputation among virtually all deputies. He is regarded as straightforward and trustworthy (and was seen as such in the last parliament, when he was a leader of the communist faction). His interests seem to be the good of the institution and stability of the political system, rather than personal power aggrandizement. Rybkin was elected chairman by a narrow majority, having been opposed by the democratic forces; but now his support is considerably wider. He has gained in stature within the legislature through his skill in engineering compromises that enable the passage of major bills and are acceptable to the president. Although the resources at his disposal are limited, his influence is reinforced by the higher degree of party organization within the parliament. For these reasons—the existence of a more consistent set of constitutional and procedural rules that were already in place when the new parliament began work; the much greater importance of party; and the different political personality of the parliament's leadership—the new legislative arrangements have a better chance of surviving the turmoil of the early postcommunist era than did the last two.

Notes

I would like to express my appreciation to Steven Smith, Gerhard Loewenberg, Jeffrey Hahn, and Alexander Sobianin for valuable comments on this paper. Research for the paper was underwritten in part by a grant from the National Council for Soviet and East European Research, which of course bears no responsibility for its content or conclusions.

1. R.I. Khasbulatov, "O povyshenii roli mestnykh Sovetov v protsesse podgotovki i priniatiia novoi Konstitutsii Rossiiskoi Federatsii," mimeographed text distributed at conference of local soviet deputies, Parliamentary Center, Moscow, June 1, 1993.

2. I am indebted to Nikolai Petrov of the Institute of Geography of the Academy of Sciences for this data.

3. The following is drawn from A. Sobianin, E. Gel'man, and O. Kaiunov, "Politicheskii klimat Rossii v 1991–1993 godakh," (Moscow: Nezavisimaia Informatsionno-Analiticheskaia Gruppa, 1993), p. 8

4. See Leonid Margolis's interview with Alexander Sobianin, "Effect 55-i paralleli," *Vek*, no. 20 (39) (1993).

5. I.M. Kliamkin, "Postkommunisticheskaia demokratiia i ee istoricheskie osobennosti v Rossii," *Polis*, no. 2 (1993) p. 16.

6. The charges of falsification have been widely aired in the Russian press. See A. Sobianin and V. Sukhovol'skii, "V korolevstve krivykh zerkal," *Segodnia*, March 10, 1994; V. Vyzhutovich, "Tsentrizbirkom prevrashchaetsia v politicheskoe vedomstvo," *Izvestiia*, May 4, 1994; Larisa Aidinova, "Fal'shivye vybory, mertvye dushi?" *Vek*, May 13–19, 1994; T. Sukhomlinova interview with A. Sobianin, "Ministerstvo demokratii: svoia ruka vladyka," *Rossiia*, May 4–10, 1994. A response to the Sobianin charges is Iu. Vedeneev and V.I. Lysenko, "Vybory–93: Uroki i al'ternativy," *Nezavisimaia gazeta* (June 28, 1994).

7. Avgust Mishin, "Ideia parlamenta i Verkhovnyi sovet Rossiiskoi Federatsii," *Politika i Mysl'*, no. 1 (November–December 1992). (California: Russian Political Review, 1992), p. 76.

8. Alexander Sobianin, "Political Cleavages among the Russian Deputy Corps," in Thomas F. Remington, ed., *Parliaments in Transition: The New Legislative Politics in the Former USSR and Eastern Europe* (Boulder, CO: Westview, 1994), pp. 181–215.

9. Nineteenth Party Conference in 1988. See Giuletto Chiesa with Douglas Taylor Northrop, *Transition to Democracy: Political Change in the Soviet Union, 1987–1991* (Hanover, NH: University Press of New England, 1993), pp. 14–26.

In his book *More Power to the Soviets*, Michael Urban cites a few criticisms of Gorbachev's proposal that were made in the course of the brief discussion in the fall of 1988. The USSR system was taken over and modified in the amendments to the Russian constitution the following year. The most important change was to drop the provision for reserved seats for members named by public organizations. Other important features were preserved, however, including the roughly 1:4 ratio of membership between the Supreme Soviet and the parent Congress, the dominant Presidium comprising all committee chairs, the strong post of chairman of the Supreme Soviet, and the weak bicameralism where the two chambers were equal in size, terms, and powers but distinct as to composition and specialization.

Thus the original structural design made by the Gorbachev inner circle in 1988 for a USSR legislative system continues to dominate the Russian legislative system long after the USSR's demise. The question that needs to be asked, though, is why: How is it that it has persisted when so many other structures in Russia have changed?

See Michael E. Urban, *More Power to the Soviets: The Democratic Revolution in the USSR* (Aldershot: Edward Elgar, 1990), esp. pp. 72–73; and Brendan Kiernan, *The End of Soviet Politics: Elections, Legislatures, and the Demise of the Communist Party* (Boulder, CO: Westview, 1993). Also on the transitional USSR legislative system, see Robert T. Huber and Donald R. Kelley, eds., *Perestroika-Era Politics: The New Soviet Legislature and Gorbachev's Political Reforms* (Armonk, NY: M.E. Sharpe, 1991).

10. Russian constitutional scholars and practitioners often assume that the principle of separation of powers applies to all democratic systems, rather than to presidential systems. They therefore have difficulty understanding the role of a parliament in a system in which the government controls parliamentary proceedings and outcomes. It is important to remember, therefore, that in such a system parliament's power to grant or deny its confidence in government is a far more important power than its nominal power to make laws.

11. Andranik Migranian, "Prezidentskii proekt—garant stabil'nosti," *Nezavisimaia gazeta*, 5 June 1993.

12. Alexander Sobianin, "Metamorfozy s"ezda," (n.p., n.d.), p. 13.

13. Regina Smyth, "Ideological vs. Regional Cleavages: Do the Radicals Control the RSFSR Parliament?" *Journal of Soviet Nationalities* 1:3 (Fall 1990), pp. 112–157; Jerry F. Hough, "Yaroslavl," in Remington, ed., *Parliaments in Transition:* pp. 75–96.

14. Gavin Helf and Jeffrey W. Hahn, "Old Dogs and New Tricks: Party Elites in the Russian Regional Elections of 1990," *Slavic Review* 51:3 (Fall 1992), pp. 511–530.

15. Here I am adding 11 komsomol and trade union officials to the 309 CPSU, soviet, and executive branch members that he defines as officials. He leaves the 43 military servicemen, however, as a separate category. Gregory J. Embree, "RSFSR Election Results and Roll Call Votes," *Soviet Studies* 43:6 (1991), pp. 1065–1084, esp. pp. 1068–1069.

16. L. Efimova, A. Sobianin and D. Yur'ev, "Are the People and the Nomenklatura United?" *Argumenty i fakty*, no. 29 (1990), p. 2. This article is based on the early research of the Sobianin group.

The methodology worked out by the Sobianin group, which they continue to use, is as follows. Selecting a set of crucial roll-call votes as indicators of political position, the group calculates a rating, or score, for every deputy based on the number of times the deputy voted for or against the reform position. If a deputy votes for the reform position 100 percent of the time, his score is accordingly +100. Correspondingly, opposition to this position 100 percent of the time yields a score of −100. The number of times a deputy voted against the reform position is subtracted from the number of times he voted for it to yield a score between +100 and −100. If a deputy did not participate in voting, this does not affect his score, but an abstention is treated as equivalent to a "nay."

The mean scores of various groupings of deputies are then calculated. In particular, the Sobianin group monitors the ratings of deputy fractions, regional delegations, and social/occupational status categories.

This method, analogous to that frequently used to calculate the political stance of American congressmen by such interest groups as the the ADA or ACA, requires informed judgment as to which votes are bellwethers of the dimension in which the observer is interested. In this case, Sobianin's scores should be seen as accurate measures of the level of deputy support for the Yeltsin position: radical economic change and strong presidential power.

The votes selected to generate political ratings are indicated in the Sobianin group's publications. The number varies by Congress. Ten were used for the first Congress (before the electronic tallying system was installed), twenty for the second, fifty-five for the third, and forty for the sixth.

17. Regina Smyth finds confirmation of this point when she extends Sobianin's analysis of roll-call voting in the first congress to another fourteen votes. Smyth, "Ideological vs. Regional Cleavages," p. 137.

18. A. Sobianin and D. Yur'ev, *S''ezd narodnykh deputatov RSFSR v zerkale poimennykh golosovanii: rasstanovka sil i dinamika razvitiia politicheskogo protivostoianiia* (Moscow: n.p., 1991), pp. 62–65.

19. A useful discussion of the problem of cycling and the way institutions may help induce stability in representative bodies may be found in Kenneth A. Shepsle, "Institutional Equilibrium and Equilibrium Institutions," in Herbert F. Weisberg, ed., *Political Science: The Science of Politics* (New York: Agathon Press, 1986), pp. 51–81.

20. This assessment is based on my interviews with a number of deputies and close observers of the legislature. In a survey of 32 deputies that I conducted in spring 1993, answers to the question "Would you wish to be elected again as deputy?" broke down as follows: 5 answered "Yes, if I am elected"; 11 responded "No"; and 16 answered "It depends on circumstances."

21. Moreover, of the 135 former deputies who ran for the Duma, 47 ran simultaneously on a party's list and in a territorial district, thus greatly increasing their chances of winning a parliamentary seat.

22. Three hundred sixty-nine at the beginning of April 1992 and 381 at the same time in 1993.

23. These data are drawn from three sources: reports of the Information-Analytic Group (March 29, 1993, and May 6, 1992), and a printout of the deputies and their current jobs that was generously done at my request by the Information Department of the Supreme Soviet on June 14, 1993.

24. For instance, thirteen blue-collar workers had shifted an average of 84 points toward the opposition end of the spectrum. The average shift in the same direction for the thirty-two physicians was 67 points. The ten college professors shifted in an antireform direction from +46 to −7.

25. A deputy can hold a paid position as committee member and yet not be a member of the Supreme Soviet. He or she may then vote in committee but not on the floor. One committee chair I interviewed happened not to be a member until recently, and claimed membership an annoying burden that distracted him from his important duties as committee chair. Another deputy had recently resigned as Supreme Soviet member in protest over Khasbulatov's

authoritarian reign, but continued to work contentedly as a paid committee member.

26. Interview with staff of the Information Department.

27. Ibid. The figures are for those individuals holding the given jobs as of the ninth Congress and indicate the ratings for those individuals at earlier Congresses whether or not they held the same positions. The figures thus reflect a sharp trend for the same deputies rather than the result of turnover in these job categories. The figures therefore understate the actual trend.

28. Thomas F. Remington, Steven S. Smith, D. Roderick Kiewiet, and Moshe Haspel, "Transitional Institutions and Voting Alignments in Russia, 1990–1993," in Remington, ed., *Parliaments in Transition*, pp. 159–180. Our factor analysis of roll-call votes finds the same high degree of left–right bipolarity across the great majority of issues at the first four Congresses that Sobianin's group observes.

29. Ibid., pp. 170–171.

30. Ibid., pp. 5–6.

31. Information-Analytic Group, "Politicheskie pozitsii i sostavy deputatskikh fraktsii na VIII i IX S"ezdakh," (Moscow: n.p., n.d.), p. 8.

32. Cf. Sobianin, "Political Cleavages," in Remington, ed., *Parliaments in Transition*, p. 186.

33. Information on the biographies of the members of the Supreme Soviet is to be found in A.S. Barsenkov, V.A. Koretskii, and A.I. Ostapenko, eds., *Politicheskaia Rossiia Segodnia: Vysshaia predstavitel'naia vlast'* (Moscow: Moskovskii rabochii, 1993), pp. 181–182, 231–232. I have drawn other information from conversations with both.

34. That is, deputies holding committee or commission chairmanships as of the ninth Congress. Ratings for the earlier Congresses are for the same deputies whether they held committee chairs then or not. A few chairmanships turned over between the third and eighth Congresses, but not enough to produce an appreciable effect in aggregate voting scores.

35. *Nezavisimaia gazeta*, July 1, 1993.

36. Thomas F. Remington and Steven S. Smith, "The Early Legislative Process in the Russian Federal Assembly," *Journal of Legislative Studies* 3:1 (1996), forthcoming; idem, "The Development of Parliamentary Parties in Russia," *Legislative Studies Quarterly* 20:4 (1995), forthcoming.

II

Legislative Development at the Local Level

6

Conflict and Consensus in Russian Regional Government: The Importance of Context

Kathryn Stoner-Weiss

In comparative politics, the claim that changing institutions changes the behavior of the actors that operate within these institutions is not particularly controversial. Indeed, institutional reform in post-Soviet Russia has been implemented with the understanding that democratic institutional change should produce concomitant societal and elite behavioral change necessary to bring about a consolidated democracy. Yet the experience of regional government performance in the first Russian republic[1] indicates that while changing institutions does indeed change elite political behavior, this change is not always in line with our expectations of the political outcomes that the imposition of democratic institutions should bring. Preexisting norms of behavior derived from the remnants of the former planned economy and command administration clearly influence the behavior of new institutions.

As Martin Malia recently noted with regard to the first few years of Russia's transition, "although the old regime had been decapitated with the dissolution of the central Communist Party apparatus and the Union in 1991, its detached limbs and sinews were everywhere. . . ."[2] Because context varies, however, the effects of the residue of old institutions on the behavior of new institutions were not uniform throughout First Republic Russia. Through an examination of some aspects of regional government behavior in two very different Russian oblasts (Nizhnii Novgorod and Saratov), this chapter demonstrates the general point that the operation of new representative governments was heavily influenced by the transitional context. Specifically, the degree of inter- (between city and oblast) and intragovernmental (within and between branches of government) conflict or consensus that existed in regional governments was determined by the varied relationships between oblast political and economic elites. This, in turn, appears to be influenced by economic context.

In this chapter I will first briefly review the comparative politics literature on the study of institutions and institutional behavior, emphasizing the importance of context. I will then compare the institutional behavior of the Nizhnii Novgorod and Saratov oblast governments—the former was consensually ruled and accomplished much in its first years of operation, while the latter was inhibited by ongoing and frequently immobilizing conflict. I will then offer an explanation as to why institutional behavior varied across these oblasts by focusing on elite attitudes and behavior and the variations in the transitional contexts. This explanation emphasizes the importance of behavioral norms derived from old institutional frameworks, conditioned by economic context, that influenced the operation of new institutions.

The Study of Institutions

Transitional contexts, note Philippe Schmitter and Guillermo O'Donnell, are marked by uncertainty of outcomes, processes, and institutions.[3] During the transitional stage, actors are aligning and realigning in the interest of self-preservation and in the face of imperfect information. Political and economic institutions provide a road map to the incentives for actors to align in one way or another. In the language of "rational choice neo-institutional" analysis, institutions shape incentives.[4] Thus, the logic goes, if we change institutions—from authoritarian to democratic, for example—we change actors' incentives and, thus, change their behavior. This has been described as the "structure–agency" problem (where structure determines the behavior of the agent).[5]

For rational-choice institutionalists, the role of institutions is to resolve problems of collective action. Collective action dilemmas are, of course, situations where cooperative behavior would benefit all actors involved, yet no such behavior takes place.[6] The "tragedy of the commons" and the well-known "prisoner's dilemma" are illustrative of problems of collective action. The classic dilemma of collective action is the lack of enforceable commitments. Institutions provide these commitments and thus make collective action possible. Institutions accomplish this task by providing information that makes commitments between actors enforceable and credible. As a result, actors who would otherwise not cooperate opt to do so because they recognize that they will gain from this behavior. In sum, by providing information about the behavior of other actors, institutions reduce uncertainty.

Yet in provincial Russia, identical institutions were planted in different transitional contexts, making the resolution of collective action dilemmas more or less likely. If we hold the structure of regional government institutions constant, rational-choice institutionalist analysis is not really capable of explaining this variation in institutional behavior. As a result, it is necessary to introduce into the analysis of institutional behavior the benefits of what Peter Hall and Rosemary Taylor refer to as "historical institutionalism" and the "new institutionalism of sociology."

Historical institutionalism and sociological institutionalism stress the importance of historical and cultural context respectively. These traditions note that "new institutions are adopted in a world already replete with institutions."[7] In contrast to rational-choice institutionalism, where institutions are thought to be chosen as a result of a rational cost–benefit analysis by actors, historical and sociological institutionalisms stress that existing institutions (social, political, and economic) structure the selection of new institutions. It is important to note as well that they may also structure the way in which new institutions behave.[8]

In the tradition of historical institutionalism, Douglass North argues that "the major role of institutions is to reduce uncertainty by establishing a stable (but not necessarily efficient) structure to human interaction."[9] But, as a historical institutionalist, North also notes that institutions (and the behaviors they encourage) change incrementally:

> even discontinuous changes (such as revolution and conquest) are never completely discontinuous [as] a result of the embeddedness of informal constraints in societies. Although formal rules may change overnight as the result of political or judicial decisions, informal constraints embodied in customs, traditions and codes of conduct are much more impervious to deliberative policies. These cultural constraints not only connect the past with the present and future, but provide us with a key to

explaining the path of historical change. They also assist us in explaining divergent paths of historical change across societies.[10]

The point of origin of historical institutionalists is not, therefore, "one of freely-contracting individuals, but one based on institutional landscape that already embodies fundamental asymmetries of power."[11]

The emphasis on the importance of context, or "embeddedness," is a recurrent theme in research on institutions by sociologists like Mark Granovetter. Granovetter and other sociological institutionalists emphasize the importance of cultural context and symbols to institutional behavior noting, for example, that the behaviors of institutional actors "are embedded in concrete, ongoing systems of social relations."[12]

Thus, new institutions are filters through which leak preexisting understandings of appropriate behavior.[13] Behavioral norms derived from context are also important in the work of political scientists like Robert Putnam and Robert Bates.[14] Putnam and Bates note that solutions to collective action dilemmas are frequently provided by "soft" behavior—like symbols, cooperative communities, and reputations among actors for trustworthiness. These resources enhance actors' abilities to make credible commitments to one another, allowing for collective action to take place.

In sum, the important corrective that these authors make to a straight rational-choice neo-institutionalist analysis is that new institutions, and political actors that operate within them, do not start with a tabula rasa. Behaviors emanating from institutional context and history influence the way in which actors respond to the incentives provided by new institutions. Yet in the Russian case, scholars thus far have not done much to explore how "shades of the past" influence the operation of new protodemocratic institutions. This chapter attempts to remedy this shortcoming through a brief foray into the operations of new regional government institutions in two Russian provinces.

Russian Regional Government Reform

Before describing and explaining the variations in the behavior of new regional government institutions in two provinces—Nizhnii Novgorod and Saratov—a brief review of the changes made to Russian regional governments in 1990 and 1991 and descriptions of the two provinces will be helpful. The evidence provided here is drawn from extensive research done between 1990 and 1993 on the performance and behavior of new Russian regional government institutions.[15]

Substantive change to regional government institutions began with the March 1990 free elections of regional soviets. For the first time, voters across Russia went to the polls freely to elect representatives to regional (oblast) and local (city and raion) government soviets, or councils.[16] Not long after the elections, these newly elected regional soviets began to insist on more autonomy. Not surprisingly, nor perhaps unreasonably, if provincial politicians were going to be held accountable in successive elections for the political and economic situations of their regions, they wanted increased policy control.

Following the August 1991 failed coup attempt against Mikhail Gorbachev, and the disbanding of the CPSU across Russia, provincial governments gained increased authority. Even Yeltsin's efforts to change regional political institutions further in order to curb growing provincial power—by creating the posts of governor and presidential representative—failed to constrain the more aggressive regions from pursuing increased authority over local affairs.[17] Further, although falling short of the expectations of regional politicians, the March 1992 Federative Agreements devolved more power to regional governments to control the reform process.

The pace, nature, and reaction of political and economic reform varied greatly across the Russian expanse, however. In no small part, this was due to the varied contexts in which these reforms were transplanted and the degree of conflict and consensus within and between new regional government institutions. The counterargument to this interpretation is that legislative-executive conflict was endemic across Russia's regions and was reflective of parallel developments in the center. The evidence demonstrates that this is not a very nuanced interpretation of events, as a comparison of events in Nizhnii Novgorod and Saratov demonstrates.

Two Oblasts

Nizhnii Novgorod and Saratov vary economically and geographically and are generally representative of different types of Russian provinces. While Saratov has some important defense and consumer goods factories, located in southern Russia some 450 miles due south of

Moscow (bracketed between the northern border of Kazakhstan and the southern edge of the fertile Black Earth Zone), agriculture is a key component of the regional economy. Saratov has long been famous for its high-quality wheat. The oblast stands at the crossroads of trade routes connecting central Russia to the Urals and to Central Asia in the south. The Volga River splits Saratov oblast into two roughly equal halves. The oblast's population in the 1989 census was reported to be approximately 2.7 million.

Although Saratov's residents voted over 55 percent in favor of Yeltsin's presidency in June 1991, the oblast leadership supported the attempted putsch in August of that year. As a result, there was a partial turnover of political elites in the fall of 1991. On the whole, Western observers generally considered the oblast soviet to be rather conservative.[18] Ironically, however, the oblast soviet elected in Nizhnii Novgorod, usually considered to be politically progressive, had a slightly higher proportion of deputies who had been members of the CPSU in 1990 (88 percent versus 80 percent in Saratov) and industrial managers (29 percent versus 23 percent in Saratov), with a rather comparable rate of incumbency (16.1 percent versus 19.8 percent).[19] Thus, by these measures of political complexion, the Nizhnii Novgorod oblast soviet also appeared rather conservative relative to Saratov's.

In some contrast to Saratov, the capital city of Nizhnii Novgorod oblast is located about 250 miles southeast of Moscow in the heart of European Russia. Both the Volga and Oka rivers flow through the province. According to the 1989 census, the population of the province was about 3.7 million. Although the province has a modest agricultural sector, the soil quality does not compare favorably with Saratov's and the provincial economy is largely devoted to heavy industry—specifically, defense. Thus, the wheat fields of Saratov are juxtaposed with Nizhnii Novgorod's high-tech defense factories.

Throughout the first Russian republic, these two oblasts gained varied political reputations. Among analysts of Russia, Nizhnii Novgorod undoubtedly conjures up impressions of a progressive oblast government, led by a democratically oriented and young regional governor, Boris Nemtsov. Nizhnii Novgorod is the darling of the Western media, largely as a result of its success in rapid privatization and its apparently aggressive embrace of market reform. Conversely, Saratov is far less progressive on economic reform and has been classified as conservative because of its legislature's opposition to Yeltsin's actions in April 1993.

More significantly for the argument advanced here, these oblasts are also distinguishable from one another by the degree to which politics in each region during the First Republic was marked by conflict versus consensus. Whereas, in interviews with the author, political actors in Nizhnii Novgorod described their most important accomplishments in such turbulent times in Russia as "consensus" and "stability," in Saratov, government suffered deadlock and repeated conflict between the legislative and executive branches, within the legislature itself, and between the capital city government and the oblast. Thus, despite the fact that the two regions had identical political institutions on paper, in practice the degree of collective action between and among political (and economic) actors varied considerably. The question this chapter seeks to answer, therefore, is, why were some regions consensually governed while others were marked by conflict? More generically, in the face of identical political institutions, what explains variations in institutional behavior?

The argument here is that relative conflict or consensus within the new regional government institutions was determined by economic context. The transitional economic context determined the degree to which political and economic actors cooperated outside of and then within the new regional government institutions. While the intention of installing representative government was to encourage conflict management within predictable confines, in fact, behavior was determined less by the structure of the new institutions than by the contexts—specifically the relationships between economic and political actors—in which these institutions operated. In short, the behavior of the new institutions reflected relationships outside these institutions. Before describing this more fully, it is worth quickly reviewing why the role of economic interests in provincial Russian politics was so crucial in the period 1990–93.

The Political Power of Economic Elites

Since the late 1980s and especially since 1990–91, Russia has undergone massive economic and political change. This precipitated remarkable societal, economic, and political dislocation. Significantly, remnants of the old economic order persisted (specifically, large factories dominated by powerful directors), while new political institutions were still relatively weak. The continued importance of the workplace to the average post-Soviet citizen, and the fact that the enormous influence of enterprise directors over regional economies and regional politics remained more or less intact, suggests the need to look at how (or whether) these economic interests were represented and accommodated by new regional political institutions.

Further, the simultaneous processes of democratization and marketization caused severe political and economic strain. This, coupled with the presence of politically influential enterprise directors and a weakly organized civil society (as evidenced, for example, by the dirth of enduring political parties across the country), meant that institutional behavior (conflict or consensus) depended on the incorporation of especially dominant economic interests into policy making.

With the final collapse of the Soviet Union in late 1991, the domineering central ministries fell further into disarray. Regional party organizations were completely abolished. Their property was generally taken over by the local soviets, popularly elected a year earlier. Similarly, enterprise directors found themselves free from party oversight and much of the domination of their respective ministries.[20] In short, the authority of enterprise directors, including directors of *kolkhozy* and *sovkhozy*, increased considerably. They had established themselves as de facto owners. Further, the process of privatization of many of these enterprises largely failed to separate enterprise ownership from management—making enterprise directors not only de facto, but also de jure owners—during the first three years of the existence of representative government at the regional level.[21]

This is particularly significant in view of the fact that in many provinces—for example, Nizhnii Novgorod—the economy was dominated by a particular economic sector (high-tech and defense) and a few particularly key enterprises. This fact handed a small number of regional enterprise directors a significant amount of influence over, and also dependence on, regional government actors. Consensual behavior in regional government institutions stemmed from the rational realization of the dependence of enterprises on regional policy instruments in the face of a withdrawing center and dwindling subsidies, and the dependence of regional governments on enterprises as primary employers of constituents.

Evidence in these two provinces of consensual (Nizhnii Novgorod) and conflictual (Saratov) behavior stemming from economically determined norms of engagement appears below.

Nizhnii Novgorod

In Nizhnii Novgorod, the presence of a core group of about twenty directors of particularly large and economically important defense enterprises quickly crystallized as a formidable political force. In 1990, they were able to gain almost 30 percent of the seats in the oblast soviet, and they were among the first group of industrialists in Russia to form an enterprise association.[22]

Indeed, a pattern of broad consultation began relatively early. Recognizing the importance of opening a dialogue with this group of economic actors, shortly after taking office Governor Nemtsov and oblast soviet chair E. Krestianinov cruised for a few hours down the Volga on a riverboat with the region's leading industrial enterprise directors. Their purpose was to present their policy platforms and to convince this core group of enterprise directors that only through collective action could they achieve these goals.[23] In return, this core group of regional employers was assured access to regional policy instruments and resources—specifically: relief from the burden of social welfare requirements that diverted scarce defense enterprise resources from investment in conversion to civilian products; development of foreign and domestic trade ties to sell enterprise products; and worker retraining programs. Although many of these enterprises were to be privatized, and some enterprise directors saw this as a threat to their control, in fact privatization in the region was conducted in such a way that political authorities were able to steer enough shares to labor collectives and enterprise directors so that most were able to retain their positions. Moreover, in return for giving business actors privileged and systematic inclusion in the policy process, political actors were able to borrow the authority of enterprise directors in implementing key policy initiatives and of course at election time.

Evidence of the cooperative relationship between political and economic actors in Nizhnii Novgorod is abundant. In late 1991 and early 1992, the political leadership began negotiating semiformal agreements. These documents were referred to as "social guarantees."[24] Some were specifically designed to soften the burdens of key economic actors. In return, these economic actors were to provide political support and legitimacy to the political leadership.

Further evidence of the cozy relationship in Nizhnii Novgorod can be found in the formal incorporation of enterprise interests into oblast political organs. For example, to address the enterprise need for increased trade and access to foreign markets for local products, one of the assistant directors of Gorky Automobile Factory (GAZ), the single largest employer in the region (with over 100,000 workers), was appointed by Governor Nemtsov as deputy governor in charge of foreign economic relations.

Collective action in Nizhnii Novgorod was facilitated by credible commitments that were undergirded by norms of trust and reciprocity, stemming from a closely intertwined and overlapping political and economic community. These norms were, as noted above, the by-products of a concentrated regional economy. In Nizhnii Novogorod, political actors were drawn from a more narrow elite pool. Many had strong professional links to the key sectors of the regional economy. For example, not only the governor and the chair of the oblast soviet were graduates of the Nizhnii Novgorod Radio Physics Institute (a VUZ, or *vyshii uchebnii zavedenie*—the equivalent of a technical specialty university), but so was the chair of the oblast soviet committee on the economy as well as the chair of the oblast administration's department of economic prognosis. In addition, a more recent graduate of the institute was the chair of the Nizhnii Novgorod Banking House. This is significant because virtually all of the founding members of the Banking House were the largest defense enterprises of the region. The bank itself, as the brainchild of the region's political actors, was intended expressly to assist them in funding defense conversion.[25] Finally, the fact that the region's economy was concentrated in a declining sector may also have served to enhance business–government interdependence in Nizhnii Novgorod. The decline of the defense sector following the end of the Cold War meant that orders for defense products were declining and these cutbacks meant possible factory closures.

Political actors' links to the radio-physics industry—which produced electronic communications and measurement technology with defense applications—is particularly significant considering that at least ten of the one hundred largest enterprises in the oblast were devoted to producing radio-communications and electronic measurement systems. These included Nitel, a defense enterprise employing 13,000 workers that was the world's leading producer of VHF air surveillance missile systems during the Cold War; Krasnoe Sormovo

Shipyard, a submarine plant and the second largest employer in the region (with 19,600 workers); and Popov Communications Equipment, employing 8,000 workers and producing aviation communications equipment.[26]

Undoubtedly these links supported collective action between political and economic elites in Nizhnii Novgorod. One example of this was the privatization of enterprises in Nizhnii Novgorod. While many enterprise directors were initially hesitant to implement the region's aggressive privatization scheme because they feared a loss of control over their enterprises, through ongoing negotiations the political leadership was able to promise various forms of compensation in return for privatization. One observer from the International Finance Corporation revealed that in negotiations with enterprise directors, Governor Nemtsov had certainly "played to his economic constituency" in promising to limit access to the bidding for shares of privatizing enterprises in return for the cooperation of the enterprise directors and work collectives.[27]

Saratov

In contrast to Nizhnii Novgorod, in Saratov there was little evidence of either economic interest group formation or concerted collaboration of economic interest groups with political elites. Economic interests that did collaborate found themselves in competition with other industries and sectors. In short, the dispersion of the economy across sectors, industries, and smaller enterprises promoted competition for access to political resources rather than collective action.

With respect to formal economic interest group collaboration, deputies in the oblast soviet elected from large enterprises complained in interviews that competition among enterprises for political resources was the norm.[28] Further, in contrast to the horizontal consultations between enterprises and political actors in Nizhnii Novgorod, in Saratov vertical patron–client ties (*sviazi*) between enterprises and political actors (specifically the governor and the presidential representative) decided which enterprises would get policy aid and which would not. While one of the key enterprise directors persistently worked on his own rather than in conjunction with others, several others allied themselves with the presidential representative, or the deputy mayor of the city of Saratov. Vladimir Golovachev, the presidential representative, of course, was not officially supposed to play a role in policy making, but in this case he was able to interfere in the processes of government. Because he had formerly been the Saratov city (*gorkom*) chair before the party organization was abolished and he was named presidential representative, Golovachev was able to build the position of presidential representative into an independent seat of power through old patron–client ties.

A split between industrial and agricultural interests was also discernible. These competing factions produced divisions between branches and levels of government (the city versus the oblast) and contributed to factionalization within the oblast soviet. Among oblasts in Russia, Saratov was among those that suffered most from factionalization within the regional legislature (the soviet actually insisted that factions register themselves and declare their members), and suffered virtual policy immobility from divided government.[29]

Divisions within the soviet and between legislative and executive branches of government simply reflected deep divisions among economic interests in the oblast. The agricultural lobby, for example, was at least partially responsible for the appointment of Iurii Belikh as governor of the oblast in February of 1992. Belikh had been the director of a poultry factory and had no real political experience. Perhaps more importantly, he did not have any strong professional ties to actors in the region's other key economic sectors.[30] The chair of the oblast soviet, Nikolai Makarevich, was similarly politically inexperienced and, as a lawyer, had no strong formal ties to the region's disparate economic interests. In short, the divergent professional experiences of Makarevich and Belikh attest to the diverse pool from which political elites were drawn in Saratov.

Makarevich bitterly opposed Belikh's appointments to the departments of the administration, complaining that a few were too strongly linked to the old Communist Party apparatus and that others were corrupt.[31] Conflict between and within branches of government in Saratov was so intense that Makarevich threatened to resign no fewer than three times in fourteen months.[32]

Thus, whereas in Nizhnii Novgorod commitments between economic and political actors and consensus within regional government institutions were upheld by overlapping professional horizontal networks and trust, in Saratov this pattern of interaction was absent. Instead, competing economic actors were vertically linked to different factions and particular actors within regional government institutions.

As a result, access to political resources was distributed as a reward for political support on an individual, patron–client footing. In interviews, many deputies accused the governor of Saratov of selling favors and subsidies to individuals on a particularistic basis.[33] Moreover, collective action between economic and political interests was inhibited by pervasive distrust between fiercely competing interests. Any collaboration that did take place was narrow and personalistic. As a result, those interests left out of these narrow exchanges defected to the political opposition (either another faction in the soviet, or a different branch or level of government), thereby condemning the political process to an ongoing cycle of sharp conflict. This had a negative effect on what the regional government was able to accomplish in its first few years of operation and may set the pattern for its future performance.

Conclusion

This chapter began by noting that while changing institutions changes political behavior, in the presence of preexisting and contextually derived norms of interaction, behavioral change is neither completely predictable nor anticipated. The extent of consensus or conflict that was observed in the regional government institutions of Nizhnii Novgorod and Saratov, at this stage of research, appears to be derived from the economic context. That is, in the face of the de facto and de jure economic power of enterprise directors during this initial transitional phase, the relationship between economic and political elites had a particularly important influence on the behavior of new regional government institutions such that some regional governments were governed by consensus, while others were governed conflictually (rendering them rather ineffectual). This, in turn, likely affected what these regional governments were able to accomplish in the first few years of their existence—Nizhnii Novgorod aggressively pursued privatization and various other ambitious trade initiatives, while Saratov built up a record of policy immobility and intransigence.[34]

The implications of these claims are potentially troubling. While the consensus among elites that was pervasive in Nizhnii Novgorod provided the region with a stable environment in otherwise turbulent political and economic times in Russia, too much elite consensus in the future could lead to a freezing out of other elites wanting to enter the political process. That is, while the intention of installing representative governments at the regional level was to encourage democracy through political pluralism, in fact, the long-run development of pluralism may be undermined by the influence of the soft-behavioral residues of the previous economic order.

As we are warned by historical and sociological institutionalists, like it or not, these norms will likely continue to influence regional government performance. The contribution of this finding is that it guides us in explaining how context and norms of behavior of residual former institutions affect current institutional behavior and may aid us in understanding the future behavior of new protodemocratic institutions in Russia. In sum, the evidence here recommends a more nuanced interpretation of the relationship between institutional change and resulting institutional behavior.

Notes

1. I take the first Russian republic to have existed from March 1990 and the election of republic and regional soviets until October of 1993, when Yeltsin disbanded the Russian parliament and regional soviets.
2. Martin Malia, "Russia's Democratic Future: Hope against Hope," *Problems of Post-Communism* (Fall 1994), p. 34.
3. Guillermo O'Donnell and Philippe Schmitter, *Transitions from Authoritarian Rule: Tentative Conclusions about Uncertain Democracies* (Baltimore, MD: Johns Hopkins University Press, 1986). Peter Hall and Rosemary Taylor, in "Political Science and the Four New Institutionalisms" (Center for European Studies, Harvard University, unpublished mimeo, 1994), classify the study of institutions into historical, rational-choice, sociological, and economic categories. I employ their classification scheme throughout this chapter.
4. Peter Hall and Rosemary Taylor, in "Political Science and the Four New Institutionalisms," (Center for European Studies, Harvard University, unpublished mimeo, 1994), classify the study of institutions into historical, rational-choice, sociological, and economic categories. I employ their classification scheme throughout this chapter.
5. Ibid., p. 1.
6. Seminal works on collective action dilemmas include, Mancur Olson, *The Logic of Collective Action: Public Goods and the Theory of Groups* (Cambridge, MA: Harvard University Press, 1965 and 1971); Russell Hardin, *Collective Action* (Baltimore, MD: Johns Hopkins University Press, 1982); and Elinor Ostrom, *Governing the Commons: The Evolution of Institutions for Collective Action* (New York: Cambridge University Press, 1990).
7. Hall and Taylor, "Political Science and the Four New Institutionalisms," p. 20.
8. Robert D. Putnam, in *Making Democracy Work: Civic Traditions in Modern Italy* (Princeton, NJ: Princeton University Press, 1993), argues, for example, that in the regions of Italy, the performance of new regional government institu-

tions varied. High performance was positively influenced by preexisting institutions of associational life (choral societies and birdwatching clubs), which gave rise to norms of conduct within regional government institutions.

9. Douglass C. North, *Institutions, Institutional Change and Economic Performance* (New York: Cambridge University Press, 1990), p. 6.

10. Ibid.

11. Hall and Taylor, "Political Science and the Four New Institutionalisms," p. 20.

12. Mark Granovetter, "Economic Action and Social Structure: The Problem of Embeddedness," in Mark Granovetter and Richard Swedberg, eds., *The Sociology of Economic Life* (San Francisco: Westview Press, 1992), p. 58.

13. See, for example, Fritz Scharpf, "Decision Rules, Decision Styles and Policy Choices," *Journal of Theoretical Politics*, vol. 1, no. 2 (1989), pp. 149–176.

14. Putnam, *Making Democracy Work*; and Robert Bates, "Contra-Contractarianism: Some Reflections on the New Institutionalism," *Politics and Society*, vol. 16, nos. 2–3.

15. The larger study is of four provinces including Nizhnii Novgorod, Tiumen', Yaroslavl, and Saratov. See Kathryn Stoner-Weiss, *Local Heroes: Political Exchange and Governmental Performance in Provincial Russia* (Harvard University, Department of Government, Ph.D. dissertation, 1994).

16. For a full description of these elections and analysis of some electoral outcomes, see Timothy J. Colton, "The Politics of Democratization: The Moscow Elections of 1990," *Soviet Economy*, vol. 6, no. 4 (October–December 1990), pp. 285–344; Jeffrey W. Hahn, "Local Politics and Political Power in Russia: The Case of Yaroslavl," *Soviet Economy*, vol. 7, no. 4 (1991), pp. 322–341; Gavin Helf and Jeffrey W. Hahn, "Old Dogs and New Tricks: Party Elites in the Russian Regional Elections of 1990," *Slavic Review*, vol. 51, no. 3 (Fall 1992) pp. 511–530.

17. See, for example, "Irkutsk Refuses to Pay Taxes into the Federal Budget," *Nezavisimaia gazeta*, May 22, 1992; "Siberians Push for Economic Autonomy," *Current Digest of the Post-Soviet Press*, vol. 14, no. 13 (1992).

18. Jeffrey W. Hahn, "Counter-Reformation in the Provinces: How Monolithic?" Paper prepared for the Annual Meeting of the American Association for the Advancement of Slavic Studies, Phoenix, Arizona, November 19–22, 1992.

19. These statistics come from reports of the Nizhnii Novgorod and Saratov oblast soviets' mandate commissions. Further, the protocol departments in each of the oblast soviets themselves provided the author with lists of deputies by profession.

20. I have qualified this statement because many formerly all-union ministries quickly found new homes in Russian federal ministries. Still, their abilities to instruct managers were severely circumscribed.

21. For further confirmation of this, see also Vitali Naishul, "Institutional Development in the USSR," *Cato Journal*, vol. 11, no. 3 (Winter 1992).

22. Irina Starodubrovskaia notes that there is a misconception that the bulk of Russian enterprises were members of such associations. In a survey of enterprise managers, she notes that slightly more than 50 percent of respondents belonged to these associations. In some cases, these associations were local branches of the old Soviet industrial ministries and their departments. While they no longer had any official governmental authority, they were in some cases effective lobby groups. See Irina Starodubrovskaia, "Attitudes of Enterprise Managers Toward

Market Transitions," in Michael McFaul and Tova Perlmutter, eds., *Privatization, Conversion and Enterprise Reform in Russia* (Stanford, CA: Center for International Security and Arms Control, 1993), p. 62.

23. Author's conversation with Evgenii Gorkov, vice governor, Department of International Relations, Nizhnii Novgorod Oblast Administration, May 1994.

24. *Nizhegorodskaia pravda*, January 25, 1992; see also *Nizhegorodskaia pravda*, March 5, 1992, regarding the governor and the chair of the oblast soviet meeting with representatives of trade organizations and unions about the privatization of retail trade.

25. Author's interview with Boris Brevnov, director of the Nizhnii Novgorod Banking House, 1992.

26. U.S.-Russia Defense Conversion Subcommittee, U.S. Department of Commerce, November 1992 and September 1993. Documents PB93–101509, PB93-18366, and PB94-100211.

27. Author's interview with International Finance Corporation representative in Nizhnii Novgorod who preferred not to be named, Nizhnii Novgorod, November 1992. Sometimes promises made by the political leadership were not always enough to reassure enterprise directors. The most striking example of (illegal) resistance to privatization was at GAZ—Gorkii Automobile Factory. In this case, the director of the enterprise, Boris Vidaev, panicked that he would not receive enough shares in the enterprise and thus appropriated funds intended for the development of a new product to purchase shares in the enterprise. Governor Nemtsov succeeded in having Vidaev removed as director, but Vidaev retained a seat on the new corporation's board of directors by a vote of the labor collective. See *Nezavisimaia gazeta*, January 21, 1994, p. 1.

28. Author's interviews with deputies of Saratov Oblast Soviet of People's Deputies, April 1993.

29. See Stoner-Weiss, *Local Heroes*, chapter 3 for a comparison of the specific policy initiatives of Saratov and Nizhnii Novgorod. Saratov was among the last oblasts in Russia where Yeltsin appointed a governor. The difficulty was largely due to disagreements in the oblast legislature regarding appropriate candidates to recommend to Yeltsin. See Stoner-Weiss, *Local Heroes*, p. 95.

30. Iurii Belikh's biography appears in *Saratovskii vesti*, February 28, 1992.

31. See *Saratovskii vesti*, July 16–20, 1992, for examples.

32. *Saratovskii vesti*, June 20, 1992, and *Saratovskii vesti*, June 24, 1992.

33. In one case, for example, Governor Belikh ordered regional banks to pay credits to one factory in order to pay employee wages. Belikh was then allowed to campaign in the factory during the December 1993 election when he ran for (and won) a seat in the Federal Assembly.

34. See Stoner-Weiss, *Local Heroes*, chapter 3.

7

The Development of Local Legislatures in Russia: The Case of Yaroslavl

Jeffrey W. Hahn

The Problem

The purpose of this chapter is to explore the process of democratization at the local level of government in Russia. In particular, it will focus on the development of local legislatures, called soviets, from 1990, the year in which major reforms of local government were introduced, until 1993, when the soviets were abolished by presidential decree. At first glance, such a focus might now seem more appropriate to the study of Russian history. However, if the political transformation under way in Russia since 1988 is understood as a continuing process in which Gorbachev's perestroika, ending in late 1991, was the first phase, and the dissolution of the old system by Yeltsin marked the end of the second, then an analysis of what was (or was not) achieved in these phases becomes highly pertinent, both for those trying to understand the political transformation of Russia and for political scientists who want to understand how political systems become democratic. In the hope of contributing something to both concerns, this chapter will address two related, although analytically distinct, questions: To what extent did local legislatures in Russia, starting in 1990, become institutionalized? Did these institutions, in the same period, become more democratic?

Conceptual Framework

The concepts of institutionalization and democratization were discussed at some length in the introductory chapter to this book. By institutionalization we mean the development over time of a set way of doing things, of increasingly specific and universal rules and procedures that distinguish one organization from another. With respect to conceptualizing institutionalization there appear to be three criteria particularly useful to the present analysis. One of these is autonomy, by which we mean that identifiable boundaries exist between political institutions that are recognized and respected by all political actors. Another is the idea that as institutions develop they acquire greater organizational complexity. Finally, as institutionalization takes place, norms of organizational behavior become more and more "universalistic rather than particularistic and discretionary" (Polsby 1962, p. 145). The development over time of greater autonomy, complexity, and universalistic norms, then, are the criteria of institutionalization used in this paper.

With respect to democratization, despite the divergence of views about why and how democracies come about, there is a broad consensus that at some level in a democracy the authority to make decisions for society is derived directly and solely from the members of that society. There is also general agreement on what minimal conditions need to be achieved if the political institutions of a country are to be judged democratic. Of these, free, fair and competitive elections are considered central. In the words of Samuel Huntington, "Elections, open, free, and fair, are the essence of democracy, the inescapable sine qua non." As to *becoming* democratic, Huntington argues that "the critical point in the process of democratization is the replacement of a government that was not chosen in this way by one that is selected in a free, open and fair election" (Huntington 1991, p. 9).

Yet while elections are a necessary condition for the emergence of democracy, they are clearly not sufficient. Except for cases of direct democracy in which members of the society participate directly in decision making, the development of democracy also depends on the emergence of representative institutions of government.[1] Just as not all elections are democratic, however, neither are all legislatures. What distinguishes *democratic* legislatures is how well they perform their representational function or what Loewenberg and Patterson call "linkage" (Loewenberg and Patterson 1979, ch. 5). Popular consultation requires some means by which the concerns of citizens can be expressed to those making decisions. Moreover, there is the expectation that those making decisions will in some way be responsive to these concerns. In discussing responsiveness, Lyn Ragsdale writes, "Legislative elections all rest on a simple premise: that they link the legislature and the citizenry, allowing citizens to participate, albeit indirectly, in legislative decision making" (Ragsdale 1985, p. 58). In addition to influencing the making of decisions, linkage between citizens and their representatives can also take the form of constituency service, the delivery of public goods, and what Loewenberg and Patterson call "symbolic responsiveness" (Loewenberg and Patterson 1979, pp. 183–191). The main criterion used in this paper to determine whether a legislature is democratic will be how well it performs this "linkage" role. What mechanisms are available for the communication of citizen demands to those who make decisions? How well do they work? In summary, this chapter will analyze three variables deemed central to the process of democratization of local government in Russia: elections, legislative institutionalization, and linkage.[2]

Methods

Preliminary answers to the questions raised in the foregoing are based on a case study of the political development of Yaroslavl, a Russian province located on Russia's historic "Golden Ring," about two-hundred miles northeast of Moscow. The provincial capital of the same name was founded in 1010 and today is an industrial city of about 650,000 people. The population of the province as whole is about twice that size. The author made ten trips to Yaroslavl from 1990 to 1993 varying in length from one week to six. During these visits, he was able to attend sessions of both the provincial (oblast) and city legislatures, to interview major political actors in and out of government, to conduct formal surveys of public opinion and of the legislators themselves, and to get to know the views of Yaroslavl's citizens through informal conversations.

To what degree can observations made on the basis of a single case be generalized for understanding the development of democratic institutions at the local level elsewhere in Russia? No claim to representativeness is made here, but there appears to be no a priori reason to believe that the experience of Yaroslavl is so different from other regions of central Russia that it constitutes a unique case. On the contrary, by most criteria, it is quite similar. In any event, the purpose of this study is to develop hypotheses and generalizations that may be helpful as guides to understanding the process of democratization in Russia and that are subject to verification by future research. A case study that is more "thickly descriptive" and offers a close look at what has transpired in one area of Russia over a period of four years can serve this purpose.

The findings presented in what follows are based on several diverse data bases. The study of *elections* uses voting data gathered by the author in March 1990, at which time detailed results for all Russian republic, oblast, and city elections in the province were published in the local press. In addition, access was made available to all voter lists, as well as to the complete list of nominees, by the Yaroslavl Election Commission. The section dealing with *changing institutions* of local government relies to a great extent on the official minutes of the oblast and city soviets collected for almost all sessions during the period of 1990–93. These and other relevant documents are supplemented by the author's field notes from attendance at several oblast and city soviet sessions and by interviews with deputies, as well as with the chairmen of both soviets, the mayor, the governor, and the presidential representative.

To better understand how Russians participate in politics, the author conducted an opinion survey in 1990 of 975 respondents drawn from voter lists using a skip interval random sample. Every effort was made to ensure that results would be representative within a margin of error of plus or minus 3 percent at a 0.95 level of confidence.[3] The section on *linkage* between constituents and representatives presented here draws on those data and on a replicate study carried out in April–June 1993. In the latter survey, a sample of 1,336 people was taken from voting lists; 1,019 were actually interviewed. The procedures used were virtually identical to those of the first survey, resulting in what the author believes is an equally high level of confidence; that is, it provides a truly representative picture of voters' political attitudes and beliefs in one Russian city. Supplementing these data are data from a survey of 183 Yaroslavl city and oblast deputies conducted in May 1992. The survey consisted of 171 items intended to elicit information on deputies' activities, on their views of their office, and on relations with members of the executive bodies and with their constituents.

Findings

The presentation of findings will be organized in the order suggested in the methods section above. The topics covered include elections, institutional development, and representational linkage. In order to provide a contextual baseline against which change can be measured, a brief look at how the old system worked is in order.

The Historical Baseline

Political institutions in Yaroslavl prior to 1990 did not differ significantly from what existed elsewhere in the Soviet Union (Friedgut 1979; Hahn 1988). In principle, the system was based on the primacy of local legislative institutions called "soviets." The word soviet, which can be translated innocuously as "council," came to denote a system of local government peculiar to Leninist communist organization. Deputies to the Yaroslavl soviets were elected directly by 99 percent of the eligible voters every two-and-a-half years in what Soviet propaganda called the most democratic elections in the world, but which lacked any element of competition. In Yaroslavl, 230 deputies were elected to the oblast soviet and 200 to the Yaroslavl city soviet.

At the first session after their election, Yaroslavl deputies elected an executive committee, known as an *ispolkom*. The ispolkom was in charge of the daily administration of local government. Since the ispolkom was elected by the deputies and legally accountable to them, in theory at least, legislative primacy was assured. The reality was quite the opposite. In practice, the deputies met in session four times a year for a few hours each session to unanimously approve whatever items were placed on the agenda by the organizational-instructional department of the ispolkom. This same department was responsible for all other matters of business before the deputies as well. No detail was left to chance, not even the deputies' speeches, which were often scripted beforehand. While deputies may have had some marginal opportunity to influence policy in the standing committees of the soviet, and apparently could (and occasionally did) act as something of an "ombudsman" for their constituents in their dealings with the administration (Hahn 1988, p. 194), their impact on local politics was minimal, at best.

Real political power in Yaroslavl, as elsewhere in the Soviet Union, did not, of course, rest with any governmental institution, but with the Communist Party. The Yaroslavl oblast party organization in 1985 represented about 114,000 party members in an oblast with 1.4 million inhabitants. At the top of this organization was the oblast committee (*obkom*) first secretary, whose control over appointments and political recruitment assured him of all but unlimited authority within the region, a position Jerry Hough has called "the Soviet prefect" (Hough 1969). Indeed, Fedor I. Loshchenkov, the obkom first secretary in Yaroslavl from 1964 to 1986, was widely, if discreetly, known as "Tsar Fedor." Nothing of significance was done in Yaroslavl without his approval.

Central to the party's ability to control local government (known as *podmena*) was its control over the nomination of candidates to the local soviets. In the old system, all nominations were made at the place of work. No one was nominated at the workplace without the support of the secretary of its party committee, a person appointed by the obkom. In single-candidate elections, therefore, the party was assured that only those compliant with its policies would be elected. By controlling elections to the soviets, the party also controlled the composition of the executive committee. At the first "organizational" session of the soviet, the deputies voted unanimously for a slate of candidates for the ispolkom that was put before it, also subject to party approval. Unlike the composition of the deputies as a whole, which was broadly representative demographically and typically included more than 50 percent non-Communists, the composition of the executive committee was almost exclusively made up of party members, usually drawn from the upper ranks of the party organization.

The point to be made here is that prior to the reforms of local government proposed by Gorbachev in 1988 and introduced in 1990, the legislative system that existed at the local level in Russia failed to meet the criteria of either institutionalization or democracy outlined in the earlier sections of this paper. With respect to institutionalization, although arguably the soviets had a clearly identifiable structure, they lacked any real autonomy, organizational complexity, or universalistic procedures. Their activities were completely dominated by the executive branch and, beyond it, by the Communist Party. If by organizational complexity we mean not only the number and variety of subunits (Huntington 1968), but scope of work and difficulty of issues dealt with (Loewenberg and Patterson 1979), then clearly the local soviets did not do much, if any, real governing. As to norms of procedure, these were highly particularistic and largely defined in terms of personal connections with, and loyalty to, the obkom first secretary. As to democracy, there was no electoral competition; the deputies' ability to represent the interests of their constituents was limited to helping them beg favors from those who really held power in the ispolkom and the party.

Elections

It is against this backdrop that we must understand the significance of the elections to the local soviets that took place in Yaroslavl in March 1990. Were they "open, free, and fair"?[4] Laws were adopted on October 27, 1989, for the 1990 Russian republic and local elections. They provided for direct elections to all local soviets on the basis of equal and universal adult suffrage and by secret ballot. No seats were to be assigned to public organizations and there was no requirement that candidates be approved at preelection meetings of district election commissions, as had been the case in the 1989 elections to the USSR Congress of People's Deputies. Candidates could be nominated at the workplace, as under the old system, by officially registered public organizations, or at places of residence. The number of candidates per single-member district was "unlimited," thus making uncontested seats possible.

As in the 1989 elections, in order to be elected a candidate had to receive more than 50 percent of the votes cast, with no fewer than 50 percent of the eligible electorate turning out to vote. Since it was clearly possible that no one would emerge victorious in a district with several candidates, provisions had to be made for runoffs (*povtornie golosovanie*) and repeat elections (*povtornie vybory*). Runoffs occurred in districts where three or more candidates were running and none got 50 percent. Repeat elections (including new nominations and time for campaigning) were held in districts where there were one or two running and none got 50 percent. As a result, the election law for the 1990 local elections was cumbersome, to say the least. By not allowing the winner to take all and by requiring that 50 percent of those eligible vote, the possibility for virtually endless elections was created; and from the standpoint of the average voter, the process was unnecessarily complicated. A simple majority without a required level of turnout would have been equally democratic. Despite its many shortcomings, however, the election laws provided a legal basis for comparatively democratic elections.

The first round of elections was held in Yaroslavl (as in the rest of the Russian Republic) on March 4, 1990. The number of seats in both the city and in the oblast soviet numbered 200. Runoff elections were held two weeks later on March 18 and repeat elections on April 22. Did they meet the requirements of a free election noted earlier? The first of these requirements, meaningful choice, has both a quantitative and a qualitative dimension. *Quantitatively*, there must be at least two candidates for each position. Generally speaking this was the case in Yaroslavl. In the city soviet, 565 candidates were registered for the 200 seats although 52 of these withdrew before election day, making an average of 2.7 candidates per district. For the 200 seats available in the oblast soviet (of which 85 were located in the city of Yaroslavl), there were 597 candidates, an average of 3.0 per district. There was considerable variance from the mean, however. Twenty of the city districts had between 5 and 7 candidates, while in 47 there was only 1. In oblast races, there were as many as 9 candidates per district, while 27 were uncontested. Running unopposed, however, did not guarantee election. In 7 of the city districts, and in at least 3 of the oblast districts, more than 50 percent of those voting defeated single candidates by crossing their names off the ballot; among the defeated were the first and second secretaries of the Yaroslavl city party committee (*gorkom*).

As this last point suggests, the local elections in Yaroslavl provided some degree of meaningful choice in a *qualitative* sense as well. In the first place, voters could voice their opinions on the old party–state apparatchiki by voting them out of office. To a considerable extent, this happened. In city elections, 65 members of the apparat[5] were on the ballot on March 4; only 27 of the 179 seated for the first organizational session of the city soviet that met on May 10 were from this group. In oblast elections, apparatchiki contended in 102 districts, and although 31 of them lost in the first round, in the end they did rather better than in the city, electing 47 by the time of the first session. In this sense, some voters do appear to have exercised a degree of choice by voting *against* candidates of the old elite.

There is a second way in which the voter's choice was meaningful qualitatively. For those opposed to the continued political domination of the apparat, the Yaroslavl Popular Front (YPF) represented an alternative that people could vote *for*.[6] The YPF supported 67 candidates in the city elections, winning 22 seats to the first session of the soviet, which was convened on May 10, 1990. Although this does not, at first glance, compare favorably with the ratio of winners to losers among the apparat, appearances are deceiving. In fact, enough of the other deputies elected were sufficiently sympathetic to the YPF that they formed a voting bloc of 44 deputies called "Democratic Yaroslavl," which, in coalition with two other reform-minded deputy groups, easily controlled the election of the chair and vice chair of the city soviet. The YPF did not fare as well on the oblast level, although they won more seats (33). The reason for this is that in the oblast soviet, the 47 members elected from among the apparat were able to form a working majority with deputies who were enterprise managers or collective farm chairs. Deputies holding these positions accounted for a much higher portion of seats in the oblast soviet than in the city; appointments to both had been subject to the "nomenklatura" of the obkom first secretary (Helf and Hahn 1992, p. 518).

Despite its limited success and limited resources, the YPF acted like a protoparty. Not only did it recruit and support candidates, it organized mass demonstrations on February 25 and on March 17. It disseminated information to the public by maintaining a kiosk in the center of town next to the city bus terminal. Although not always efficiently, the leadership provided a measure of internal discipline. At an organizational meeting attended by the author on the eve of the March 4 elections, much of the discussion turned on getting out the vote, giving out telephone contact numbers, going over the mechanics of voting, reading telegrams of support from "Democratic Russia" leaders Yeltsin and Popov—in short, the sort of precinct politics familiar to this author from eight years in elective office in a city government in suburban Philadelphia.

There were also important differences from the American experience of local politics, however. Some of these help account for the fact that the YPF did not do better than it did, and must be acknowledged in any assessment of meaningful choice. Pomper's model of free elections specifies that choices should be manageable and that voters have the opportunity to know and discuss these choices. It is hard to conclude that these requirements were met. The first reason has to do with the lack of a legal basis for registering political parties. Candidates could not run on a party ticket. The only hint of partisan identification was whether candidates were members of the CPSU. If not, they were identified as nonparty (*bezpartiinyi*). Since 70 percent of the candidates were party members, including many supported by the YPF, these labels had little meaning. The absence of legislation by which alternative parties could register and identify their candidates meant that voters had to rely on word of mouth and other forms of mass communication to know which candidates stood for what.

It is in connection with this last point that the second problem arises. At the time the elections were held, the local party officials had an overwhelming advantage in resources: they commanded a fleet of cars, telephones, finances, offices, and the main means of mass communication, including access to radio, television, and the press. In short, they had an effective organization. The YPF had none of these advantages. How were they to make their case known to the voter? Demonstrations, word of mouth, and a kiosk were hardly sufficient to allow YPF-supported candidates to publicize their names and policy positions so that voters could make an informed choice. In retrospect, it is surprising that the YPF did as well as it did.

The other three requirements for free elections identified by Pomper—equal weighting of votes; free registration of choices; and accurate registration, counting, and reporting of ballots—appear to have been largely fulfilled in Yaroslavl. With respect to equal weighting, the average number of voters registered in each district for the first round was 2,312. In the oblast, it was 5,434. In the city, the range varied from a low of 1,299 voters in district 163 to a high of 3,455 in district 154, a clear violation of the principle of one man, one vote. However, the standard deviation from the mean was only 295, indicting that in two-thirds of the districts the actual number of eligible voters was less than 13 percent larger or smaller than the norm. A similar pattern held true for the oblast soviets. Forty-two districts fell outside of one standard deviation, only 12 of them seriously (Helf and Hahn 1992, p. 524).

Procedures followed for the registration of voters and for the counting and reporting of votes also seemed to meet at least minimal standards for a free election. In precincts visited by the author, voters went first to a table where ten to fifteen members of the election commission sat and verified their names on a voter list. They were then given five differently colored ballots, one for each level of government where seats were to be filled: borough, city, oblast, and RSFSR national and territorial.[7] In the city, the polls were open from 7:00 A.M. to 8:00 P.M., during which time 283,691 voters cast their ballots—a 62 percent turn-out. The turnout for elections to the oblast soviets was higher (70 percent), apparently because voting in rural districts was greater. It was substantially so in some districts (Hahn 1991a, p. 328), raising the possibility that fraudulent practices may have been more common there. While fraud may have been easier to perpetrate in rural districts, however, the evidence suggests it was not widespread (Helf and Hahn 1992). Rather, greater rural turnout seems to be a feature of Russian voting behavior. It also occurred in the presidential election of 1991.[8]

After the polls closed, ballot boxes were sealed by the chair of the election commission, unused ballots were destroyed, and counting began. The author received permission to be present on March 18 when this was done for precinct 9/174, which was located in the ship-building area of the Frunze borough (*raion v gorode*). Sixty-three per-cent of the eligible electorate in this district had voted, down from about 70 percent who came out for the first round of voting on March 4. While the work had to be done by hand in the absence of voting machines, all results were confirmed independently by at least two counters. Although it was legally possible for the someone from the YPF to be present, the only observer there, aside from the author and a colleague, was the secretary of the factory party committee. He did not, however, interfere in any way with the proceedings. At the end, the chair read the results, asked for objections, and, hearing none, sealed the ballots, signed the proper forms, and sent the results to the city's Central Election Commission.

From the point of view of election mechanics, were the elections honest? Clearly there were opportunities for fraud and manipulation. The author himself witnessed a number of minor violations. Numerous complaints of election irregularities were made at a postelection meet-ing of the YPF on March 20. However, the evidence presented here suggests that on the whole the results were honest. At they same time, they cannot be said to have fully met the requirements of free elec-tions. In large part this is because of the absence of a multiparty sys-tem. Moreover, it is not clear that all those contending for office had the equal opportunity to persuade the voters, largely because they lacked the resources to do so. This left the local party organization with an unfair advantage to indirectly help those it favored—for example, by providing a good buffet in districts where it wanted to mobilize the vote. To a large extent, however, the legitimacy of an election is in the eyes of the voters. Voters' attitudes on this question were measured in the survey conducted by the author in Yaroslavl in 1990. The results show that nearly 70 percent of the electorate felt that the March 4 elections had been fair; only 16 percent thought they had not been. In response to the same question in 1993, the latter figure was 13 percent, suggesting that three years later, most voters still felt that their local representatives had been chosen in a fair manner.[9]

Institutional Development

The following sections offer an analysis of the institutional development of oblast and city legislatures in the period 1990–93, using Yaroslavl as a case study. The chief criteria for institutionalization have already been identified: the development of autonomy, organizational complexity, and universalistic norms and procedures. While these criteria come almost exclusively from the literature on the institutionalization of national legislatures, there does not seem a priori to be a reason why they cannot be applied to local legislatures as well. Since the failed coup attempt of August 1991 marks a watershed in the evolution of Russian political institutions, the analysis offered here will be divided into two parts, before and after the August "putsch."

Part I (1990–1991)

The structures of both oblast and city soviets were established at the first "organizational" session of the deputies held after the elections of March–April 1990. Organizational sessions represented a major departure from previous practice. Both legislatures made it clear that henceforth their role in the formation of the executive branch was no longer a formality. In the city, 14 candidates for chairman of the soviet were nominated from among the deputies, but only 4 remained when 10 of them withdrew their names from consideration. Three of the four were sympathetic to, or supported by, the democratic bloc; the fourth was L.L. Karnakov, the first secretary of the city's party committee (gorkom). After the first three presented their platforms, Karnakov also withdrew his candidacy, citing the pressures of his duties as head of the city party committee.[10] In reality, he faced almost certain defeat by the coalition of forces sympathetic to the democratic bloc, which controlled a working majority among the 179 deputies elected by May 10. After Karnakov's withdrawal, L.L. Kruglikov, a specialist on criminal law from Yaroslavl State University, was elected easily in the first round, winning 132 votes.

In terms of the dominance of deputies sympathetic to the democratic movement, similar results were produced in balloting for first vice chairman of the city soviet and for chairman of its executive committee (ispolkom). In both cases, Kruglikov's endorsement appears to have been decisive. V.N. Bakaev was chosen as vice chairman, receiving 95 votes. The selection of the ispolkom chair proved more controversial. Five candidates were nominated, with three remaining prior to the final vote. One of them was V.V. Volonchunas, who had been chairman of the ispolkom under the previous system, and as such, a member of the old apparat. He was ultimately elected with 125 votes out of 166, but only after Kruglikov intervened on his behalf, arguing that Volonchunas's professional background and experience made him indispensable for running the government. "Not all apparatchiks are bad," said Kruglikov. "They should be judged first of all by their performance, and Viktor Vladimirovich [Volonchunas] is a capable, thoughtful, and calm man." While noting that the criticism directed at Volonchunas might have some merit, Kruglikov concluded by saying: "I simply don't see any other candidate."[11] Other positions were then filled, including chairs of the sixteen standing committees. Along with Kruglikov, Bakaev, Volonchunas, and the chair of the People's Control Committee, they comprised the Presidium of the soviet.

The organizational session of the oblast soviet proved to be rather more complicated. Here, too, the legislature established real authority with respect to the executive. However, unlike the city soviet, the results of the voting demonstrated that those sympathetic to the democratic bloc were far weaker and the old guard stronger in the oblast soviet. Of nineteen candidates originally nominated to chair the legislature, only four remained when the vote was finally taken. Among them were I.A. Tolstoukhov, then obkom first secretary, V.G. Varukhin, a candidate supported by the democratic bloc. In the first round of voting, Varukhin got 56 votes and Tolstoukhov got 70, both short of the majority of 84. Two more rounds of balloting failed to resolve the issue, however. Tolstoukhov could do no better than 73 votes for, 84 against, and he withdrew his candidacy.[12]

Ultimately, A.N. Veselov, the first secretary of the Pereslavl'–Zalesskii gorkom, was chosen out of four candidates to chair the oblast soviet, receiving 105 votes. The candidate favored by the democratic forces, Iu.Ya. Kolbovskii, could capture only 40 votes. Kolbovskii was, however, elected vice chairman of the soviet, winning 117 of the votes cast. The ability of the coalition of apparat and nomenklatura deputies to dominate the proceedings was further demonstrated in the selection of a chairman for the executive committee. A.E. Kovalev was elected easily, receiving 126 votes in the first round.[13] Kovalev had been first vice chairman of the old ispolkom and a standard-bearer of the party–state apparat in the elections to the RSFSR parliament from the Yaroslavl national-territorial district, a race which he won. Three deputy vice chairmen endorsed by him also were elected by the deputies—significantly, without opposition. As in the city, along with the chairs of the standing committees and the head of the People's Control Committee, these officials made up the Presidium of the oblast soviet.

Relations between legislative and executive branches in Yaroslavl were set forth in the regulations (*reglamenti*) of the soviets. On paper, it was made clear that the executive branch was to be bound by the decisions of the legislature. In the case of the city soviet, article 84 specified, "The fulfillment of the decisions of the soviet and of its presidium is obligatory for all ispolkom officials. The soviet has the right to overrule any decision of the executive committee."[14] In addition, the soviet had the exclusive power to pass the budget and to receive reports about its fulfillment by the ispolkom, a right reaffirmed by article 17 of the Law on Local Self-Government adopted in June 1991. Legislative oversight (*kontrol*) was to be exercised by the chair of the People's Control Committee, a full-time position elected by the deputies and by the standing committees of the soviet. Deputies were also guaranteed broad access to information used by the ispolkom. In principle, when combined with the accountability of executive officials before the legislature established at the organizational sessions, a basis for the institutionalization of democratic local legislatures was in place.

In-depth interviews with about fifteen deputies conducted in June–July 1991 suggested that in practice, despite the new institutional arrangements, the balance of power between the two branches still favored the executive. All those interviewed were asked directly which body was more important in resolving Yaroslavl's problems and who had more influence over this process, the chairman of the Presidium or of the ispolkom. Virtually all confirmed the preeminence of the executive. In the words of one, "We may pass the budget, but it is the ispolkom that spends it." Another was more hopeful: "The ispolkom is involved more with current, everyday issues; the soviet with general policy, so the ispolkom has more power, although this is changing." A third concluded: "The chairman of the soviet was a law professor one year ago. He doesn't know all the old connections. The heads of the executive departments are almost all old nomenklatura. They know how to get things done."

The strong impression this author received during these interviews, and in the course of the sessions of the soviets he observed, was that the executive branch continued to dominate the governing of Yaroslavl, not because of its total control over the organization of the work of the deputies as before, but because of the expertise and experience of its leaders in running the government. In this context, it is significant to understanding the evolution of executive-legislative relations in the two years of the new system that those chosen to exercise executive authority in both the oblast and the city were those who had exercised it previously. As the power of the local party organization began to wane, many party professionals sought, and found, positions in the ispolkom, especially at the oblast level where their deputies were able to form a working majority. There they could use experience and personal connections to their advantage. Among state officials, then, the old elites had managed to survive the institutional changes aimed at reducing their influence, at least in Yaroslavl.

One other development of crucial importance to the emergence of local legislatures as viable institutions in Yaroslavl and elsewhere in Russia was the diminished influence of the Communist Party. As discussed earlier, the absence of legislative institutionalization in the old system was due in large part to complete control of all institutions of government by the party through its control over political recruitment. By 1991, the situation had changed dramatically. In part, the decline of the CPSU came about as a result of decisions made nationally, notably the 1989 decision to introduce competitive elections, and the removal of article 6, which guaranteed the party a "leading role" in political affairs, from the USSR constitution in spring 1990. The factionalization of the CPSU, which had become visible at the twenty-eighth (and last) Congress of the CPSU in July 1990, also contributed.

In Yaroslavl, the party's increasing inability to control local politics was apparent well before the party was abolished in the wake of the failed coup of August 1991. Party membership had declined by 25 percent and only 40 of the 140 members of the apparat from a year earlier remained. Most of their office space in the huge modern white headquarters built in the middle of town by former obkom first secretary Fedor Loshchenkov were now occupied by members of the soviets. Despite the fact that a majority of those elected to both soviets were party members (63 percent in the city; 77 percent in the oblast), party discipline in the soviets was negligible, as demonstrated by the inability of deputies from the apparat to elect the city and oblast first secretaries as chairmen of their respective soviets. Interviews with deputies in June 1991 found almost universal agreement that the party lacked influence, an assessment confirmed, at least for the city soviet, in conversation with the last obkom first secretary, Sergei Kalinin.

Part II (1992–1993)

The evolution of local political institutions after the dissolution of the USSR on December 25, 1991, was very much affected by events surrounding the attempted coup a few months earlier. Broadly speaking, this evolution is chiefly characterized by the growth of executive authority at the expense of legislative institutions and by the growing polarization (and politicization) of executive-legislative relations from top to bottom as a result. The ultimate denouement of this conflict, of course, was Yeltsin's abolition of legislative institutions altogether, locally as well as nationally, in October 1993. The most visible assertion of executive authority in the wake of the coup was the appointment of "presidential representatives" in virtually all the provinces of Russia. As originally conceived, the presidential representatives were to act as a link between the president and local authorities. They were to oversee (*kontrol*) the implementation of the acts of the federal government and to make recommendations about removal from office in the event of violation of federal acts by local executives (Vladimirov 1993). In practice, not surprisingly, those appointed were Yeltsin loyalists, most being deputies to the Russian parliament affiliated with the Democratic Russia political movement despite the legal proscription that they not belong to a political party (Slider 1994).

The other major way in which executive authority was strengthened was through the establishment of the office of chief of administration (*glava administratsii*). This new institution represented a fundamental change in the previous institutional balance because it removed the leadership of the executive branch of government from the control of the legislature. In conception, the chief of administration was to be elected directly by the people living within a particular territorial unit. At the oblast level chiefs would be known as governor (*gubernator*), while at the city level they would be called mayor (*meyr*). They, and not the local legislature, would be responsible for appointing other members of the administration, which was to replace the ispolkom in the day-to-day running of government. As it became clear to Yeltsin that his opponents stood a good chance of winning elections to these posts, especially at the oblast level, he persuaded the fifth session of the Russian Congress of People's Deputies in October 1991 to declare a moratorium on them for one year. Local soviets could nominate candidates for the position, but the president would have the final say as to which of them would hold office. Moreover, since the CPD had given him control over all matters affecting the structure of local executive authority, Yeltsin also had the right to remove officials he determined were not acting "legally."[15]

How did these institutional changes play out in Yaroslavl? In the winter of 1991 there were meetings of both the city and oblast soviets to nominate candidates for Yeltsin's consideration. In a session of the city soviet held on November 18, 1991, the incumbent chair of the ispolkom, Viktor Volonchunas, received the most votes among three candidates and was "presented" to President Yeltsin for appointment as mayor. At the oblast level, the incumbent head of the oblast ispolkom, and a deputy of the Russian parliament, Vladimir Kovalev, received by far the most votes from the soviet. He, however, was passed over by Yeltsin on the recommendation of the presidential representative, Vladimir Varukhin, in favor of Anatolii Lisitsyn, a former ispolkom chair from Rybinsk. Lisitsyn had gotten only a few votes at the meeting of the oblast soviet, and the few he did get came from deputies associated with the local democratic movement, but they were enough to ensure that his name was on the list sent to Yeltsin. Yeltsin's rejection of Kovalev was based on Kovalev's strong ties to the old apparat and his apparent support for the coup attempt. For his part, Lisitsyn promptly used his authority to replace the old ispolkom, including, of course, those with links to the old elite, and named a new team loyal to himself and predictably to the president.[16]

At the same time that executive institutions were being reorganized, changes were also under way in the legislative branch. The most important of these was the formation of a small soviet (*malyi sovet*) comprised of members elected by the soviet as a whole. The reason for this institutional change was obvious. Under the old Soviet system, conducting legislative business with two hundred or more deputies was possible only because all decisions were unanimous; in conditions of free debate, it had become impossible. Therefore, a smaller legislative body that met more frequently (once or twice a month) was needed. Having derived its authority from the larger body, the small soviet could take over the policy-making functions of the legislature and report its decisions to quarterly sessions of the body as a whole. If the deputies at a session of the whole disagreed with the decisions of the small soviet, they could rescind them.[17] The small soviet also was given authority to act in place of the soviet as a whole in relations with the executive branch, especially in approving the budget and local finance. If the local executive issued regulations that the small soviet felt contradicted its own, or which it considered illegal, the small soviet could rescind them.

In Yaroslavl, the formation of the city's small soviet took place on November 21, 1991. Out of 31 candidates, 16 were elected, with only the chairman, L.L. Kruglikov, serving ex officio. Among those elected, 10 were chairs of standing committees and had served on the old Presidium, thereby ensuring some sense of continuity. The city's small soviet held its first meeting (*zasedaniie*) on January 23, 1992. In addition to 11 of its members, the meeting was attended by 7 members of the permanent staff and 11 invited guests. The first item on the agenda was approval of the city budget. Other matters varied from approving the structure of the city administration to changing the prices of municipal transport. The oblast formed its small soviet on January 18, 1992. Considerable debate over its composition occurred as a result of jockeying for position between the urban and rural deputies, a harbinger of conflicts to come. In the end, 40 deputies were elected, rather large for a "small" soviet. Two of these, the oblast soviet chair A.N. Veselov and the vice chair Yu.Ia. Kolbovskii, were ex officio. The oblast small soviet held its first meeting in February 1992.

During the course of 1992, the focus of legislative activity in Yaroslavl clearly shifted to the small soviets. Meetings of the city's small soviet in 1992 were held on an average of more than twice a month, and the agenda grew in size and complexity. In general, this was also true of the oblast soviet, although it met less often (once or twice a month), presumably because of its larger size. By contrast, sessions of the deputies as a whole became less frequent. City sessions were held only twice in 1992, the minimum required by regulation; at the oblast level, only one session was held between July 1992 and March 1993. It would be reasonable to conclude that the small soviets represented an improvement from the standpoint of legislative efficiency. And so they did. In the end, however, they represented an effort to make the system inherited from the Soviet period work better: newly designed bottles holding old wine.

In evaluating whether local legislatures in Russia became institutionalized in 1990–93, we must first decide if they became more autonomous as institutions. The evidence presented here is mixed. As compared with the old soviets, there was undeniable progress. For one thing, deputies were no longer dependent on the local party organization for holding office. For another, local legislatures no longer served as a "rubber stamp" for decisions presented to them already made by the executive branch. If all decisions were previously made unanimously, now none were. Debate, criticism, and divided votes became the norm. At least in the initial period of reform, it was clear that the members of the executive branch of government were accountable for their positions before the legislators. Most importantly, some perception of a division of labor between the legislators and administrators seemed to be emerging, at least in Yaroslavl.[18]

At the same time, institutionalization was very much impeded by the growing struggle for power at the national level. The amendments to the Russian constitution of 1991 grafted a presidential system of government onto what was structurally a parliamentary one. In the fall of 1991, as we have seen, Yeltsin extended this institutional miscegenation to the local level. His decision, in the face of what he considered "conservative" soviets, to create an independent source of executive authority from top to bottom had the effect of creating not one local authority, as intended, but five, each with its own institutional prerogatives: the chairs of both oblast and city soviets; the heads of administration at both levels (mayor and governor); and the presidential representative. The chairs of the small soviets interfered with the work of the administrators, and the presidential representative interfered with both.[19] In the ensuing struggle for power, it became increasingly clear in 1992–93 that real power at the local level was steadily shifting away from the legislative institutions to the executive. The autonomy of legislative institutions was in danger of becoming more apparent than real.

Another criterion of institutionalization discussed in the theoretical section of this chapter was the growth of organizational complexity. To some extent, this can be said to have occurred. Legislative committees were established with impressive rights on paper to oversee executive branch activities. Rules and procedures for the work of the soviets were adopted and clearly set forth in their regulations (*reglamenti*). The issues debated by the deputies were significant ones and not easily resolved. There were permanent staff. In these respects the local legislatures that emerged after the reforms of 1990 differed from their predecessors. At the same time, it was clear that the soviets lacked the kind of differentiated internal organization that would enable them to exercise effective power relative to the executive branch. Members of the small soviet served without pay, administrators were full-time. On paper, the staff of the soviets numbered about thirty, administrative staff numbered in the hundreds. The functions performed by administrators were clearly delineated and continuous over time, those of the deputies were not. While the deputies could and did debate any and all matters, it was the executives who governed. Compared to those in the executive branch, the deputies were amateurs.

This brings up another point that is central to the inability of the legislatures to institutionalize—the absence of well-developed norms of legislative behavior. The rules governing legislative behavior were not universalistic, or even particularistic; they were chaotic. This conclusion is based on the author's attendance at sessions of the soviets and small soviets at both levels (most recently at the session of the city's small soviet in June 1993). These meetings revealed a number of rather serious shortcomings from the standpoint of institutional development. In the first place, while there was a lot of participation, much of it was not very productive. Speakers frequently and freely introduced subjects that were trivial or irrelevant to the matter at hand, debate degenerated into shouting matches, and matters related essentially to constituency service were put up for votes by the body as a whole (a good thirty minutes were spent discussing a bus rerouting necessary to service one district). In many respects, the executive institutions took over by default. Someone, after all, had to govern.

In principle, the introduction of a small soviet was supposed to increase the efficiency of the legislature's operation. But the impression made on this observer during the small soviet's meeting of June 16, 1993, was quite the opposite. Toward the end of the meeting, procedure seemed nonexistent. Votes were taken while half the deputies were still engaged in discussion. Some voted, some did not, but a decision to send a delegation of deputies to other cities was deemed "passed" by the presiding officer, the vice chairman of the soviet. To this observer's dismay, chaos, rather than calm deliberation, had also characterized much of the work of the June 1991 session. Unfortunately for the development of local legislative institutions, matters had changed little two years later. Despite all that had been accomplished in bringing about the establishment of viable legislative institutions, Russia still had a long way to go.

Linkage

One of the primary functions of legislative institutions is representation. They act as a link between the people and their government. Democratic legislatures may be distinguished by how well they perform this function, that is, by the degree to which, in the words of Hannah Pitkin, "the people of a nation are present in the action of its government" (Pitkin 1967, p. 235). For linkage to take place, it is obvious that there must be mechanisms by which people can participate politically. There must also be some evidence that those representing them heed this participation. One important way in which linkage is maintained is through voting, but since this subject has already been discussed at some length, we need not return to it here. In assessing other forms of linkage, it is helpful to distinguish between individual participation and participation through groups. In what follows, we present some evidence about each mode of participation and how effectively they are performed in Yaroslavl.

Meaningful (as opposed to ritual) popular participation in government under the old Soviet system was negligible, but not nonexistent. In fact, there were a number of mechanisms available to citizens for communicating their preferences to power holders, some of them quite novel (Hahn 1988). Among them was the use of what were called

"voters' mandates" (*nakazy izbiratelei*), which took the form of requests voted for by constituents at the time of election which elected
deputies were pledged to fulfill. Deputies were expected to hold at
least four meetings a year with constituents both in the district they
represented and in the workplace that nominated them to report on
their activities. Deputies were also expected to hold office hours
(called *priyom*) at least once a month in the district, during which
constituents could come with their problems. Beyond these formal
requirements, deputies were also expected to be responsive to informal
constituent contact. Although not widely used or necessarily heeded,
these various mechanisms established a basis for political participation
that has continued into the post-Soviet period.[20] Given the fact that
deputies must now compete for voter support, have they become more
responsive? Are voters taking advantage of opportunities for contact-
ing their representatives since their votes now carry real weight? In
short, what evidence is there that individual political participation has
become more "meaningful" since 1990?

The levels of popular political participation in Yaroslavl are reported in Table 7.1. The statistics for 1990 represent levels of activity
up to March 1990, and so must have been included under the old
system, with the exception of electoral activity and political demonstrations.[21] What seems clear from the table is that few Yaroslavl
citizens took advantage of the mechanisms for constituent contact
available under the old system, and that this has not changed after three
years of local political reform. If anything, it decreased somewhat.
Partly, this may be a function of political alienation. Levels of political
efficacy are generally low. When asked if deputies lose contact with
their constituents after elections, 86 percent of respondents said "yes."
Another explanation may be that most voters simply do not know
about these mechanisms. When asked how many times a year a deputy
is required to report to constituents, only 35 percent answered correctly. Whatever the reason, political participation in Yaroslavl has not
grown. Only 10 percent of the respondents in 1990 indicated that they
had ever "tried to influence local legislation"; in 1993 the figure was
9 percent.

With respect to the question of responsiveness, however, it is not
only the level of political participation that causes decision makers to
take public concerns into account. In fact, numerous studies of political
participation in Western democracies, including the United States,

Table 7.1

Political Participation Levels in Yaroslavl, 1990 and 1993
(rank order, percent)

	1990	1993
1. Voted in March 1990 elections for deputy to Russian CPD	81.9	99.0*
2. Voted in March 1990 local soviets elections	78.0	99.0*
3. Discussed political issues in meeting of work collectives	55.1	63.3
4. Attended preelection meetings	35.5	44.0
5. Participated in election work	32.7	30.1
6. Took part in political demonstrations	12.8	13.2
7. Attended deputy meeting with constituents	12.4	23.4
8. Wrote to deputy about political opinion	7.0	6.7
9. Met with deputy in reception hours	6.4	7.6
10. Met with deputy on personal problem at another time	5.5	7.8
11. Met with deputy on a matter of public concern at another time	4.5	5.4
12. Made formal complaints to deputy for attention by city government	2.7	4.2
13. Expressed political opinion in media	2.7	4.4

Source: Data reported or gathered by the author using survey research in Yaroslavl, 1991, 1993.

* Estimates; voter turnout for elections prior to 1990 was 99 percent, as was customary in old-style soviet elections.

have shown that, except for elections, most people, most of the time, do not participate politically (Verba and Nie 1972). At the same time, this does not mean that representatives are inattentive or insensitive to the views of their constituents. Quite to the contrary, their preoccupation with reelection ensures both (Mayhew 1974). Consequently, even though most voters may not be paying attention to politicians, most politicians play close attention to what the voters in their district have to say. On highly visible issues, they are also likely to act on it.

What about deputies in Yaroslavl? Although we have no comparable data from before 1993, there is evidence to suggest that most deputies do take their constituent duties fairly seriously (see Table 7.2). If the "don't know/no answer" category is dropped, a majority appear to meet or better the regulatory standard for contact with those they represent. Moreover, when asked which of several deputy activities occupied the most time, easily the most frequently mentioned was the "protection of the district's interests" (46 percent). The next most frequent was helping constituents with the local administrators (36

Table 7.2

**Economic Attitudes Related to Political Reform—
Citizens and Deputies, Yaroslavl, 1992–93** (in percent)

Questions	Citizens (1993) (S = 1,019) (N = 1,019)	Deputies (1992) (N = 183)
1. The complexity of today's problems allows only the simplest questions to be exposed to public scrutiny.		
Agree	58	40
Disagree	42	60
2. A high level of public participation in making decisions often leads to unwanted conflicts.		
Agree	76	58
Disagree	23	42
3. All citizens should have equal opportunity to influence government.		
Agree	80	77
Disagree	20	23
4. Talented, strong-willed leaders always achieve success in any undertaking.		
Agree	81	45
Disagree	19	55
5. A few strong leaders could do more for their country than all laws and discussion.		
Agree	76	49
Disagree	25	51
6. There are situations when a leader should not divulge certain facts.		
Agree	81	83
Disagree	12	17
7. When deciding important problems, a leader should not pay attention to how the community feels about his position.		
Agree	42	43
Disagree	59	57
Summary Scales (mean score*)		
1. Popular Participation (1.00 is most favorable) (variables: 1, 2, 3 [R])	$x = 1.919$	$x = 1.798$
2. Strong Leader (1.00 is unfavorable) (variables: 4, 5, 6, 7)	$x = 2.095$	$x = 1.745$

* The range is 1.00–3.00. Scale reliability lists were performed for all scales. No scale items that correlated negatively were included. A minimum mean inter-item correlation of .088 was required. All scales exceeded this level substantially.

percent). Paying attention to constituents, however, does not necessarily translate into doing what they want. This depends on the "style" of representation adopted by the legislator (Loewenberg and Patterson 1979, p. 178–182). What happens when there is a difference of opinion between the representative and his constituents about what is best for the community? When we asked our deputies about this, 57 percent indicated that such differences had indeed arisen. When asked what they should do about it, 49 percent said constituent preferences should prevail and 39 percent said they should do what they thought best. The remaining 12 percent could not make up their minds.

There appears to be a lack of consensus between voters and those they elect on questions of public policy. Although respondents were not asked to evaluate specific policies adopted by the government, they were asked a series of questions designed to measure their attitudes on political and economic reform. Since the same questions had been asked in a survey of 183 Yaroslavl deputies, comparing the two sets of answers could tell us something about the congruence (or lack thereof) between mass and elite policy perceptions. In addition to comparing answers on individual items, additive scales were constructed to provide a summary measure of four attitudinal dimensions. They summarized favorable or unfavorable orientations on: political participation, the desirability of a "strong leader," a free market economy, and the accumulation of wealth. The data are presented in Tables 7.3 and 7.4.

While there is a lack of consensus on all scaled items, those pertaining to the economy may be particularly significant since the dominant question of public policy since Yeltsin introduced his "shock therapy" in January 1990 has been the introduction of a free market. On this question, the views of elected officials appear to be far more positive than those of their constituents. This seems especially true when it comes to the accumulation of wealth. Legislators appear willing to accept the notion that free markets benefit some, more than others. But among voters, there is resistance to the idea that the accumulation of wealth is a good thing if everybody does not benefit. There are also danger signals for reformists on questions of political reform. Public support for the idea that "a few strong leaders would do more for the country than all laws and discussion" runs to 73 percent; among deputies to less than 50 percent. Such attitudes suggest that support in the Russian political culture for policies promoting democracy and a free market may still be very much in the formative stage. They also sug-

Table 7.3

**Economic Attitudes Related to Economic Reform—
Citizens and Deputies, Yaroslavl, 1992–93** (in percent)

Questions	Citizens (1993) (S = 1,019) (N = 1,019)	Deputies (1992) (N = 183)
1. An upper limit should exist on earnings so that no one accumulates more than anyone else.		
Agree	51	20
Disagree	50	80
2. If some live in poverty, the government should react so that no one can become wealthy.		
Agree	63	32
Disagree	37	68
3. Wealthy people should pay more than the poor should.		
Agree	93	92
Disagree	7	8
4. A system based on profit brings out the worst in human nature.		
Agree	50	26
Disagree	50	74
5. A system of private enterprise is effective.		
Agree	68	33
Disagree	32	67
6. State regulation of business usually brings more harm than good.		
Agree	55	45
Disagree	45	55
7. The share of the private sector in business and industry today should be increased.		
Agree	70	86
Disagree	31	14
8. People accumulate wealth only at the expense of others.		
Agree	60	41
Disagree	40	59
Summary Scales (mean scores*)		
1. Accumulation of Wealth (1.00 is unfavorable) (variables: 1, 2, 3)	x = 1.948	x = 2.12
2. Free Market (1.00 is favorable) (variables: 4[R], 5, 6, 7, 8[R])	x = 1.950	x = 1.918

* The range is 1.00–3.00. Scale reliability tests were performed for all scales. No scale items that correlated negatively were included. A minimum mean inter-item correlation of .088 was required. All scales exceeded this level substantially.

Table 7.4

Yaroslavl Deputies—Reported Frequency of Meetings with Constituents, 1992* (in percent)

	Once a year	Every 6 months	Every 3 months	Every 2 months	Once a month	Once a week	More often	Don't know/ no answer
Meeting at a residence	41	26	9	2	1	1	0	21
Deputy's office hours	7	7	26	18	27	4	2	10
Meetings at the workplace	22	22	18	6	10	1	2	19
Rallies	18	7	0	1	0	1	1	74
Informal meetings with people about affairs	7	7	13	4	18	13	13	27

* The question asked was: How often do you use the following forms of organization to meet with voters?

gest that the voter approval of Yeltsin's economic and social program in the April 1993 referendum may be more a vote of support for the man than for his programs.

While levels of individual political participation may be low in many democratically governed countries, it can be argued that participation through groups is a more effective way for communicating the concerns of citizens to those who govern. In pluralist theories of politics, democracy is ensured by the contention of competing groups for political influence. "Public contestation" is one of the dimensions by which Robert Dahl measures the achievement of "polyarchy," and, in modern democracies, public contestation generally takes place between groups. Groups need not be primarily political to exert influence politically. The notion of "civil society" is widely used to refer to the presence of independent social or economic groups (churches, labor or business organizations, communities of scholars, and so forth) whose existence is considered essential for the emergence of democratic institutions. The central defining characteristic of groups in a civil society is their autonomy from government control. In his study of Italian regional politics, Robert Putnam found that the absence or presence of a lively "associational" life was a critical variable in determining whether democratic government worked well (Putnam 1993, pp. 89–116).

In looking at the development of group participation in political life in Yaroslavl since 1990, one is struck not only by how many groups emerged in this period, but by how poorly organized most of them are. In the first blush of liberalization released by Gorbachev's policy of glasnost, informal (*neformalnyi*) groups sprung up like mushrooms in September after a heavy rain. In Yaroslavl, the most prominent independent political group was called the Yaroslavl Popular Front, whose origins were discussed earlier. From 1988 until the election in 1990, the YPF acted as a sort of umbrella organization for most of the emerging independent (and by definition, opposition) groups, including movements concerned with ecology and labor and civil rights (such as the group Memorial). With the elections over and diversity of opinion not only established, but glorified, the YPF broke up into factions. So did many other groups. The only organization to show a semblance of organizational discipline in 1990–91 was the Communist Party, but it too was disintegrating even before its abolition in the wake of the 1991 coup attempt.

By the end of 1992, there were perhaps thirty identifiable groups of all stripes actively involved in Yaroslavl politics. In an effort to provide a forum in which they could discuss their differences peaceably and, perhaps, establish a clearinghouse for independent organizations, the Council of Civic Union (Sovet Grazhdanskogo Soglasiia) was formed in January 1993. It included "nonpolitical" groups such as trade unions, veterans, women, Memorial, charities, youth, the Russian Orthodox Church (old and new believers), a Union of University Teachers, and a group called the Consciousness of Krishna. Groups whose concerns were explicitly political were, among *liberals*: the ·Russian Democratic Party, Democratic Russia, Democratic Reform, the Russian Social Democratic Party, the Republican Party of Russia, and Free Russia; among *Communists*: the Russian Communist Worker's Party, the United Labor Front (OFT), the Russian Party of Communists, and the Socialist Workers' Party; on the *nationalist* right: Pamiat and the Russian National Assembly (*sobor*).

Despite this lengthy list of politically relevant groups, only a few are well enough organized to have much political impact. Among "civil society" organizations, this would include the Orthodox Church, which has moved quickly to take back church property, and the group Memorial, which is dedicated to accounting for the crimes of the Stalin period, and which received 50,000 rubles for its activities from the oblast soviet in October 1992.[22] Even among well-organized groups, however, it is not clear that their articulation of interests is viewed favorably. When asked about being contacted by public organizations, nearly 50 percent of the deputies denied having any. Among the embryonic political parties, only Democratic Russia, Democratic Reform, and the Russian Communist Party were registered by summer 1993. Nationalist parties do not appear to have much following in Yaroslavl and have failed to elect any candidates at the local level, although Zhirinovsky's Liberal Democratic Party did receive about 18 percent of the party list vote in 1993. Support for a multiparty system is widespread in Yaroslavl but does not appear to be deep. There is little evidence of party identification among the deputies or the public. When asked which of nineteen protoparties they supported, 78 percent of the public said none; among deputies, the figure was 60 percent. In short, groups, whether explicitly political or not, do not yet seem to be a very effective mode of political communication in Yaroslavl.

Overall, to what extent does linkage exist between the voters of Yaroslavl and those who represent them? What evidence is there that it has grown? The evidence presented here indicates that rates of individual political participation in Yaroslavl remain fairly low, despite mechanisms to promote such participation. Political participation through groups also does not appear particularly effective. Most seem to be poorly organized, with membership lists that are limited, if not downright fictional. As indicated above, there is little attachment to political parties among voters and deputies alike. Most of the latter seem almost proud that they are independent of the influence of parties or other social organizations, perhaps overcompensating for memories of the communist period.

At the same time, it would be incorrect to conclude that no change has taken place. Under the old system, linkage was largely a fiction in which citizens pretended to participate and those in office pretended to listen. It was a system in which there were no autonomous groups. This simply is no longer true. Moreover, legislators do appear to be genuinely attentive to constituent concerns, and political parties have begun to emerge, even if their organizational base is weak. This weak base may change. Among the main reasons for the poor development of parties in Yaroslavl and elsewhere in Russia is that there was no party competition in the 1990 elections and most nominations were still made at the workplace. But, elections to half the seats in the Russian State Duma of December 1993 were conducted on the basis of a party list system, and despite the large number of different parties that competed (thirteen) some degree of party identification seems to have resulted. Also encouraging was the fact that in Yaroslavl political participation remained fairly high: 54 percent of the Yaroslavl electorate took part. In contrast, however, elections to the city and oblast legislatures (now called Municipalitet and Duma, respectively), which were held in February 1994, attracted a much smaller turnout (20–30 percent) and were dominated by candidates who ran as "independents" without party affiliation. This suggests that progress toward creating real linkage between constituents and representatives is likely to be slow and tentative.

Conclusions

This chapter sought answers to two questions. Over the period 1990–93, did local legislatures in Russia become institutionalized? Did these same institutions, during the same period, become more democratic? In order to provide preliminary answers to these questions, research findings were presented based on the experience of a single Russian province, Yaroslavl, and its capital city. Conclusions based on the diachronic analysis of the development of political institutions in one region cannot be applied with any certainty to other regions of Russia. They can, however, suggest potentially fruitful lines of inquiry in trying to understand the political transformation under way in that country. It is also hoped that they may be useful in establishing testable hypotheses relevant to our understanding of how democratic institutions come into being more generally.

The short answer to these two questions is that both institutional and democratic development were evident after the reforms of local legislative institutions were introduced in 1990. Those who dismissed the local soviets as vestigial relics of a bygone Leninist communist era, as Yeltsin and most of the Western press did in 1993, failed to appreciate just how different these institutions were after three years of reform. Nowhere was this more evident than in elections. In contrast to elections under the old Soviet system, the elections of local deputies in 1990 were competitive both quantitatively and in the sense of offering the voter a meaningful choice. Moreover, they generated strong voter interest and high levels of participation even without the ritual mobilization efforts characteristic of the old regime. Most importantly, perhaps, these elections were generally viewed as fair, giving the new soviets a degree of legitimacy unknown under the old system. Nevertheless, they were not entirely satisfactory. There were simply too many candidates running for too many seats in too many elections for even the well-informed voter to make informed choices. The absence of a multiparty system ensured confusion and also meant that deputies who were elected lacked any organizational incentive to vote cohesively on issues before the councils.

On the question of institutional development, the evidence is also mixed. By comparison with the old system, local legislatures for the first time exercised real authority. Autonomy from executive institutions (and, of course, from party control) did begin to emerge. The principle of executive accountability to popularly elected representatives was established on paper and in practice. Legislators began to play a real role in policy making, setting their own agendas, deliberating, and overseeing implementation. Even the right to vote negatively and to openly oppose measures must be regarded as a major step forward when compared with the enforced unanimity of the old soviets. Over time, however, legislative authority began to erode. For one thing, by 1992, institutional confusion characterized local government in Yaroslavl; instead of effective leadership, there were five leaders, each clinging to his prerogatives, even if it meant things did not get done. Inexperienced and amateur deputies proved incapable of governing well, thereby laying the groundwork for the reemergence of executive dominance. Above all, perhaps there was a failure to develop what Nelson Polsby calls "universalistic" norms of procedure. To the extent that government and politics worked in Yaroslavl (and compared with other regions, it worked rather well), it was because of personal relations between the major players, not because of established procedure.

With respect to political participation, the survey data revealed no increase over three years; individual and group participation remain low. Levels of voter turnout that had exceeded 70 percent in the first blush of competitive voting in 1990 had dropped to about 25 percent in the local elections of spring 1994. More optimistically, however, there is evidence to suggest that legislators nevertheless take their constituency concerns seriously. One departure from past practice favorable to democratization is the existence of independent organizations and political parties. Unfortunately, support for these as vehicles for the expression of public views on politics does not seem well developed. Despite their support for a multiparty system, for instance, few voters or legislators have a party affiliation. The absence of political partisanship and low levels of participation are not encouraging signs for the further development of representative legislative institutions.

Notes

The author wishes to thank the Carnegie Corporation of New York for the financial support that made this research possible. The grant supported a four-year study of democratization in Russia starting in January 1990. The author was joined in this research by Timothy Colton, Jerry Hough, and Blair Ruble, whose insights often proved very helpful and to whom he is also grateful. Additional support for the author's work on Yaroslavl came in the form of a travel grant from IREX and a grant from the National Council for Soviet and East European Research, which gave him a semester free from the distractions of teaching. It is a pleasure to acknowledge their assistance.

1. In this paper, the chief criteria of whether local Russian legislative institutions have become more democratic are (1) the degree to which elections were free and fair and (2) the degree to which local legislatures were representative.

These are minimal criteria. Other factors, it may be reasonably argued, need to be present if a political system is to be considered democratic. Among those commonly identified in the literature are a rule of law, a free press, guaranteed civil and minority rights, and autonomous civic associations.

2. In addition to elections and responsive legislative institutions, much of the literature on democratic transitions suggests that successful democratization is unlikely to succeed in the absence of a political culture that is supportive of democratic institutions. For an excellent review of the development of this concept and an explanation of how it has returned as a mainstream concept in political science, see Larry Diamond, ed., *Political Culture and Democracy in Developing Countries* esp. pp. ix–xii. Diamond argues that "it is, by now, a cardinal tenet of empirical democratic theory that stable democracy also requires a belief in the legitimacy of democracy" (p. 13).

In 1990, the author of this chapter conducted a representative opinion survey in the city of Yaroslavl to evaluate the argument that Russians lacked a political culture that could sustain democratic institutions due to their long historical experience with exclusively autocratic ones. The findings provided little support for the "cultural continuity" thesis and suggested that the political culture of Russia was not so different from those found in other Western industrial democracies in terms of support for democratic institutions (Hahn 1991b). Other studies have come to similar conclusions (Gibson, Duch, and Tedin, 1992; Finifter and Mickiewicz 1992). A replicate survey conducted in 1993 showed some erosion of this support, but far less than might have been expected given the Russian government's poor economic performance in the intervening three years (Hahn 1995).

3. The results of this research were initially written up in an article published in 1991. A more detailed discussion of the survey procedures used may be found there (Hahn, 1991a, pp. 323–341).

4. According to Gerald Pomper, at least six requirements need to be met before an election can be regarded as truly free: meaningful choices, the freedom to know and discuss the choices, a manageable number of clear choices, the equal weighting of votes, free registration of choices (a secret ballot), and accurate registration, counting, and reporting (Pomper 1968, pp. 263–266).

5. For the purposes of this paper, a member of the apparat is defined as anyone holding a full-time position working in the party or in the state, including full-time officials of party-controlled "public organizations" such as trade unions.

6. The YPF originated as a protest movement against the election of former obkom first secretary Fedor Ivanovich Loshchenkov (often referred to locally as "Tsar Fedor") to the nineteenth Party Conference in the summer of 1988 (*Izvestiia*, June 18, 1988). Although the movement was initiated mostly by those in the party committed to Gorbachev's policies of perestroika, it became radicalized over time and by the time of the local elections, it was openly campaigning against the local party establishment, even though four of its five co-chairs were party members (*Izvestiia*, January 10, 1990). Although splintered by the emergence of a more radical group called the Movement for Popular Rule, the YPF had managed to elect Boris Shamshev to the USSR Congress of People's Deputies and had become broadly affiliated with the Interregional Group of Deputies (of which Shamshev was a member) and the national democratic movement, Democraticheskaia Rossiia.

7. The critical condition for the free registration of choices is a secret ballot. In contrast to previous practice, Russian voters were now required to take their paper ballots into a curtained booth to be marked. Personal observation at several precincts randomly chosen during both the March 4 and March 18 elections gave the impression that this procedure was routinely followed, although a few older voters tried to go directly to the red ballot boxes on the other side of the booths to deposit their unmarked ballots as in the old days and had to be gently reminded that things were different now.

8. The author was unable to personally observe elections in oblast districts located outside of the city. There is reason to suggest, however, that the rural constituents in Russia are politically more conservative and that their support of greater numbers of deputies from among the old elite reflects real differences with their more liberal city "cousins."

9. The proportion of those concluding the elections were "fair" dropped from 69 percent to 54 percent (still a majority), with most of the change going to the "don't know/no answer" category (28 percent). Some of the 1993 respondents in 1993 were ineligible to vote in 1990.

10. As reported in a special edition of the Yaroslavl city newspaper *Gorodskie novosti*, May 15, 1990, p. 3.

11. Special edition of *Gorodskie novosti*, May 16, 1990, p. 2.

12. The results are reported in the oblast newspaper, *Severnyi rabochii*, April 22, 1990, p. 4. Varukhin later became Yeltsin's "presidential representative" in Yaroslavl—a position discussed below.

13. Kovalev would lose this position in the fall of 1991 because he failed to support Yeltsin during the August coup attempt. He was replaced by Anatolii Lisitsyn, a Yeltsin supporter.

14. *Reglament gorodskogo soveta narodnykh deputatov*, Yaroslavl, 1991, article 84. In the case of the oblast soviet, the ispolkom is bound by the decisions of the soviet and by those of higher bodies of state power (article 81 of the *Reglament Yaroslavskogo oblastnogo soveta*).

15. For further information about the development of executive authority in this period, see Jeffrey W. Hahn, "Latest Developments in Russian Local Government," unpublished manuscript presented at the Mid-Atlantic Slavic Studies Conference, Harriman Institute, New York, March 15, 1995; and William A. Clarke, "Central Authority and Local Governance in Post-Communist Russia," unpublished manuscript presented at the twenty-sixth annual meeting of the American Association for the Advancement of Slavic Studies, Philadelphia, November 17–20, 1994.

16. The information on the personnel changes in the Yaroslavl oblast and city soviet come from the minutes of meetings that were made available to the author during his visits, and from interviews conducted with those involved and with other deputies in January and April of 1992.

17. The small soviets differed from the old "presidiums" not only in their ability to make policy, but also in their composition. Presidium members were drawn ex officio from the chairs of the standing committees, while members of the small soviet were elected at large from among the larger body. The small soviet did, however, retain the organizational functions of the Presidium.

18. The author was struck by a remark made by the mayor of Yaroslavl during

a meeting of the small soviet he attended in June 1993. Discussing how to better fund (and house) the local militia, the mayor said: "There are functions of the soviet and there are functions of the mayor. We will fulfill your decisions; you have the budget. If you make a decision to increase housing space, we'll figure out how to do it, how much it costs; if you support it we'll carry it out, even if it means there will not be enough for other projects. You must choose."

19. Rolf Theen quotes Anatolii Lisitsyn's speech to a gathering of administrators at Cheboksary, Chuvashia, in September 1992, which complained of the "absurdity" of the oblast small soviet's rescinding the administration's decision to help someone whose house had burned down simply because the soviet had not authorized it. Rolf Theen, "Russia at the Grassroots: Reform at the Local and Regional Levels," *In Depth*, vol. 3, no. 1 (Winter 1993), p. 72. An example of the presidential representative's complicated relations with both can been found in Gennadii Vladimirov, "Rossiiskii tsentr i mestnaia vlast' " *Politicheskii monitoring*, no. 4 (April 1993), p. 12. My thanks to Darrell Slider for bringing this valuable article to my attention.

20. Evidence of the continued use of these mechanisms *after* the end of the Soviet system can be found in the minutes of both oblast and city soviets. At a meeting of the city's small soviet on July 15, 1992, a decision was taken on how well deputies had been conducting their constituent meetings, and at the tenth session of the city soviet held on February 21, 1992, deputies received a report on the fulfillment of voters' mandates. A similar report was made to deputies of the oblast small soviet on August 27, 1992.

21. The data reported here come from representative opinion surveys conducted in Yaroslavl in 1990 and 1993. For details regarding sampling see Hahn (1991b) and Hahn (1993). Preparation for the March 4, 1990, election had been under way since January 1990 and since respondents were not asked to distinguish between old and new elections it is impossible to say whether this figure is for the new competitive elections. Since many voters had been "mobilized" into serving in some electoral capacity under the old system, it is possible that a similar response could have been obtained.

22. Labor unions are another group that could press political demands, and there have been strikes in Yaroslavl. These seem confined to particular grievances at particular workplaces, however, and the author knows of no single organization representing labor. The agrarian workers appear to be organized as well and have exerted considerable influence on local politics, especially at the oblast level, where they have demanded higher prices for their products.

References

Almond, Gabriel A., and Sidney Verba. 1965. *The Civic Culture*. Boston, MA: Little, Brown and Company.

Clarke, Harold D., and Nitish Dutt. 1991. "Measuring Value Change in Western Industrialized Societies: The Impact of Unemployment." *American Political Science Review*, 85, no. 3 (September): pp. 905–920.

Dahl, Robert. 1971. *Polyarchy: Participation and Opposition*. New Haven, CT: Yale University Press.

Diamond, Larry. ed., 1993. *Political Culture and Democracy in Developing Countries*. Boulder: CO: Lynne Rienner Publishers.

DiPalma, Giuseppe. 1990. *To Craft Democracies*. Berkeley, CA: University of California Press.

Easton, David. 1965. *A Framework for Political Analysis*. New York, NY: Prentice-Hall.

Fenno, Richard. 1973. *Congressmen in Committees*. Boston, MA: Little, Brown and Company.

Finifter, Ada W., and Ellen Mickiewicz. 1992. "Redefining the Political System of the USSR: Mass Support for Political Change," *American Political Science Review* 86, no. 4 (December): pp. 857–874.

Friedgut, Theodore H. 1979. *Political Participation in the USSR*. Princeton, NJ: Princeton University Press.

Gerlich, Peter. 1973. "The Institutionalization of European Parliaments." In Allan Kornberg, ed., *Legislatures in Comparative Perspective*. New York, NY: David McKay.

Gibson, James L., Raymind M. Duch, and Kent L. Tedin. 1992. "Democratic Values and the Transformation of the Soviet Union." *Journal of Politics* 54: pp. 329–374.

Hahn, Jeffrey W. 1988. *Soviet Grassroots*. Princeton, NJ: Princeton University Press.

———. 1991a. "Local Politics and Political Power in Russia: The Case of Yaroslavl." *Soviet Economy* 7, no. 4 (October–December): pp. 322–341.

———. 1991b. "Continuity and Change in Russian Political Culture." *British Journal of Political Science* 21: pp. 393–421.

———. 1995. "Changes in Contemporary Russian Political Culture." In Vladimir Tismaneanu, ed., *Political Culture and Civil Society in Russia and the New States of Eurasia*. Armonk, NY: M.E. Sharpe, Inc.

Helf, Gavin, and Jeffrey W. Hahn. 1992. "Old Dogs and New Tricks: Party Elites in the Russian Regional Elections of 1990." *Slavic Review* 51, no. 3: (Fall) pp. 511–530.

Hough, Jerry. 1969. *The Soviet Prefects*. Cambridge, MA: Harvard University Press.

Huntington, Samuel P. 1968. *Political Order in Changing Societies*. New Haven, CT: Yale University Press.

———. 1991. *The Third Wave*. Norman: University of Oklahoma Press.

———. 1991–1992. "How Countries Democratize." *Political Science Quarterly* 106, no. 4: pp. 579–616.

Kornberg, Allan, ed. 1973. *Legislatures in Comparative Perspective*. New York, NY: David McKay.

Kornberg, Allan, and Harold D. Clarke. 1992. *Citizens and Community*. New York: Cambridge University Press.

Linz, Juan J. 1990a. "The Perils of Presidentialism." *Journal of Democracy* 1 (Winter): pp. 51–70.

———. 1990b. "Transitions to Democracy." *Washington Quarterly* (Summer): pp. 143–164.

Linz, Juan J., and Alfred Stepan, eds. 1978. *The Breakdown of Democratic Regimes*. Baltimore: Johns Hopkins University Press.

Lipset, Seymour M. "Some Social Requisites of Democracy." *American Political Science Review* 53: pp. 69–105.

Loewenberg, Gerhard, and Samuel C. Patterson. 1979. *Comparing Legislatures.* Boston: Little, Brown and Company.

March, James G., and Johan P. Olson. 1984. "The New Institutionalism: Organizational Factors in Political Life." *American Political Science Review* 78: pp. 734–749.

Mayhew, David R. 1974. *Congress: The Electoral Connection.* New Haven, CT: Yale University Press.

Mezey, Michael L. 1979. *Comparative Legislatures.* Durham, NC: Duke University Press.

———. 1993. "Legislatures: Individual Purpose and Institutional Performance." In Ada W. Finifter, ed., *The State of the Discipline II.* Washington, DC: American Political Science Association.

Mishler, William, and Richard Rose. 1993. "Public Support for Legislatures and Regimes in Eastern and Central Europe." Paper presented at the International Conference on the Role of Legislatures and Parliaments in Democratizing and Newly Democratic Regimes, Paris, France (May).

Moe, Terry. 1990. "Political Institutions: The Neglected Side of the Story." *Journal of Law, Economics, and Organization* 6 (Special Issue): pp. 213–253.

Pitkin, Hannah F. 1967. *The Concept of Representation.* Berkeley: University of California Press.

Polsby, Nelson W. 1962. "The Institutionalization of the U.S. House of Representatives." *American Political Science Review* 62, 1 (March): pp. 144–165.

———. 1975. "Legislatures." In Fred I. Greenstein and Wilson W. Polsby, eds., *Handbook of Political Science: Government Institutions and Processes* Vol. 5. Reading, MA: Addison-Wesley.

Pomper, Gerald M. 1968. *Elections in America.* New York: Dodd, Mead and Co.

Przeworski, Adam. 1986. "Some Problems in the Study of the Transition to Democracy." In Guillermo O'Donnell, et al., *Transitions from Authoritarian Rule.* Baltimore: Johns Hopkins University Press.

Putnam, Robert. 1993. *Making Democracy Work,* Princeton, NJ: Princeton University Press.

Olson, David M., and Michael L. Mezey, eds. 1991. *Legislatures in the Policy Process.* New York: Cambridge University Press.

Olson, Mancur. 1993. "Dictatorship, Democracy, and Development." *American Political Science Review* 87, 3 (September): pp. 567–576.

Ragsdale, Lyn. 1985. "Legislative Elections and Electoral Responsiveness." In Gerhard Loewenberg, Samuel C. Patterson, and Malcolm E. Jewell, eds., *Handbook of Legislative Research.* Cambridge, MA: Harvard University Press.

Schumpeter, Joseph A. 1947. *Capitalism, Socialism, and Democracy.* New York: Harper.

Sisson, Richard. 1973. "Comparative Legislative Institutionalization: A Theoretical Exploration." In Allan Kornberg, ed., *Legislatures in Comparative Perspective.* New York: David McKay.

Skocpol, Theda. 1985. "Bringing the State Back In." In Peter Evans, Dietrich Rueschmeyer, and Theda Skocpol, eds., *Bringing the State Back In.* Cambridge: Cambridge University Press.

Slider, Darrell. 1994. *"Federalism, Discord and Accomodation: Intergovernmental Relations in Post-Soviet Russia."* In *T.H. Friedgut and Jeffrey W. Hahn, eds., Local Power and Post-Soviet Politics*. Armonk, NY: M.E. Sharpe.

Steinmo, Sven, Kathleen Thelen, and Frank Longstreth. 1992. *Structuring Politics: Historical Institutionalism in Comparative Analysis*. New York: Cambridge University Press.

Susser, Bernard, ed. 1992. *Approaches to the Study of Politics*. New York: Macmillan Publishing Company.

Rostow, Eugene. 1960. *The Stages of Economic Growth*. London: Cambridge University Press.

Rustow, Dankwurt. 1970. "Transitions to Democracy: Towards a More Dynamic Model." *Comparative Politics* (April): pp. 337–363.

Theen, Rolf. 1993. "Russia at the Grassroots: Reform at the Local and Regional Levels." *In Depth* 3, 1 (Winter): pp. 53–90.

Vanhanen, Tatu. 1990. *The Process of Democratization: A Comparative Study of 147 States, 1980–88*. New York: Crane Russack.

Verba, Sidney, and Norman H. Nie. 1972. *Participation in America*. New York: Harper and Row.

Verba, Sidney, Norman H. Nie, and Jae-on Kim. 1978. *Participation and Political Equality*. Cambridge, NY: Cambridge University Press.

Vladimirov, Gennadii. 1993. "Rossiiskii tsentr i mestnaia vlast'." *Politicheskii monitoring*, 4 (April).

8

Local Policy Making: Lessons from Urban Planning in Yaroslavl

Blair A. Ruble

The simultaneous devolution of power from the executive branch of government to the legislature as well as from central administration to regional agencies has become a principal focus both for those who seek to foster a more democratic political order in Russia and for those who seek to analyze a perceived transition from a more authoritarian Soviet past. The orderly delegation of duties and authority away from the national executive lies at the core of any sustained attempt to democratize the inheritor states of an excessively centralized Soviet state.

The traditional Russian state suffered simultaneously from hyperinstitutionalization and underinstitutionalization. Historically, the Russian state has been hyperinstitutionalized in the sense that hardly a sphere of human activity fell outside the purview of central state institutions. Nevertheless, the Russian state remained underinstitutionalized in that few intermediary institutions were either created or wielded sufficient resources to mediate between state and society. Present-day efforts to empower legislative agencies at all levels and to strengthen regional and local governmental institutions seek to resolve this historic inconsistency.

This chapter will not explore such interrelated processes through a discussion of the extensive theoretical and comparative literature examining either democratization or the devolution of power within centralized states. Rather, it will be merely descriptive in an attempt to illustrate the tangible repercussions of such processes for a single community—the provincial Russian city of Yaroslavl—during the early 1990s. Even more circumspectly, this chapter will draw lessons from a finite set of issues revolving around the planning and use of real property—land, buildings, factories, domiciles—in that city. In so doing, this chapter endeavors to highlight the practical consequences of national reform efforts at the local level.

Yaroslavl, a historic city founded in 1010 at the confluence of the Volga and Kotorosl' rivers some 150 miles northeast of Moscow, is home to approximately 650,000 residents employed primarily in medium and heavy industrial production. A number of physical changes have occurred in the spatial organization of the city over the course of the past half-decade as a consequence of an expansion of property rights on the one hand, and a diminution in the influence of central planning authorities on the other. These complex processes have merged into a cluster of policy issues that includes both the privatization of state housing and the use of urban space. The implementation of policies relating to these questions highlights the labyrinthine impact on local institutions of policies intended to devolve power from the executive branch to the legislature as well as from central administrative agencies to regional governments.

Housing Privatization

Housing patterns in post-Soviet Yaroslavl are now being determined by the market. The initial guidelines for the privatization of housing were announced by the USSR Council of Ministers in December 1988, and were expanded by a joint decree of the Council of Ministers and the All-Union Central Council of Trade Unions four months later.[1] By May 1990, privatization proposals stood at the center of Mikhail Gorbachev's Presidential Decree on housing issues.[2] The Russian Federation government launched its own, more aggressive privatization initiatives following passage of a July 1991 law on housing privatization.[3]

The July 1991 Russian Federation law established the principle that resident families were eligible to receive free of charge no less than nine square meters per family plus eighteen square meters per family member.[4] Municipalities were required to determine the precise means for title transfer, including compensation requirements for those families occupying less space than the minimal norm, and payment requirements for those inhabiting a larger area. The law exempted or partially protected enterprise housing, housing controlled by social organizations, as well as collective and state farm housing from privatization regulations.

It is important to recall at the outset of this discussion that a private housing sector existed in Russia throughout the Soviet period.[5] Fifteen percent of all urbanites in the Russian Federation in June 1990 lived in "housing owned by individual citizens," including 12 percent inhabiting "single-family dwellings."[6] These were almost exclusively private wooden houses. In addition, a limited but vibrant cooperative apartment market existed in nearly every Russian city. While the actual percentage of all Soviet-period urban housing in cooperatives was a low 3.8 percent in the Russian Federation at the close of 1990, this housing stock long provided an important alternative to the clutches of state monopolies.[7] By 1993, cooperative associations in Moscow were beginning to band together to protect mutual interests.[8] In Yaroslavl, both the private and cooperative housing sectors are likely to expand regardless of the disposition of the city's public housing.

The 1991 Russian Federation legislation left a number of technical issues that were to be resolved by local officials in the wake of the Federation's statutes and regulations concerning such questions as the transfer of title, the eligibility of collective farm and state enterprise housing for privatization, the rights of family members to a share of privatized title, and payment of required capital repairs.

Yaroslavl city officials and legislators reviewed these various procedures governing housing privatization in late 1991.[9] Claiming authority over all state housing—even that built by individual state enterprises for their own employees—the city soviet enacted its own privatization initiatives in early 1992.[10] Apartments smaller than or equal in size to established norms were to be transferred to private ownership free of charge.[11] Special provisions were also designed to expedite the transfer of title to the families of military officers and survivors of the Chernobyl' nuclear accident who had moved to the region.[12]

Yaroslavl standards were moderately more generous than those of the Russian Federation law: ten square meters per family plus an additional twenty square meters per resident.[13] Seventy-eight percent of the city's state-controlled housing stock qualified for free title transfer.[14] Residents of larger apartments would have to pay an additional fee of

698 rubles per square meter (approximately U.S. $6.00 in April 1992). Once title had been obtained, a resident would be able to rent or resell the unit as he or she pleased. Maintenance fees of 0.1 percent of the estimated value of the unit remained strikingly low.[15] Yaroslavtsy, however, were terrorized by the specter of ever-increasing maintenance fees and taxes in a period of galloping inflation and remained loath to privatize.[16] Trade unions opposed the abandonment of a state commitment to free housing.[17] Major enterprises and ministries resisted privatization of their apartment inventory through what they claimed to be "yet another round of state expropriation in Russian history."[18]

The initial three months of housing privatization in Yaroslavl saw the tortuous transfer of only a handful (156) of housing units.[19] Most of those apartments—spacious units located near or on the prestigious Volga Embankment—were likely inhabited by the old Communist Party elite. Privatization was also popular in the Bragino district, where many middle-level managers reside.[20] Privatization of housing gained speed throughout April 1992 with 560 units being privatized at month's end.[21] Then, during the course of the summer, 3,812 apartments were fully privatized, and the residents of another 6,100 apartments had requested that their units be privatized.[22]

Some officials had predicted such a rapid acceleration during the spring of 1992.[23] What accounts for their prediction becoming fulfilled? Why did privatization in Yaroslavl take such a positive turn while the process remained tormented by bureaucratic and political intrigue in other cities such as Moscow and St. Petersburg?

Leadership appears to have made a difference in the Yaroslavl case. Mayor Viktor Volonchunas made a number of television appearances during June and July 1992 in which he made the case for privatization of housing.[24] Volonchunas explained that he was privatizing his own apartment in order to ensure that he would be able to pass a valuable resource on to his children. He said that the city would continue to maintain apartments at a minimal cost, and that the new owners could rent or resell their apartments for income. Pensioners almost immediately began to privatize their apartments in large numbers—both to be able to offer an inheritance to their children and to generate income. Unconfirmed rumors abounded that private firms were supplementing pensioner incomes for the right to assume control of apartments following the new owner's death.[25] Others soon followed the pensioners and, by summer's end, workers were demanding that their trade unions drop their resistance to privatization and help city officials move the program forward as swiftly as possible.

Leadership mattered in a second way. In expectation of a rising wave of housing privatization, the *malyi sovet* (small soviet) established a seven-member independent commission to supervise and manage the transfer of apartment titles.[26] The commission was designed to bring together representatives of the mayor's office, city council, city housing office, construction associations, major enterprises, and trade unions in an attempt to diminish conflict by bringing representatives of major social groups together to oversee the city's housing privatization program. This strategy reflected a growing desire among city leaders to find common ground among competing interests so as to advance their community's position within an increasingly threatening national environment.[27]

At the same time—on May 6, 1992—the malyi sovet named Iurii Verbitskii as commission chair.[28] Verbitskii, a feisty and savvy politician known for his strong independent—some would argue ornery—streak, was elected to the city council in 1990 with the support of prodemocracy forces. He never shied away from controversy, as was the case when he used his position as chair of that council's Commission on Culture to challenge the transfer of the Church of Elijah the Prophet to the Russian Orthodox Church.

Verbitskii's commission replaced a similar body established to supervise housing privatization by the mayor's office on February 28, 1992, in violation of Russian Federation law.[29] Russian Federation legislation passed on February 17, 1992, specified that housing privatization was to fall within the purview of the city soviet rather than the municipal executive branch. Once under way, Verbitskii's group began meeting at least once a week and had been given responsibility for improving the procedures and standards used in housing privatization. The commission's charge was to place the interests of individual citizens and their families at the center of local privatization efforts. Verbitskii reported on the commission's performance both to the city soviet through the malyi sovet and directly to the mayor's office.

Conflicts over valuation of property began almost immediately. The operational legislation used in housing privatization called for the application of a number of variables in the establishment of a price for a given apartment. Verbitskii and his commission determined how they were to be applied and, quite naturally, some residents did not quite agree with their decisions. Appeals were made directly to the malyi sovet and, eventually, to the city council for adjudication. Iurii Verbitskii explained the procedures in the following manner.[30]

Each square meter of housing space initially had a base value of 698 rubles (U.S. $3.40 in September 1992) to which various coefficients were added or subtracted according to building material (+0.5 percent for brick, –0.5 percent for wood, no change for panel structures), size of kitchen space, whether or not there is a balcony, transportation service to the neighborhood, the age of the building, and, of course, location. The range of value was from 85 percent of 698—or 593 rubles for units in wooden structures in poorly serviced districts such as Krasnoperekopskii—to 135 percent (942 rubles) per square meter for the best housing in the city center.

Each citizen received twenty square meters free value, plus an additional ten square meters for family unit, plus two square meters for 15–20 years in the work force, three square meters for 20–25 years, four square meters for 25–30, and five for more than 30 years of work service. Hence, a three-member family in which the mother had worked for 18 years, and the father for 21, with a minor daughter would have had the right to the free transfer of title to an apartment encompassing:

20 + 20 + 20 = 60 sq. meters for individual family members,
10 sq. meters for the family unit,
2 sq. meters for the mother's labor service, and
3 sq. meters for the father's labor service,

for a total of 75 sq. meters valued at 698 rubles, or a transfer of 52,350 rubles' (U.S. $255) worth of housing at the then current (September 1992) market rate. If an apartment was valued at more than that amount following the application of the various coefficients mentioned above, the family paid the difference. Many residents disputed the application of the coefficients and denied, with some frequency, that location should make any difference in the valuation of their property. The hoary American expression that, in real estate transactions, all that matters is "location, location, location" would have come as a surprise to many Yaroslavtsy. Nonetheless, over three-quarters of the city's apartment residents qualified for the free transfer of title under this program.

Once an apartment was privatized, the citizen could do with it whatever he or she pleased. Taxes were set at .001 percent of value. Hence, a 40,000 ruble apartment had a 40 ruble tax incumbrance (or 19 cents). In addition, there was a monthly *kvarplata* for maintenance—also a minimal charge at 13 kopeks per square meter per month. Eventually, a *tovarishchestvo*, or fraternal association, was to have been established to handle maintenance after an entire building had been privatized.

All of the Verbitskii Commission's grand plans came crashing to a halt in early 1993.[31] On January 10, 1993, the Russian Federation Supreme Soviet passed a law "supplementing" existing privatization legislation. The changes seemed to be rather innocent at the time, but the new law turned out to contain some rather deleterious provisions that undercut local Yaroslavl initiatives in the housing privatization area. Given the new signals coming from Moscow during a period of political retrenchment, the Yaroslavl city government turned away from its privatization campaign while popular opinion and action followed suit. If leadership had been critical in launching the privatization initiative the previous spring, the absence of political will subverted the program during the winter.

The January 1993 supplemental legislation fundamentally altered the process of title transfer. All public housing units were to be privatized for free. This would appear to have encouraged the process, except that it favored residents of large apartments while the remainder— and majority—of the population had already been entitled to free privatization in any event. The switch to free privatization also had the somewhat perverse effect of convincing public opinion in Yaroslavl that title must be worthless, or why else would the state merely be giving it away?[32] As demand slackened and Yaroslavtsy no longer had to wait in line to initiate privatization of their apartments, public opinion polls showed that local citizens were losing interest in the program. Yaroslavtsy became skeptical of the need to obtain a document—formal title—that did not require a lengthy period of standing on line in some dark and dank government office.[33] As the administrative structure implementing the program was intended to be supported on a "pay-as-you-go basis" (*khozrachet*), the elimination of fees and charges merely reduced the financial basis for the city's privatization effort.[34]

The January 1993 legislation went even further, abolishing all housing commissions subordinate to local soviets, including the one chaired by Iurii Verbitskii. This move left supervision of the program to executive branch agencies. Moreover, title documents were no longer to be notarized, undercutting their legal authority and opening the way for intense battles over competing claims that would be adjudicated by housing administrators thought by many to be for sale to the higher bidder. In a surprising move that went beyond the Supreme Soviet's minimal intent, the Yaroslavl malyi sovet voted to *return* all funds that had previously been collected from those who had already privatized their apartments.[35]

The move by the Russian Federation Supreme Soviet was but a small skirmish in a larger battle for power between the antireform majority in the national legislature and the proreform Yeltsin administration. It nonetheless reveals just how vulnerable local reformers remained in the provinces during the early weeks of 1993. Iurii Verbitskii's independent city commission presided over the privatization of some 14,000 apartments—or almost 10 percent of the city's total public housing stock—during the nine months of its existence (May 6, 1992, to February 1, 1993).[36] It established a number of procedures and principles that served the city well. Verbitskii and his colleagues attempted to place privatization programs within the context of an overall housing policy at the local level. As Nadezhda Erzhova, the head of the Mayor's Housing Privatization Office, noted in frustration in April 1993, there is no national housing policy in Russia and, without such a policy, "privatization programs are meaningless."[37]

Housing privatization continued in Yaroslavl, though at a reduced pace. By April 4, 1993, 22,422 apartments had been privatized, while another 4,445 requests were being processed (recall that only 156 had been privatized just a year before).[38] Yet, as in many other Russian towns and cities, the privatization program ground to a halt during the latter half of 1993 as ordinary Russians waited for clear signals from the politicans over the long-term meaning of newly issued ownership documents.

Those citizens requesting title for their apartments tended to fall into two rather distinct groups: those who were privileged, and pensioners who required new sources of income.[39] Such trends are evident in a district-by-district accounting of housing privatization for the period March 1992 to March 1993 (see Table 8.1).

According to district-level data, privatization rates in the Kirovskii District of central Yaroslavl—which is the venue of much of the housing occupied by the old Communist Party apparat—surpasses all other

Table 8.1

Privatization of Housing by Urban District, City of Yaroslavl, March 1992–March 1993

City district	Total no. of units	Percentage state units	Total privatized	Percentage of city privatized	Percentage of district privatized
Dzerzhinskii	47,560	29	4,757	22	10
Zavolzhskii	26,073	16	2,582	12	10
Kirovskii	25,489	16	4,797	22	19
Krasnoperekopskii	16,502	10	1,548	8	9
Leninskii	23,965	14	3,890	18	16
Fruzenskii	25,125	15	3,923	18	17
CITYWIDE	164,714	100	21,497	100	16

Sources: Iaroslavskii gorodskii otdel statistiki, *Statisticheskii Biulleten'. Dannye o zhilishchnom fonde goroda Iaroslavlia za 1989 goda* (Yaroslavl, February 1990); Meria goroda Iaroslavlia, Otdel privitizatsii zhil'ia, "Dannye po privatizatsii zhil'ia grazhdanami g. Iaroslavlia za period s 01.03.92 po 26.03.93."

districts both in terms of its percentage of the privatized housing stock for the entire city and in terms of the percentage of its own housing stock that has been privatized. Large numbers of units have been privatized in the Dzerzhinskii district, primarily in the Bragino area, which is home to many middle-level managers. More proletarian districts—such as the Krasnoperekopskii—straggle behind. The relatively small number of privatized apartments in the Zavolzhskii district is somewhat deceptive, as many cooperative apartment buildings were built together with state housing when the area was developed during the 1980s. As a result, the number of Zavolzhskii residents living in nonstate housing is among the city's highest.

In addition to the privatization of municipal housing, Verbitskii's commission worked on a contract basis to manage the privatization of factory housing. Several enterprises became interested in releasing their housing to private control during 1992 as managers began to realize that bankruptcy might be looming on the horizon.[40]

Beyond privatization of existing housing, state construction firms in Yaroslavl have begun building new apartments further out from the city center with the intention of offering the new units at market-based rents.[41] City officials have been exploring the possibilities of offering older buildings to the construction trusts for restoration, although Russian Federation guidelines prohibit privatization of communal (multi-family) apartments and of units located within historic districts. Even if pursued, sale of inhabited buildings to new owners will require the approval of *all* residents.[42]

Changes in Russian Federation legislation during 1991 also permitted the construction of new private homes in urban areas for the first time since 1961.[43] A few rather substantial single-family dwellings have been constructed in Yaroslavl, with the final price of a three-to-five-room, one-to-two-story brick house originally running between 200,000 and 500,000 rubles at the end of 1991 (between U.S. $5,000 and $12,500 at the time).[44] New homes were being built on lots within previously existing settlements of wooden houses in order to facilitate provision of city services. This practice brought some of the city's richest and poorest residents into immediate proximity. Previous residents have expressed dissatisfaction with their haughty new neighbors, and some local officials anticipate increasing social tensions from these arrangements.[45] Such programs were expanding quickly, with new districts being set aside for single-family housing construction quite far away from previously existing districts—in newly developed areas to the northeast, southeast, and west.[46] Architects in Yaroslavl and elsewhere in Russia are delighted to have the novel experience of working closely with private clients to design single-family dwellings.[47]

The initial municipal response to the new housing market in Yaroslavl has been hindered by the absence of financial institutions.[48] There is a critical need for a functioning mortgage lending program through which credit would be made available to potential homeowners on a commercial basis.[49] Otherwise, privatization will be nothing more than a meaningless transfer of state obligations to a Russian citizenry lacking the basic resources required to accept such responsibilities. Preliminary interest in just the promise of an expanding private housing market indicates that the privatization of housing—and perhaps of urban property later on—will reshape how Yaroslavtsy imagine their community, live out their lives, and reinvent the physical character of their city in the post-Soviet era.

Land Use Planning

Local authorities across Russia also gained unprecedented control over local urban planning decisions in recent years as a consequence of the general disintegration of central authority that proceeded apace during the early 1990s. New land use regulations and taxes approved by the Russian Federation's parliament in 1991 promised local officials even more powerful leavers for curtailing land consumption by industrial enterprises.[50] Russian Federation laws permitting foreign ownership of nonagricultural land initially proposed in June 1992 would further alter land use patterns.[51] The very mechanisms of land use management will change further as economic and political decentralization continue.

In March 1992, Yaroslavl officials seized the opportunities being created by the Russian government for local initiative to reimagine the physical form of their city. They sponsored an inventory of land use patterns and established a new system of land use tax rates as a first step toward reinventing land use patterns.[52] Initial tax rates ranged between 3.71 and 7.77 rubles (between U.S. $.03 and $.06 at the time) per square meter of land occupied by enterprises and between 0.11 and 0.23 rubles per square meter of land occupied by housing and da-chas—or cottages—occupied by individuals. These charges were accompanied by fines ranging from a low of 50 rubles for organizations and 1 ruble for individuals (between U.S. $.41 and $.008 at the time) illegally occupying building sites to 1 million rubles for organizations and 5,000 rubles for individuals (between U.S. $8,000 and $50) destroying valuable subsoils through pollution or inappropriate land use.[53]

Turning next to physical planning, the Yaroslavl City Executive Committee engaged the services of Central Scientific Research and Design Institute for City Construction in 1990 to prepare a new city-wide general development plan.[54] According to the joint agreement of the local executive committee with the Moscow-based institute, the two parties would seek to formulate the new "social-production and legal-ecological basis" for a new general plan before the end of 1993. Planners were asked to view the city and a region within 50 kilometers of its boundaries as a single, integrated region. Several alternative projections of future development were to be proposed, with greater flexibility expected in plan implementation than in the past. Traditional concerns for cultural, economic, social, and physical development would be joined with a greater emphasis on ecological issues. Local officials sought expanded authority over monitoring and directing urban development, and also proclaimed an intention to expand community participation in the planning process.[55]

By late 1992, the planning team had agreed to develop a number of alternative plans for the city, which would be presented for public discussion within approximately one year.[56] The city's elected agencies would consider these competing concepts for the future of Yaroslavl, presenting them to the public for discussion. Once general objectives had been established, elected officials would turn the planning process back to the professionals for elaboration. The entire process was to be completed before the end of 1994.

In March 1993, the Moscow-based consultants reported back to Yaroslavl municipal authorities, proposing three radically different conceptions of future city development.[57] The first was predicated upon the continuation of Soviet-era levels of population growth, projecting a population increase of 60,000 to 700,000 over a twenty-year period. Ten percent of all new housing construction would be in the form of free-standing individual homes.

The second plan foresaw the maintenance of the current status quo, with little or no population increase. However, the planners urged local officials to take advantage of stability to shift the profile of new housing construction slightly away from large apartment houses. Hence, the second conception called for a 20–80 percent distribution of new housing construction between houses and apartment buildings.

The third proposed conception for the Yaroslavl of 2014 foresaw a radical deindustrialization and deurbanization of the entire region. The city's population would decline by some 60,000 residents to around 580,000 inhabitants, while 40 percent of all new housing would take the form of single-family houses with garden plots. Financial incentives would be used to encourage city residents to return to the countryside and "reruralize" the province.

All of these various options were discussed when the city's malyi sovet took up the new general plan in September 1993.[58] The Moscow authors of various alternative development strategies presented their projections for Yaroslavl's future. A hearty discussion followed, with a great deal of sympathy being expressed for a reduction in the city's size. However, deputies dismissed the idea of a smaller city as unrealistic. Instead, they instructed the Office of the Chief Architect to work with their Moscow consultants to produce more detailed projections of physical and economic trends under both the "no growth" and the "moderate growth" strategies. Additional documentation was to be prepared for further discussion on October 15, 1993.

The suspension of the Russian parliament in late September—followed by the insurrection of October 3–4, 1993—further delayed consideration of local general plans in Yaroslavl. With the city soviet disbanded and public attention directed toward the December 1993 constitutional referendum, Mayor Volonchunas shied away from resolving the debate on his own. Municipal survival rather than urban planning dominated the local political scene in early 1994, so that no further progress was made on developing a new general plan following the September 1993 malyi sovet session. As of May 1995 the plans still lie in the Office of the Chief Architect collecting dust until such time as "normalcy" returns to local politics.

Unlike the past, Yaroslavl city planners did not consult with economic officials before reimagining their city's form. At the same moment that urban planners were beginning to consider the implications of radical deindustrialization, Regional Chief Administrator (or Governor) Anatolii Lisitsyn and Deputy Chief Administrator Anatolii Guseev were inviting the consulting firm of former Russian prime minister Egor Gaidar to undertake development planning for the entire oblast.[59] Lisitsyn and Guseev's growth-oriented approach stood in contrast to the recommendations of lower regional officials, who spoke in rather dramatic terms of draining the massive Rybinsk reservoir, closing down that reservoir's hydroelectric dam, and returning to the flax and dairy farm–dominant regional economy of the pre-Soviet period.[60] For their part, urban planners were asking what kind of city they wanted first, and turning to the economic consequences of their decisions only later. This pattern reversed the Soviet-era pattern, according to which all physical planning decisions were held in abeyance until after the adoption of a general plan's economy-dominated "technical-economic foundations" (*tekhniko-ekonomicheskie osnovy—TEO*).

All of these projections have a bit of an air of unreality about them. As Chief Architect Bobovich noted during an interview, any attempt to reorganize living patterns around individual houses faces immediate economic and technological obstacles.[61] A local housing industry oriented toward single-family houses has yet to develop and requires legal and technical support that would cost millions of scarce rubles. More importantly, projections of rustic semirural city dwellers tending to their gardens by night and their country cousins milking cows and cutting flax by day ignore the terrible environmental degradation of the Soviet era. Heavy metal soil pollution would have to be attacked at considerable expense before Yaroslavtsy could even contemplate tending their own gardens. Finally, population projections are erroneous at times of great social upheaval.[62] Whether the city's population expands or contracts will depend on the future success of Russian economic and political reform, as well as the country's capacity to absorb tens of thousands of demobilized soldiers and refugees fleeing ethnic conflicts to the south and east.

Regardless of these difficulties, the variety and inventiveness of the various physical and economic conceptions for Yaroslavl city and region under discussion throughout the early 1990s demonstrated an intense desire to use the opportunity posed by the collapse of central authority in Moscow to chart a unique course for local destiny that would serve Yaroslavtsy and not Muscovites. Whatever the practical difficulties of implementation, each of these projections revealed the extent to which local officials wanted to reinvent their city.

The Post-Soviet City and Russian Democracy

The politics of real property stand at the center of the conflict over the role of the state in Russia's future. Only the state can shape the city in a world without private right to ownership of land and buildings. At present, the who, what, when, and how of the ownership of real property in a new Russia have yet to be established. Yet the ultimate resolution of these questions is becoming visible in the very stones of a single provincial Russian city. Comprehending these processes in Yaroslavl may disclose valuable insights into the social, cultural, political, and economic processes that will shape Russia more generally.

Housing will be privatized as the municipality and the various enterprises that currently control and manage apartment buildings seek to divest their responsibilities to residents. Quarrels are erupting across Russia over the most just distribution of responsibility and cost among state agencies, individual citizens, and their families. Participants in these discussions appear only dimly concerned about the psychological, economic, and political consequences of private custody of the primal resource of shelter. Even those who are familiar with American debates over property taxes, mortgage deductions on income tax, and the myriad other issues that rouse homeowners can only begin to imagine the transformation of Russian political and economic life that will follow in the wake of the privatization of state housing.

Land use decisions and urban planning that have ignored financial constraints are giving way to a new preoccupation with land cost. Planners must learn how to incorporate private actors into their vision of Yaroslavl's future. Enterprise managers must recalculate how much land they need to accomplish their economic mission. Where people live and work will be quite different in the years to come as hundreds and thousands of individual and institutional decisions find expression in the city's physical form.

These policy areas demonstrate the extent to which the post-Soviet city is transitional. Privatization of housing moves forward, yet titles to well under a quarter of state apartments are being turned over to residents. Even when gaining title, individuals must deal with apartments that remain physically embedded in huge buildings and neighborhoods based on a socialized infrastructure. Single-family houses are being built, yet they remain tied to an urban infrastructure and system that was never intended to serve individual dwellings. Prices, to the extent to which they may be said to exist, are established by municipal planners as much as by market mechanisms. The transition to a private-dominated housing market will be long. Nevertheless, the physical form of Yaroslavl is already being transformed by the privatization of municipal and enterprise apartments and the construction of single-family cottage settlements. A new, decentralized, boundless urban form well familiar to urban and suburban residents of capitalist societies is coming into being. The precise contours of this future post-Soviet city may not yet be well-defined, but its vague outline may already be discerned.

The post-Soviet transition has created a valuable opportunity for citizens, officials, and planners to reinvent their towns. An entire range of physical planning issues long shrouded in Soviet-era security regulations has become exposed to public discussion. Should Yaroslavl expand or contract? Should its housing pattern remain tied to public transportation? Should rich live next to poor? Where should industry be located? If factories are to close, what should replace them? Yaroslavtsy have been presented with a rare chance to rethink their community, to reinvent its physical form, and to reimagine its future. They have pursued this opportunity with zeal, offering up an impressive assortment of economic and physical visions ranging from unrealistic longing for a lost agricultural past—complete with dismantling a major hydroelectric dam—to equally unrealistic visions of a high-tech future.

Much of the rethinking of Yaroslavl has been a consequence of the collapse of the central Russian state. The heavy hand of central bureaucracy has been lifted, leaving municipal and regional officials and legislators to deal with daily reality more or less on their own. The paralysis of power in Moscow together with the very transitional character of the post-Soviet period has created a singular opportunity for local residents to reimagine their city.

Local legislative agencies have moved to establish their jurisdiction over both housing privatization and land use policies within Yaroslavl. Their success has been somewhat measured. In privatization, the city soviet experienced some initial success. Yaroslavl legislators elaborated upon central norms to meet local conditions. The independent commission established to supervise and manage the transfer of apartment titles to private owners greatly facilitated the privatization processes. Nevertheless, local leadership could not withstand uncertainty at the national level. The housing privatization program foundered in the wake of the conservative attack on the Yeltsin administration during the weeks between the December 1992 session of the Congress of People's Deputies and the April 1993 referendum on the Yeltsin presidency.

Local legislative involvement in land use planning has proven to be more lasting. The retreat of central planning agencies during the late 1980s created an opportunity for Yaroslavtsy to reconsider the spatial contours of their community. A spirited debate has ensued, bringing together deputies, administrators, and public activists in a continuing effort to reformulate community development goals. These deliberations continue at this writing.

Some general insights may be inferred from the attempt of Yaroslavl citizens and officials to reimagine their provincial city—recognizing, of course, that caution must always be exercised when generalizing from a single case. Yaroslavtsy of all social ranks are struggling to reinvent their city and, in the process, have demonstrated an understanding that the future cannot be like the past. They may want to proceed to a new post-Soviet city slowly, they might want to be respectful of Soviet-era social programs, they may resist privatization of their apartments. Nevertheless, the growth of civil society and democratic political institutions is apparent in their efforts. It is precisely at the level of a single provincial town that the potential for a new democratic Russia is most unmistakable. In reimagining the physical form of their city, Yaroslavtsy are also reinventing the political form of their society.

Local Lessons About Reform in Russia

Modest though they may be, the small interactions among Yaroslavl citizens and politicians described in this chapter suggest possible lessons about reform more generally in Russia. Local Yaroslavl political leaders have viewed their primary responsibility during the first post-Soviet republic as "cushioning the negative impact of reform."[63] These very same politicians have simultaneously been remarkably creative in their approaches to making reform initiatives from above actually work in their community. Conservative by temperament, local officials—and citizens—seek to preserve as much as possible of familiar ways. They proceed quietly and cautiously, realizing all the while that fundamental change must take place if their community and nation are to thrive politically and economically. Such tangled attitudes exist in a region and a city that consistently supported first Gorbachev and then Yeltsin in various elections. These are politicians and citizens open to reform, resourceful in their response to reform initiatives, but who simultaneously retain a deep provincial conservatism.

On a more general level, the actions reported in this chapter suggest that successful reform in Russia cannot come exclusively from either above or below. Realization of reform programs requires many levels of Russian society to move more or less in the same direction. National reform politicians are wrong in viewing local elites as opposed to change, while reform-minded Yaroslavl politicians are equally misguided in their belief that their community can somehow go it alone down a reform path. Yaroslavl reform initiatives in housing and urban planning moved forward with dispatch when there were clear pro-reform signals emanating from Moscow. This momentum dissipated as soon as mixed political signals began to come from Moscow. The reform impulse lost all power by mid-1993 as Russia's first post-Soviet government collapsed in the political infighting that eventually led to the storming of the Russian parliament on October 3–4 of that year.

One of the lessons of this chapter, then, is that center and periphery must work in concert for new policies to be successfully implemented. The reform impulse in Yaroslavl is too strong to be stymied by anti-reform conservatives, yet too weak to move forward in the absence of clear direction from above. Any political constellation that fails to bridge the economic and political gulf between central and regional elites will result in stalemate.

Notes

1. K.A. Glukhov, *Privatizatsiia zhil'ia (kommentarii k zakonodatel'stvu)* (Moscow: Iuridicheskaia firma "Paritet," MGU im. M.V. Lomonosova, 1991), Part 1, pp. 3–5.

2. Ibid., Part 1, p. 3.

3. "Zakon RSFSR o privatizatsii zhilishchnogo fonda v RSFSR oy 4 iiulia 1991 g.," and, "Postanovlenie Verkhovnogo soveta RSFSR o vvedenii v deistvie zakona RSFSR o privatizatsii zhilishchnogo fonda v RSFSR," in ibid., Part 2, pp. 3–15. The importance of this act is discussed in Lynn D. Nelson, Lilia V. Babaeva, and Rufat O. Babaev, "Perspectives on Entrepreneurship and Privatization in Russia: Policy and Public Opinion," *Slavic Review*, vol. 51, no. 2 (Summer 1992), pp. 270–286, esp. 275–276.

4. K.A. Glukhov, *Privatizatsiia zhil'ia*, Part 1, pp. 5–17.

5. For Western accounts of Soviet-era urban housing practices, see A.J. DiMaio, *Soviet Urban Housing: Problems and Policies* (New York: Praeger, 1974); Henry W. Morton, "Who Gets What, When, and How? Housing in the Soviet Union," *Soviet Studies*, vol. 31, no. 2 (1980), pp. 235–259; Henry W. Morton, "Housing in the Soviet Union," *Academy of Political Science, Proceedings*, vol. 35, no. 3 (1984); and Carol Nechemias, "The Impact of Soviet Housing Policy on Housing Conditions in Soviet Cities: The Uneven Push from Moscow," *Urban Studies*, vol. 18, no. 1 (1981).

6. Raymond J. Struyk, Nadezhda Kosareva, Jennifer Daniell, Charles Hanson, and Maris Mikelsons, *Implementing Housing Allowances in Russia: Rationalizing the Rental Sector* (Washington, DC: Urban Institute, 1993), p. 14.

7. Charles Hanson, Nadezhda Kosareva, and Raymond Struyk, "Housing Reform in the Russian Federation: A Review of Three Cities and Their Transition to a Market Economy," *Urban Institute International Activities Center Research Paper* (Washington, DC: Urban Institute, 1992 [March]), p. 3.

8. Vladimir Moiseev, "Istoriia ZhSK mozhet zavershit'sia v Rossii," *Nezavisimaia gazeta*, January 11, 1993, p. 6.

9. Interview, Aleksandr Vaseil'evich Vornarev, Chair, Fund of the Yaroslavl City Soviet on Municipal Property, and Aleksandr Germanevich Savinov, Deputy Chair, Committee of the Mayor's Office of Yaroslavl on the Administration of Municipal Property, Yaroslavl, April 29, 1992.

10. Interview, Lev Leonidovich Kruglikov, Chair, Yaroslavl, City Soviet, Yaroslavl, April 28, 1992; and "Polozhenie 'O poriadke privatizatsii munitsipal'ykh predpriiatii i imushchestva g. Iaroslavlia," 1991.

11. Interview, Arkady Romanovich Bobovich, Chief Architect, Yaroslavl City Executive Committee, October 14, 1991; and discussions with members of the Yaroslavl Division of the USSR Union of Architects hosted by Division Chairman Eduard Aleksandrovich Mesian on October 11, 1991.

12. Malyi sovet Iaroslavskogo gorodskogo soveta narodnykh deputatov, "Reshenie No. 65 o vnesenii dopolnenii i izmenenii v polozhenie o poriadke i usloviiakh privatizatsii zhilishchnogo fonda v gorode Iaroslavlia," April 8, 1992.

13. Interview, Lev Leonidovich Kruglikov, April 28, 1992; and interview, Aleksandr Vaseil'evich Vornarev and Aleksandr Germanevich Savinov, Deputy

Chair, Committee of the Mayor's Office of Yaroslavl on the Administration of Municipal Property, Yaroslavl, April 29, 1992.

14. Interview, Aleksandr Vaseil'evich Vornarev and Aleksandr Germanevich Savinov, April 29, 1992.

15. Ibid.

16. Interview, Tatiana Pavlovna Rumiantseva, Director, Center for the Study of Public Opinion and Sociological Research of the Yaroslavl City Soviet, Yaroslavl, April 29, 1992.

17. Interview, Lev Leonidovich Kruglikov, Yaroslavl, April 28, 1992.

18. Interview, Vasili Tikhonovich Zheltyakov, Chief Engineer, and Iuzef Iakovlevich Chervnikov, Economic Director, Yaroslavl Motor Works Avtodizel', Yaroslavl, April 29, 1992.

19. Interview, Aleksandr Vaseil'evich Vornarev and Aleksandr Germanevich Savinov, Yaroslavl, April 29, 1992.

20. Interview, Tatiana Pavlovna Rumiantseva, Yaroslavl, September 4, 1992.

21. Interview, Lev Leonidovich Kruglikov, Washington, DC, May 20, 1992.

22. Interview, Iurii Ivanovich Verbitskii, Chair of the Independent City Commission on the Privatization of the Housing Fund and Chair of the Yaroslavl City Soviet Commission on Culture, Yaroslavl, September 1, 1992.

23. Interview, Lev Leonidovich Kruglikov, Yaroslavl, April 28, 1992.

24. Interview, Tatiana Pavlovna Rumiantseva, Yaroslavl, September 4, 1992.

25. Ibid., and interview, Iurii Ivanovich Verbitskii, Yaroslavl, September 1, 1992.

26. Malyi sovet Iaroslavskogo gorodskogo soveta narodnykh deputatov, "Reshenie No. 87 o predsedatele nezavisimoi kommissii po privatizatsii zhil'ia," April 22, 1992; and Malyi sovet Iaroslavskogo gorodskogo soveta narodnykh deputatov, "Reshenie No. 94 o sozdanii gorodskoi nezavisimoi kommissii po privatizatsii zhilishchnogo fonda v gorode Iaroslavle," May 6, 1992, together with its accompanying "Polozhenie o nezavisimoi kommissii po privatizatsii zhilishchnogo fonda v gorode Iaroslavle." Also, interview, Iurii Ivanovich Verbitskii, Chair of the Independent City Commission on the Privatization of the Housing Fund and Chair of the Yaroslavl City Soviet Commission on Culture, Yaroslavl, September 1, 1992.

27. Interview, Lev Leonidovich Kruglikov, Washington, DC, May 20, 1992.

28. Interview, Iurii Ivanovich Verbitskii, Yaroslavl, September 1, 1992.

29. Ibid.

30. Ibid.

31. Interview, Iurii Ivanovich Verbitskii, Yaroslavl, April 14, 1993; and interview, Tatiana Pavlovna Rumiantseva, Yaroslavl, April 15, 1993.

32. Interview, Tatiana Pavlovna Rumiantseva, Yaroslavl, April 15, 1993.

33. Ibid.

34. Nadezhda Erzhova, Head, Housing Privatization Office of the Yaroslavl Mayor's Office, Yaroslavl, April 16, 1993.

35. Interview, Iurii Ivanovich Verbitskii, Former Chair of the Independent City Commission on the Privatization of the Housing Fund and Chair of the Yaroslavl City Soviet Commission on Culture, Yaroslavl, April 14, 1993.

36. Ibid.

37. Interview, Nadezhda Erzhova, Yaroslavl, April 16, 1993.

38. Interview, Tatiana Pavlovna Rumiantseva, Yaroslavl, April 15, 1993.

39. Ibid., and interview, Nadezhda Erzhova, Yaroslavl, April 16, 1993.

40. Interview, Tatiana Pavlovna Rumiantseva, Yaroslavl, September 4, 1992; and interview, Iurii Ivanovich Verbitskii, Yaroslavl, September 1, 1992.

41. Interview, Aleksandr Vaseii'evich Vornarev and Aleksandr Germanevich Savinov, Yaroslavl, April 29, 1992.

42. Ibid.

43. Discussion with members of the Yaroslavl Division of the USSR Union of Architects hosted by Division Chairman Eduard Aleksandrovich Mesian, Yaroslavl, October 11, 1991.

44. Cost estimates rose and fell according to the official position of the interlocutor. Those with more responsible positions—and perhaps more removed from the rough-and-tumble world of Yaroslavl construction practices—tended to quote lower prices.

45. The author witnessed one such heated exchange between city officials and local residents over four new brick houses during a city tour of Yaroslavl organized by Arkady Romanovich Bobovich, Chief Architect, Yaroslavl City Executive Committee, and Tatiana Pavlovna Rumiantseva, Director, Public Opinion Research Center, Yaroslavl City Soviet, on October 14, 1991. No issues were resolved before the visiting dignitaries were forced to flee the scene.

46. Interview, Arkady Romanovich Bobovich, Yaroslavl, September 1, 1992.

47. See, for example, A.Ts. Dychinskii, "Chelovek i sreda obitaniia," *S. Peterburgskaia panorama*, 1992, pp. 26–29. Dychinskii was the Chief Architect of the Leningrad Region (*oblast*) at the time the article appeared.

48. Interview, Eduard Aleksandrovich Mesian, Chairman, Yaroslavl Division of the Russian Union of Architects, Yaroslavl, September 2, 1992, For an expanded discussion of this issue in relation to St. Petersburg, see N.A. Malinina and Iu.A. Iakovleva, "Rossiiskii rynok zhil'ia," *S. Peterburgskaia panorama*, 1992, no. 7, p. 7.

49. Chuck Hanson and Raymond Struyk, "USAID Technical Assistance Strategy for the Russian Federation in the Shelter Sector," *Urban Institute International Activities Center Research Paper* (Washington, DC: Urban Institute, 1992 [May]), pp. 9–10; and Struyk, et al., *Implementing Housing Allowances in Russia*, pp. 34–36.

50. Interviews, Iurii Bocharov, Chairman, Soviet Society of Urbanists, Washington, DC, March 22, 1991, and May 9, 1991; Boris Nikolaeshchenko, Chief, Scientific Research and Design Institute of the Master Plan for the Development of the City of St. Petersburg and Leningrad Region, St. Petersburg, September 13, 1991; Valentina Vladimirovna Istomina, Chief, Financial-Budget Department, Yaroslavl City Executive Committee, Yaroslavl, October 11, 1991; Arkady Romanovich Bobovich, Yaroslavl, October 14, 1991; Vladimir Ivanovich Polunin, Chair, Kiev District Council (Moscow), Moscow, October 17, 1991; Olga Kaganova and Nikita Maslennikov, Advisers on Land Use, St. Petersburg City Soviet, Washington, DC, October 22, 1991; and Valentin Fadeev, Deputy, Moscow City Council, Washington, DC, December 12, 1991.

51. Fred Hiatt, "Yeltsin to Let Foreigners Buy Russian Land," *Washington Post*, June 13, 1992, p. A15.

52. Malyi sovet Iaroslavskogo gorodskogo soveta narodnykh deputatov,

"Reshenie No. 41 o provedenii inventarizatsii zemli i stroenii i utverzhdenii stavok zemel'nogo naloga na territorii g. Yaroslavlia," March 18, 1992.

53. Malyi sovet Iaroslavskogo gorodskogo soveta narodnykh deputatov, "Reshenie No. 12 o poriadke obsushchestvleniia kontrolia za ispol'zovaniem i okhranoi zemel' v g. Yaroslavlia," January 23, 1992.

54. "Programma-Zadanie na razrabotku general'nogo plana g. Iaroslavlia, utverzhdanno Presedatel'iem ispolkoma Iaroslavskogo gorodskogo Soveta narodnykh deputatov i TsNIIPgradostritel'stva," Yaroslavl, 1990.

55. Given the extensive literature on the planning process in other societies, this newfound openness in Russia expands the possibilities for genuinely comparative scholarship on the nature of urban planning in a variety of social, economic, and political environments.

56. As reported by Arkady Romanovich Bobovich, Chief Architect, Yaroslavl City, in an interview in his office on September 1, 1992.

57. Interview, Arkady Romanovich Bobovich, Yaroslavl, April 15, 1993.

58. Interview, Arkady Romanovich Bobovich, Yaroslavl, September 9, 1993.

59. Interview, Anatolii Lisitsyn, Chief of Regional Administration (Governor), Yaroslavl Region, and Anatolii Guseev, Deputy Chief of Regional Administration (Lt. Governor), Yaroslavl Region, Yaroslavl, April 15, 1993.

60. Interview, Dimitrii Ponomarev, Specialist, Yaroslavl Regional Information-Analytical Administration, and Aleksei Bushev, Deputy Chief, Yaroslavl Regional Information-Analytic Administration, Yaroslavl, April 14, 1993.

61. Interview, Arkady Romanovich Bobovich, Yaroslavl, April 15, 1993.

62. Interview, Tatiana Pavlovna Rumiantseva, Yaroslavl, April 15, 1993; and interview, Arkady Romanovich Bobovich, Yaroslavl, April 15, 1993.

63. Interview, Anatoli Ivanovich Lisitsyn and Anatolii Feodorovich Guseev, Yaroslavl, April 15, 1993.

III

The Lessons of
Legislative Development
in Russia

9

Studying Legislatures: Lessons for Comparing the Russian Experience

Michael L. Mezey

There are certain obvious weaknesses that I bring to a discussion of democratization in Russia. Except for what I read in the newspapers and what I have been able to glean from essays such as those collected in this volume, I know little about Russia or its Soviet Union predecessor. I have never visited the country and certainly do not speak the language. So, the reader might well ask, what is a political scientist like you doing in a book like this?

Answering this question requires a brief autobiographical digression. My first experience studying a legislature other than the United States Congress came when I found myself some twenty-five years ago in Thailand, a country that I had not visited previously, about which I knew very little, and where I did not speak the language. Upon arriving in Bangkok as a visiting faculty member at Thammasat University, I discovered that the first legislative session in nearly ten years was about to convene. Within two months, the students with whom I was working were in the field interviewing legislators using a questionnaire that we had designed. Eventually, they collected more than one hundred interviews, which they then translated into English so that I could analyze the results. These data, along with some informant interviews that I conducted and some background information gathered from the English-language press and U.S. State Department translations of the Thai press, provided the basis for several articles on the Thai National Assembly that I published in the early 1970s.

My work in Thailand took place at a time when many other political scientists were studying legislative institutions in other nations in what we referred to in those days as the developing world. These scholars produced articles, papers, and anthologies dealing with legislatures in Africa, Latin America, and Asia along with new research on more established legislatures in Western Europe.[1] This was also the period when the subspecialty of comparative legislative studies emerged. The Consortium for Comparative Legislative Studies was created, a Research Committee of Legislative Specialists was organized within the International Political Science Association, the Comparative Legislative Studies Newsletter was published, and the *Legislative Studies Quarterly* was launched.[2] For my part, although I maintained an active interest in the world's legislatures (see Mezey 1979), much of my scholarly attention in the 1980s returned to the political institutions of the United States.

I recount this slice of personal and disciplinary history as an introduction to my assignment for this volume, which, as I understand it, is to provide a comparative perspective for those who are studying democratization in Russia and, particularly, the role of legislatures. How can the experience of those who researched Third World legislatures during the 1970s inform our approach to the study of legislative development in Russia? What errors were made then that can be avoided now? And, most importantly, how can what we have learned over the years about the world's legislatures help us to better understand the Russian experience as well as the other new legislatures of Central and Eastern Europe and the former Soviet Union? In brief, what is the larger comparative context for the extraordinary events now going forward in Russia?

The Pitfalls

Ethnocentrism

Perhaps the most common failing of those who studied legislative institutions in the developing world was in not fully recognizing the Western or American bias that many of us brought to this enterprise. When people who had devoted their careers to learning about the United States Congress and the British House of Commons went to other nations, they either expected to find similar institutional models or they analyzed these other legislatures from the perspective of the Western models with which they were most familiar. The result, all too often, was a misunderstanding of the functions that the legislatures being examined were supposed to perform, or a finding that these legislatures seemed so unimportant that they were not really worth further study.

Those who were accustomed to a United States Congress that regularly turned down—and always amended—presidential initiatives were quick to conclude that a legislature that never turned down executive proposals was weak or inconsequential. Those who had been accustomed to the harsh and sometimes personal nature of question period in the House of Commons assumed that the absence of criticism of the government on the floor of a legislature meant the absence of legislative influence over government decisions. The hypothesis that these legislatures could be performing functions that either were not as apparent—or were less important—in the West was only occasionally entertained. Nor was much attention accorded to the possibility that in regard to policy-making power, many of these institutions might have been exercising influence in ways that were less visible than was the case in Western legislatures.

As American and European political scientists examine Russian legislative development, it is important that they recognize these biases. Much of the debate, for example, about the relative power of the Russian parliament and the Russian presidency seems to have been influenced by the American model. This has been true even though it is far from clear that the American model has ever functioned effectively elsewhere, particularly in nations with vast and pressing economic and social issues. The American model developed and became institutionalized over an extended period of time and under historical circumstances that simply cannot be replicated (Mezey 1991).

It also should be remembered that policy making is only one of the functions of a legislature and that in most of the legislatures of the world it may not even be the most important function. The United States Congress is virtually unique in terms of the leading role that it plays in making public policy. Most other legislatures play a more subtle role than the U.S. Congress, working largely at the periphery of public policy, modifying proposals initiated by the executive branch, reacting privately to proposals before they are publicly announced, and, when they do achieve changes in government initiatives, often doing so before they are even formally proposed to the legislature. In sum, the typical policy-making function of legislatures is to set parameters within which other institutions such as the executive may act. Generally, they do not initiate policy on their own or, on a regular basis, stop the executive from doing what it wishes to do.

Two points follow from this. First, studies of the new Russian parliament should not concentrate exclusively on the capacity of the institution to stop the president from pursuing his policy goals, nor should they view such a capacity as the sole standard by which the success or failure, or strength or weakness, of the institution can be judged. We should look instead for presidential actions (or inactions) that are influenced by the reactions that he anticipates from the parliament. Second, the policy influence that the Russian parliament does exercise may be much closer to the modal case for the world's legislatures than most observers have realized.

Taking the Legislature Out of Context

A significant number of those who went to study legislatures in the developing world were people like me who knew very little about either the country or the larger institutional context within which the legislature operated. Lured by the excitement of foreign travel or perhaps by the ready availability of research funds (developing nations were as "hot" then as Eastern Europe is today), we packed our bags and went. We supplemented what little we could find in English about the history and politics of our destination with the background information the local political scientists or informants could supply. But in the end, all we really knew about when we arrived was legislatures and all we really investigated was the legislature. Taking the legislature as an analytically distinct research target, we often failed to see it in historical or cultural context. Thus, we failed to connect what we were seeing in any systematic or informed manner with the nation's past political experiences or with its current cultural and social norms.

Although we might have been accurately observing and reporting what we saw, we were not seeing completely. Today, it seems to me that the list of those writing and publishing on Russian parliamentary experience and on the new legislatures of Central and Eastern Europe includes many for whom this part of the world represents an entirely new area of study. Although many of these people have distinguished scholarly credentials in legislative studies, their knowledge of Central and Eastern Europe and, even more broadly, the subdiscipline of comparative politics and its reigning paradigms, may be marginal at best. The result can be an analysis of a legislature snatched from its broader institutional, cultural, and historical context.

Reinventing the Legislative Wheel

In contrast to those itinerant scholars who only knew about legislatures, others who wrote about legislatures in the Third World were country or area specialists who knew little about legislative institutions or about the extant body of research on legislative behavior. Although a large literature existed on the United States Congress and European legislatures, the research tools and findings contained in that literature were seldom drawn upon by this group to inform their work on these "developing" legislatures. Naturally, several problems arose.

First, many misread the importance of the legislature. Because they were unfamiliar with the research on similar legislatures in other parts of the world—research that might well have relied on a more nuanced approach to the question of legislative power and influence—they looked only for the most obvious (and often ethnocentric) indicators of legislative power, failed to find them, reported the same, and moved on to other institutions and phenomena such as political parties or civilian or military bureaucracies, which seemed more central to the politics of the nation.

And when those who did take the legislature seriously reported their findings, what they said was usually disconnected from what had been discovered about other legislatures. For example, different researchers working in different locales would report that legislators had told them that they spent a great deal of their time dealing with complaints from individual constituents. The larger meaning of this finding escaped them, of course, because they were blissfully unaware of similar findings about legislatures in other countries that were outside their area of special interest. Similarly, scholars working in different settings would ask legislators the same questions about their orientations toward their representational roles, but no one would make an attempt to relate what they had found out in the country that they were studying to what others had discovered when these same questions had been put to legislators in other nations.[3]

Some of the early studies of the legislatures in Russia and Eastern Europe bear the signs of a similar innocence about what has been discovered about legislatures in other countries. This seems particularly true of findings concerning the representational activities of legislators, a topic that has constituted the reigning paradigm in research on the United States Congress for almost twenty years, and that has become increasingly prominent in studies of the British Parliament, but is barely alluded to in the studies of these new legislative institutions.[4]

There are two reasons for this. First, much of this early work is being done by the Russia specialists who understandably have had rather little experience studying legislatures and are therefore not very familiar with that literature. Second, because the big story in these countries is democratization, the question on everyone's mind is "who governs?" As suggested below, as important as that question is, for most legislatures most of the time, other functions besides policy making, particularly representation, may well be more important. And for those concerned with the development of strong legislative institutions, the ties that individual legislators are able to establish with mass publics through the performance of their representational activities may be a more crucial factor in the legislature's prospects for long-term survival than how it performs its policy-making activities.[5]

Single-Country Studies

Work by country specialists suggests another, larger problem—the tendency to avoid comparison. With some notable exceptions, scholars have studied legislatures one at a time. Of course, in being country specific, these scholars are only following the bad example of the most narrow country specialists of all—those who study American politics. For students of the United States Congress, a comparative study usually means looking at more than one committee or, occasionally, comparing the House with the Senate. Few if any congressional scholars have ever cared to ask how what was happening on the banks of the Potomac differed from, or was similar to, what was happening on the banks of the Thames, the Seine, or the Danube. Similarly, the large group of Russia specialists who have devoted their entire scholarly careers to the study of that nation and the Soviet Union have been accustomed to treating Russia as *sui generis*; it seems to me, therefore, that as these scholars turn their attention to democratization, there is a great danger that they will do so without connecting their work with the larger body of scholarship on democratization and comparative legislatures.

The cost of a noncomparative and therefore noncumulative literature is expensive, calculated primarily in terms of a paucity of theory and an omnipresence of description. Descriptive work, particularly on legislatures such as the Russian parliament, about which very little is known, is of course welcome and valuable, but it is most valuable when it helps us to compare and to make generalizations. The goal is theories and explanations that help us to understand legislatures in general. A theory or explanation that applies only to the Russian parliament (or, for that matter, only to the United States Congress) is about as useful as a theory of gravity that applies only to Chicago.[6]

The remedy is not to avoid case studies, but rather to approach case studies with a clear understanding of the work that has been done on similar institutions and similar nations. It is interesting in this connection that professional political scientists so frequently violate the first rule that they teach to their graduate students: read the literature! In the case of Russian parliamentary development, legislative specialists would be well advised to look closely at the voluminous materials on Russian politics, history, and culture; by the same token, Russian specialists should carefully examine the comparative legislatures literature.

Legislative Partisanship

Most of those who study legislatures seem to like these institutions. For these scholars, legislative strength is not something simply to be observed and measured, but something to be hoped for, often devoutly. In nations where these institutions have proven to be fragile, scholars have come to root for them—to hope not just for their survival but for their prosperity and their permanency.

There is nothing nefarious about this. Most political scientists are democrats (small d) and it is difficult to conceive of democracies without legislatures. But viewing the world through such ideological lenses may cause one to miss or downplay the pathologies that often plague these institutions. Scholars of the United States Congress in particular have tended to ignore the problems of that institution while often blithely recommending its practices to others. Critical analyses of the Congress have been exceedingly rare in the mainstream political science literature.[7]

Many who study legislatures refuse to entertain the hypothesis that legislatures are essentially conservative institutions that might be impediments to significant change, whether such change means achieving social justice, economic development, or a market economy (see Huntington 1968; Packenham 1970). Certainly this was true of the Russian Supreme Soviet from 1991 to 1993. The early history of the new Russian parliament also appears to offer some support to this conservative legislature hypothesis. The Russian State Duma has resisted the more radical market reforms advocated by Yeltsin and those close to him and, by providing a forum for Zhirinovsky and other nationalists, has forced Yeltsin toward a more confrontational approach on issues such as Yugoslavia and the Baltic states.

It is also worth saying that the survival and prosperity of the legislature may not be the most important goal for a nation. In Russia today, it is my impression that successfully restructuring the economy, modernizing industry, dealing effectively with the social costs of the shift to a market economy, pacifying rebellious minority groups and displaced military personnel, and fighting off the advances of the far right wing are among the truly major issues confronting the nation. Certainly, an effective legislature may help the nation to deal with some of these challenges, but in some instances the legislature can be counterproductive. In a sense, to be primarily concerned with strategies for strengthening the legislature in the face of these stupendous problems is analogous to rearranging the deck chairs on the *Titanic* after its encounter with the iceberg.

The Search for Prediction

It is understandable that when one grasps the story behind the development of one legislature, one seeks to apply those lessons to other legislatures. In the recent literature on democratization, there has been an assumption that if one correctly understood, for example, how Spain made the transition from authoritarianism to democracy, one could apply those lessons to nations in other parts of the world. Similarly, if one knows what makes the United States Congress a strong and stable political institution, the same factors, appropriately installed in another nation, will have the same result.

However, we are unable to make such predictive statements because we have failed to be truly comparative. Predictions come from theories that have been subjected to rigorous testing with comparative data. Our plethora of country studies and our paucity of comparative studies means that our theories are still at the embryonic stage. Thus, what we are left with are attempts to predict the future course of events in one nation from the experience of another nation with which it may have certain similarities but also certain important differences. This is analogous to predicting the weather in Rome simply by observing the weather in London. Such predictions, absent any theory linking meteorological conditions in London with those in Rome, would be extremely problematic.

Easy Data

Those who study the United States Congress have grown accustomed to the "easy" data of roll calls and election returns. Structured interviews with participants in the legislative process, although far from easy data, are less frequently used these days. But in Third World legislatures as well as the new legislatures of Central and Eastern Europe, roll calls often mean little, reliable election data are difficult to come by, and legislators are not always open to interviews. Furthermore, what these legislatures actually do, and the influence that their individual members exert on public policy, often takes place in less public arenas. Assessing this influence in any systematic manner is extraordinarily difficult, so difficult in fact that most scholars do not make the attempt. Yet clearly, just because something is difficult to assess and virtually impossible to measure in a scientific sense, does not mean that it is not important.

My fear is that when one concentrates on what is most visible in a legislature such as the Russian parliament, one will almost inevitably miss a great deal that is crucial. For example, most studies of legislatures in the Soviet Union and Eastern Europe prior to 1988 concluded that these legislatures did nothing at all. Such findings were based primarily on observing them in public session. But some investigators looked more closely, particularly at the activities in the less public arenas of parliamentary committees and commissions, and found a greater level of influence than they had expected. Certainly, these legislatures did not rival their Western counterparts in terms of their policy-making influence, but it also seemed clear that these institutions did more than a casual look at their plenary sessions would suggest (Vanneman 1977; Nelson and White 1982).

In terms of the Russian parliament, for example, it is just as important to dig beneath the activities within the parliament, which manifest themselves in the form of votes and speeches, to the less visible and likely much more important activities that take place in the committees, and to the less public negotiations between members of the government and individual legislators.

Another category of "easy" data are national constitutions. Ironically, we owe to students of the predemocratized Soviet Union and Central and Eastern Europe the insight that constitutions may obscure more than they reveal. Although the constitutions of these nations seemed to establish very strong legislative institutions, the reality, of course, was that these institutions were quite weak. Clearly, the formal allocation of power described in the constitution was less important than the informal and extra-constitutional powers exercised by the dominant single party.

It is thus surprising to see so many students of the new legislatures unduly occupied with constitutional provisions when such provisions are seldom discussed by students of more established legislatures (see Howard 1993). Certainly, these documents are useful as artifacts of the transition from authoritarianism to democracy, and the debates that took place as they were negotiated open an important window on the transition process. Nonetheless, it should be kept in mind that the words that are written on constitutional paper will not always describe the manner in which power is actually exercised.

Guideposts for Further Study

Subnational Legislatures

Much of the research on Western legislatures has focused on national institutions. Although there is a vast literature on American state legislatures, it is less frequently cited and of generally lesser stature than the work on the United States Congress. In the unitary states of Western Europe, state legislatures do not exist, but even in nations such as Germany where they do exist and are important, there has been relatively little scholarly work on them.

This nearly exclusive focus on the national level is a mistake, and would be particularly so in the case of Russia.[8] First, the deficit of experience in democratic politics that characterizes Russia today is more likely to be made up at the local level than at the more distant national level. Second, Russia's size, complexity, and diversity means that much will need to be decided locally and, therefore, regional and local political institutions will be important. Scholarly work on these subnational legislatures should be encouraged, especially as it might address the role of such institutions in the creation of a democratic political culture.

Non–Policy-Making Functions

As suggested earlier, the most important functions of most legislatures have more to do with representation and legitimization than with policy making. Representation refers to the process of articulating disparate, often geographically based interests in the national arena, seeking a fair distribution of national resources for those whom one represents, and working to resolve the local concerns of constituents as they are expressed by either groups or individuals.

There is now ample evidence that legislators the world over devote a great deal of their time and that of their staff to these activities. Individual requests to legislators for help with government agencies or for personal services of various sorts—some of which would not be characterized as political by our usual definitions—occur in every nation. Similarly, all legislators to some extent view themselves as their constituents' ambassadors to the central authorities and therefore as advocates for local economic needs, for the concerns of regionally based ethnic minorities, or for the political priorities of local officials.

In terms of legitimization, the legislature provides a symbol of popular government and citizen involvement in political decision making. Because its members are elected, the legislature conveys to larger publics the sense, if not necessarily the reality, that they are involved in policy making. Because it is a large collective body, representation can be divided among regions, salient political forces, and ethnic groups so that various segments of society can look to the legislature and know that their interests are being represented by someone who is either like them, or selected from among them. In a nation such as Russia, broad representation of this sort can have an important integrating effect and can contribute to building a degree of consensus for the new political institutions or the new economic order. Finally, members of the legislature, by explaining and defending government initiatives to those whom they represent, can contribute to the mobilization of consent for the government and its policies.

This is not to argue that the policy-making role of Russian legislatures should be ignored, or to suggest that the representational and legitimization functions of this institution are necessarily more important. It is to urge those studying Russian parliaments to broaden their horizons beyond what happens inside the legislature and in particular to include the relationship between the members of the legislature and the larger public. Ultimately, the institutionalization of Russian legislatures will depend upon their capacity to evoke a certain level of public support, and one key to developing that support will be the effectiveness with which legislators perform their representational activities.

Political Parties

It is virtually a rule of comparative legislative studies that the strength, prominence, and prospects of a nation's legislature are inextricably connected with the strength of its political party system. Party system strength is measured by a number of variables including the complexity of party organization, the strength of the connection between citizens and the parties, the degree of control that party organizations exercise over the electoral process, the dominance of government decisions by party leaders, and the number of political parties (Mezey 1994).

In single-party systems such as those found in the Soviet Union and Eastern and Central Europe prior to 1988, the power of the party was hegemonic, its connections to the public were strong although not always amicable, and its control of the electoral process and political decision making was absolute. These nations had "minimal" legislatures. All decisions were made by the governing party; and although government party legislators, typically the only members of the legislature, might under certain circumstances affect the shape of public policy at the margins, in general and certainly on major matters, they were obliged to follow the party line.

At the other end of the continuum are nations in which political parties lack internal cohesion and have very little in the way of governmental or extra-governmental organization. In such systems, parties often form and re-form from day to day, and candidates regularly shift from one group to another while many others stand outside the party system running as independents. Curiously, such parliaments are almost as weak as their one-party-state counterparts. Although such institutions may appear to exercise considerable power in the short run, in the end they tend to be vulnerable to attacks on their prerogatives and existence by nondemocratic elements, especially the military.

The trick to legislative development is the simultaneous development of political parties strong enough to allow the legislature and the government to function, but not so strong as to threaten the integrity or existence of the institution. Allowing the legislature to function means providing enough discipline to produce dependable legislative majorities for policy proposals emanating from either the government or legislative leaders. A legislature without the capacity to produce majorities is by definition without the capacity to act; unfortunately, such legislatures usually have the power to prevent the government from acting. An inability to act in the face of serious problems invites intervention from executive or military authorities, and encourages public discontent born of frustration with the failure of the government to deal with pressing issues. Such discontent may in turn be exploited by demagogues interested in aggrandizing their own power. In a very real sense then, a weak party system suggests that representative democracy itself is at risk.

In addition to facilitating government action, strong party systems also play a role in linking citizens with governmental institutions. Local party organizations can help legislators respond effectively to the particularized needs of constituents. As they provide opportunities for people to be involved in politics at the grass roots, parties can contribute to the strengthening of the democratic culture of a nation. Finally, in a large and diverse society, strong parties can play a more effective nation-building role than legislatures can. For example, the strength of democratic institutions in India during the years after independence can be more readily attributed to the strength of the Congress Party than to the strength of the Lok Sabha.

The impression one gathers of Russia today is of a nation with a weak, nearly disintegrated party system. Party coalitions shift almost daily; some parties disappear while others emerge, many of the latter being little more than the personal vehicles of ambitious leaders. Because no one force is in a position to dominate the legislature and determine its policy decisions, such an environment may create short-term legislative power. Debates in the legislature will be consequential and the outcomes of deliberations will be difficult to predict. But eventually, and probably sooner rather than later, such a situation will lead to government paralysis, an inability to address real problems, and a failure to make necessary decisions. And if parties continue to be cadre organizations located entirely in Moscow, with no local organizations or roots, they will make no contribution either to the creation of a stronger democratic culture or to the political integration of the nation.

Presidentialism

As is the case with weak political parties, it also has been argued that a presidential system of government weakens the capacity of the state to act. Advocates of parliamentary rather than presidential systems argue that the latter are characterized by policy-making inefficiency and ultimately political instability. Juan Linz (1994) suggests that in such systems both the president and the legislature enjoy "democratic legitimacy" and therefore it is not possible to resolve disputes between the two institutions by appeals to democratic criteria. Also, because the terms of both the legislature and the president are fixed and independent of each other, presidential systems are rigid. When political lines shift or new challenges confront the nation, it is not possible to adjust the personnel of government until the next scheduled election. Finally, presidential systems are prone to a zero sum politics, especially when the group controlling the presidency is different than the majority controlling the legislature. In such an event, policy outcomes are viewed as either victories or defeats for one or the other of the separated branches of government. Because of that, such systems may have a tendency toward stalemate, with difficult decisions avoided either because the executive and the legislature cannot reach agreement, or because one side sees political advantage in thwarting the plans of the other.

Critics of this viewpoint have argued, as we have earlier, that the effectiveness of government may have more to do with the presence of a majority party than with a particular constitutional form. In parliamentary systems with no majority party and a fragile governing coalition, policy making may be as slow and inefficient as in a presidential system. The term "immobilism" after all was first used to describe government under the parliamentary system of the French Fourth Republic rather than the semipresidential system of the Fifth Republic. In addition, in a deeply divided nation, an elected presidency may actually enhance stability, especially if the electoral system is designed to encourage the selection of a centrist (Horowitz 1990; Shugart and Carey 1992).

In the case of Russia, this debate seems to have been resolved in favor of a presidential system and the early results of that decision seem to confirm some of the gloomier predictions of those who are skeptical about such arrangements. Yeltsin's October 1993 confrontation with the parliament underlines the rigidity and zero sum nature of presidential systems. Although the new presidential powers established by the December 1993 elections and referendum appear to have strengthened the president's hand, this may have more to do with the current disorganization of his parliamentary opponents than with the constitutional adjustments. Certainly, the possibility of stalemate has not been eliminated and the prospect of further confrontations between the president and the parliament seem quite real.

Bureaucracy

Probably the strongest institution in the post-Soviet era (and possibly before as well) is the state bureaucracy. There is reason to believe, however, that strong bureaucracies may lead to weak legislatures. Fred Riggs (1963) argued that democratic systems have the most difficulty developing in nations where a strong bureaucracy has developed first. In such systems, the bureaucracy attracts the best people while those of lesser talent gravitate to democratic institutions such as legislatures. Bureaucratic policy making is also at odds with democratic policy making; the former is premised on the meritocratic notion that there are some policy solutions that are objectively better than others, while the latter is premised on the notion that the best policy is the one upon which the most can agree, regardless of its technical merits or its capacity to solve the problem at hand. In states with well-developed bureaucracies and new legislatures, these two different institutional cultures often mean that the bureaucracy will undermine and weaken the legislature (see O'Donnell 1979).

The Limits of Legislatures

A case can be made that as legislatures become stronger, the states with which they are associated become weaker in terms of their capacity to act. The intervening variable here is the strength of the political party system. For example, in recent years majority parties have weakened and minority governments have become more common in the established democracies of Scandinavia. These same nations have witnessed an increasing level of legislative activity as measured by such indicators as the length of parliamentary sessions, the frequency with which floor amendments are offered, more consequential committee deliberations, and greater attention paid by legislators to the concerns of their constituents. But interestingly enough, there is no indication that this rising level of legislative activity has been accompanied by an enhanced capacity to deal with policy issues (see Mezey 1994).

As suggested earlier, weak parties mean that the legislature is unable to generate dependable majorities behind either government proposals or those advanced by individual legislators. Without such majorities, the legislature may be able to stop government action that requires legislative approval but be unable to develop alternative policies of its own. The result is a weak state incapable of acting in the face of pressing problems.

Even if legislatures can develop majorities, they may not be very helpful in dealing with important issues. It is wise to remember John Stuart Mill's dictum that the proper function of the legislature is to "watch and control the government" rather than to govern; the latter, said Mill, was a function for which the legislature was "radically unfit." There are several reasons for the inability of legislatures to deal effectively with public policy problems. They are, by their very nature, slow to act. Collective decision-making bodies need a great deal of time to generate information, to allow various sides to be heard, and to construct majorities. Add to this the inclination of legislators to avoid policy options that though necessary may be politically distasteful, and to favor those options that anger the fewest people and interests. Finally, legislators may lack the competence to deal with complex policy issues, especially in those nations with new legislative institutions and few members with governing experience.

All of this means that legislatures may be unable to respond, even when the state confronts pressing problems. And when they do respond, they may respond slowly or ineffectually. Clearly, then, a strong legislature may be a mixed blessing, especially when state action is imperative. Needless to say, when a nation faces problems of the magnitude that confront Russia today, the state's inability to act can be catastrophic.

Ironically, new legislatures that play a subordinate role to the executive may contribute more to democratization and have better long-term prospects than those new legislatures that attempt to play an early, activist role. A subordinate legislature may allow the state to deal more effectively with its policy agenda. If that happens, then public support for all of the institutions of government, including the legislature, will rise. If the state is unable to respond, then support for all government institutions will erode. It may be that if democracy is to survive in Russia, a strong legislature will need to develop later rather than earlier in the process.

Legislatures are also the subject of inflated expectations. By itself, a legislature cannot bring consensus to a deeply divided society or solve enduring social and economic problems. And the legislature's capacity to contribute to democratization is also questionable. Effective legislatures, in my view, are more a product than a producer of democracy. The identity of the producers (or prerequisites) of democracy has been subject to debate. Scholars have focused on the economic requisites for democracy, the importance of a democratic frame of mind among the people, and a host of other national and international factors that are ostensibly connected with democratization.[9]

From these various perspectives, Russia has both advantages and disadvantages. As an industrialized nation with a very high level of literacy and a standard of living that is better than most Third World nations, Russia would seem to possess many of the economic requisites to democracy. On the other hand, the rapid shift to a market economy has created serious economic dislocations, a dramatic decline in the standard of living that many enjoyed under the old regime, and an apparent breakdown in public order. Even in nations with a long history of democratic politics, crises of this sort provoke people to question democratic institutions and to turn instead to men on horseback who promise simple solutions to complex problems. Given Russia's long history of authoritarianism, first under the tsars and then under the Bolsheviks, and its sparse experience with democracy, these conditions constitute a clear threat to the survival of its democratic institutions.

Notes

1. This work is contained in several anthologies: Kornberg and Musolf (1970); Agor (1971); Kornberg (1973); Boynton and Kim (1975); Eldridge

(1977); Smith and Musolf (1979); and Nelson and White (1982). See Mezey (1985) for a summary of this literature.

2. This story is well told in Morris-Jones (1983).

3. These questions and categories have been a staple of legislative research ever since they were proposed by John Wahlke and his colleagues (1962) in *The Legislative System*. See Mezey (1979, p. 172) for a summary of some of the findings from different countries where these questions have been asked.

4. On the importance of this approach to the study of the United States Congress, see Mezey (1993). For the United Kingdom, see Cain et al. (1987); Norton and Wood (1993); Searing (1994).

5. For a discussion of this point, see Kim et al. (1983) and Mezey (1985, p. 756ff.).

6. This point is well made by Patterson (1989) in his critique of research on the British Parliament.

7. The work of James Sundquist (1981) is one notable exception.

8. Encouraging in this regard is the fact that, perhaps because the old USSR Supreme Soviet was relatively powerless and inaccessible, considerably more attention was paid by Western specialists on the Soviet Union to local government. See, for example, Taubman (1973); Hill (1977); Friedgut (1979); Jacobs (1983); Hahn (1988); and Ruble (1990).

9. This is a huge literature. For a start, see Held (1993); O'Donnell et al. (1986); Przeworski (1991); Pereira et al. (1993); Liebert and Cotta (1990); and Longley (1994).

References

Agor, Westin H., ed. 1971. *Latin American Legislatures: Their Role and Influence*. New York: Praeger.

Boynton, G.R., and Chong Lim Kim, eds. 1975. *Legislative Systems in Developing Countries*. Durham, NC: Duke University Press.

Cain, Bruce, John Ferejohn, and Morris Fiorina. 1987. *The Personal Vote: Constituency Service and Electoral Independence*. Cambridge, MA: Harvard University Press.

Eldridge, Albert F., ed. 1977. *Legislatures in Plural Societies*. Durham, NC: Duke University Press.

Friedgut, Theodore H. 1979. *Political Participation in the USSR*. Princeton, NJ: Princeton University Press.

Hahn, Jeffrey W. 1988. *Soviet Grassroots: Citizen Participation in Local Soviet Government*. Princeton, NJ: Princeton University Press.

Held, David, ed. 1993. *Prospects for Democracy: North, South, East, West*. Stanford, CA: Stanford University Press.

Hill, Ronald J. 1977. *Soviet Political Elites: The Case of Tiraspol*. New York: St. Martin's Press.

Horowitz, David L. 1990. "Comparing Democratic Systems." *Journal of Democracy* 1 (Fall): pp. 73–79.

Howard, A.E. Dick. 1993. *Constitution Making in Eastern Europe*. Washington, DC: The Woodrow Wilson Center.

Huntington, Samuel C. 1968. *Political Order in Changing Societies*. New Haven, CT: Yale University Press.

Jacobs, Everett M., ed. 1983. *Soviet Local Politics and Government*. London: George Allen and Unwin.

Kim, Chong Lim, Joel D. Barkan, Ilter Turan, and Malcolm E. Jewell. 1983. *The Legislative Connection: The Politics of Representation in Kenya, Korea, and Turkey*. Durham, NC: Duke University Press.

Kornberg, Allen, ed. 1973. *Legislatures in Comparative Perspective*. New York: David McKay.

Kornberg, Allen, and Lloyd D. Musolf, eds. 1970. *Legislatures in Developmental Perspective*. Durham, NC: Duke University Press.

Liebert, Ulrike, and Maurizio Cotta, eds. 1990. *Parliament and Democratic Consolidation in Southern Europe*. London: Pinter.

Linz, Juan J. 1994. "Presidential or Parliamentary Democracy: Does It Make a Difference?" In Juan J. Linz and Arturo Valenzuela, eds., *The Failure of Presidential Democracy*. Baltimore, MD: The Johns Hopkins University Press.

Longley, Lawrence D., ed. 1994. *Working Papers on Comparative Legislative Studies*. Appleton, WI: International Political Science Association Research Committee of Legislative Specialists.

Mezey, Michael L. 1979. *Comparative Legislatures*. Durham, NC: Duke University Press.

———. 1985. "The Functions of Legislatures in the Third World." In Gerhard Loewenberg, Samuel C. Patterson, and Malcolm E. Jewell, eds., *Handbook of Legislative Research*. Cambridge, MA: Harvard University Press.

———. 1991. "Congress within the U.S. Presidential System." In James A. Thurber, ed., *Divided Democracy: Cooperation and Conflict between the President and Congress*. Washington, DC: Congressional Quarterly Press.

———. 1993. "Legislatures: Individual Purpose and Institutional Performance." In Ada W. Finifter, ed., *Political Science: The State of the Discipline II*. Washington, DC: American Political Science Association.

———. 1994. "New Perspectives on Parliamentary Systems: A Review Article." *Legislative Studies Quarterly* 19:3 (August): pp. 429–441.

Morris-Jones, W.H. 1983. "The Politics of Political Science: The Case of Comparative Legislative Studies." *Political Studies* 31: pp. 1–24.

Nelson, Daniel, and Stephen White, eds. 1982. *Communist Legislatures in Comparative Perspective*. Albany: State University of New York Press.

Norton, Philip, and David M. Wood. 1993. *Back From Westminster: Constituency Service by British Members of Parliament*. Lexington: University of Kentucky Press.

O'Donnell, Guillermo. 1979. "Tensions in the Bureaucratic-Authoritarian State and the Question of Democracy." In David Collier, ed., *The New Authoritarianism in Latin America*. Princeton, NJ: Princeton University Press.

O'Donnell, Guillermo, Philippe C. Schmitter, and Laurence Whitehead, eds. 1986. *Transitions from Authoritarian Rule: Comparative Perspectives*. Baltimore, MD: The Johns Hopkins University Press.

Packenham, Robert A. 1970. "Legislatures and Political Development." In Allan Kornberg and Lloyd D. Musolf, eds., *Legislatures in Developmental Perspective*. Durham, NC: Duke University Press.

Patterson, Samuel C. 1989. "Understanding the British Parliament." *Political Studies* 37: pp. 449–462.

Pereira, Luiz Carlos Bresser, Jose Maria Maravall, and Adam Przeworski. 1993. *Economic Reforms in New Democracies: A Social Democratic Approach.* Cambridge: Cambridge University Press.

Przeworski, Adam. 1991. *Democracy and the Market: Political and Economic Reforms in Eastern Europe and Latin America.* Cambridge: Cambridge University Press.

Riggs, Fred W. 1963. "Bureaucrats and Political Development: A Paradoxical View." In Joseph La Palombara, ed., *Bureaucracy and Political Development.* Princeton, NJ: Princeton University Press.

Ruble, Blair A. 1990. *Leningrad: Shaping a Soviet City.* Berkeley: University of California Press.

Searing, Donald D. 1994. *Westminster's World: Understanding Political Roles.* Cambridge, MA: Harvard University Press.

Shugart, Matthew Soberg, and John M. Carey. 1992. *Presidents and Assemblies: Constitutional Design and Electoral Dynamics.* Cambridge: Cambridge University Press.

Smith, Joel, and Lloyd D. Musolf, eds. 1979. *Legislatures in Development.* Durham, NC: Duke University Press.

Sundquist, James. 1981. *The Decline and Resurgence of Congress.* Washington, DC: The Brookings Institution.

Taubman, William. 1973. *Governing Soviet Cities.* New York: Praeger.

Vanneman, Peter. 1977. *The Supreme Soviet: Politics and the Legislative Process in the Soviet Political System.* Durham, NC: Duke University Press.

Wahlke, John, Heinz Eulau, W. Buchanan, and W. Ferguson. 1962. *The Legislative System.* New York: John Wiley.

10

Studying the Russian Experience: Lessons for Legislative Studies (and for Russia)

Jeffrey W. Hahn

This book was written to contribute to our understanding of how democratic legislatures emerge. It seeks to do so by analyzing why the development of legislatures in Russia from 1990 to 1993 ended the way it did—namely, in their abolition by force in October 1993. What went wrong? What lessons can we learn from an analysis of the Russian experience that may help us better understand the dilemmas of democratic consolidation? In light of what we can learn from such an analysis, what are the prospects for future legislative development in Russia? In undertaking this analysis, the editor has been mindful of the admonition expressed by Michael Mezey in the previous chapter that single-country case studies have scientific value only insofar as they are explicitly comparative. As he reminds us: "The goal is theories and explanations that can help us understand legislatures in general. A theory or explanation that applies only to the Russian parliament is about as useful as a theory of gravity that applies only to Chicago." At the same time, even as gravity in Chicago is not a matter to be taken lightly, especially for those living there, so this book is also concerned with what is happening in Russia. In what follows, then, we first try to generalize from the studies of Russian legislative development presented in this book about the factors that explain why democratic consolidation failed. Second, we look at the new Russian legislatures and speculate on whether they are likely to be more successful.

What Went Wrong?

The chapters in this book have dealt with discrete aspects in the development of Russian legislative institutions from 1990 to 1993. Yet there are common threads in each, which, taken together, form something of a tapestry. Hopefully, the larger picture that emerges tells us something about what determines whether stable democratic legislative institutions get built. What are the common threads? Sifting through the empirical studies that comprise this volume, we can identify at least four variables that seem to be critical to the process by which stable democratic institutions successfully emerge: rules, elites, linkage, and internal organization. There are almost certainly others, but these provide at least a point of departure. All seem to be necessary; none is sufficient. In the case of each there appear to have been deficiencies that proved fatal for democratic consolidation in the first Russian republic. An autopsy can prove useful if we are going to generalize beyond the Russian case.

Rules Matter

The confrontation between parliament and president that climaxed in the destruction of the first Russian republic in October 1993 was in large part the result of rules in place in 1990 and rules adopted subsequently. Consistent with neo-institutional theory, the strategies of key actors in this period were shaped by constitutional arrangements established during the Soviet era; conversely, new rules in the form of amendments and decrees were products of these strategies. As discussed in the introductory chapter, the constitution of the first Russian republic was a much amended version of the one adopted in 1978. That constitution was a clone of the Soviet constitution, which located all state power in parliament—that is, in the Supreme Soviet. In reality, as long as the CPSU retained a monopoly of real decision-making power (also constitutionally guaranteed), what parliament did did not matter much. In 1988, however, by calling for competitive elections nationally in 1989 and locally in 1990, Gorbachev changed the rules fundamentally. His goals in doing so were strategic: Gorbachev wanted to use elections to undermine his opposition in the party–state bureaucracy and replace it with those committed to his program of perestroika. The new Soviet legislative system that resulted was carefully constructed to ensure Gorbachev's political leadership; it was no accident that he was elected chair of the USSR Supreme Soviet by the Congress of People's Deputies in 1989.

The net and lasting (and probably unintended) effect of these rule changes was to create parliamentary bodies that did matter and which, in Russia, became the dominant political institutions in 1990. How did this happen? Gorbachev's mastery of the USSR Congress was a product of election rules that reserved a third of the seats for party-dominated public organizations, and of a two-stage nomination process that enabled those in charge of elections to limit the number of anticommunist candidates. To maximize their chances in the 1990 elections to be held in Russia, the leaders of the democratic movement forces, including Andrei Sakharov, Gavril Popov, and Boris Yeltsin, successfully demanded that these requirements be dropped. Although the two-tiered structure of the USSR parliament was preserved in Russia, the political composition of the Russian CPD was much more favorable to those who sought more radical reforms than Gorbachev's perestroika could accommodate. Parliament was divided more or less evenly between "conservatives" and "democrats," but enough independents joined the latter to narrowly elect Yeltsin as chair of parliament, thus making him the most powerful political figure in Russia in 1990.

In these constitutional arrangements lay the seeds of the destruction of the first Russian republic. As 1990 unfolded, it became increasingly clear that Yeltsin's ability to get the Russian CPD to do what he wanted was limited by the numbers of those opposed to more radical reforms. To overcome this opposition, his strategy was to call for another major change in the rules: a constitutional amendment creating the office of president. Here too he succeeded. Yeltsin's election to that office in June 1991 created what Thomas Remington calls in his chapter a "ménage à trois," an unstable triangle among three players consisting of two groups of deputies in parliament and the president. As a result, when the dissolution of the old USSR on December 25, 1991, ended whatever common cause existed among the Russian deputies, the struggle between a parliament dominated by conservatives and an executive controlled by radical reformers escalated. As the chapter by Remington so clearly demonstrates, the ensuing polarization of legislative-executive relations gained momentum as reform-minded deputies deserted parliament in favor of service in the executive branch while at the same time, the chair of the parliament, Ruslan Khasbulatov, used his patronage power *within* parliament to reward his allies among the conservatives. As matters became ever more contentious, especially over the question of privatization, which provided real stakes to the game, each branch asserted its institutional prerogatives ever more strongly. The rules in place were a prescription for gridlock.

The polarization of politics at the national level was extended throughout Russia in the course of 1992–93. In the fall and winter of 1991–92, Yeltsin adopted new rules—in the form of decrees—aimed at strengthening the powers of the executive branch locally and making sure that local executives would carry out the reforms dictated by the center. To this end he created two new institutions—the presidential representative and the chief of administration. While appointments to both positions were made by Yeltsin mostly from among allies in the democratic movement, the position of the chief administrator at the provincial (oblast) level, known as the governor, is of particular importance. Whereas chief executives previously had been chosen by the provincial legislatures (soviets), the new governors were not. More-over, since provincial legislatures included a substantial number of seats from rural districts, their political composition tended to be much more conservative. As a result, governors looked to Yeltsin for guidance and support, while provincial soviets increasingly aligned themselves with parliament. The institutional gridlock at the top was mirrored below. As the chapters by the editor and by Kathryn Stoner-Weiss show, these changing local institutional arrangements had a profound effect on the behavior of local elites. In the 1993 showdown between parliament and the president, the soviets supported parliament; executives, the president.

Elites Matter

While the rules in place and the rules adopted established an institutional context for growing polarization and confrontation in the first Russian republic, there was nothing inevitable about the outcome of this confrontation. On the contrary, in some respects the stage was arguably set for democratic consolidation. In his seminal article on what brings about democratic transitions, Dankwart Rustow argues that the "preparatory phase" for such a transition is characterized by "a prolonged and inconclusive struggle [between] well-entrenched forces fighting over issues of meaning to them."[1] This leads to a "decision phase" in which the leaders of the contending groups acknowledge their differences and institutionalize mutual tolerance by accepting democratic rules. His view is similar to Przeworski's notion of democracy as the institutionalization of uncertainty discussed in the introduction. A case can be made that the conditions for Rustow's preparatory phase were met in Russia in 1990–93. The struggle was between those opposed to the old regime who wanted it radically reformed economically and politically (candidates of the democratic movement), and those whose power and privileges were tied to the old regime and who sought to modify reform in ways that preserved their positions (candidates associated with the party–state apparatus). Initially, the struggle was fought out *within* the parliamentary institutions; later, between legislative and executive branches. As the chapters by Hough and Remington both make clear, the division was fairly equal, at least in the Russian CPD as originally constituted. Neither side appeared to be in a position to win decisively over the other.

If the conditions for the preparatory phase of a democratic transition appeared favorable, why did events in Russia not proceed to the next phase? For democratic consolidation (Rustow's decision and "habituation" phase) to take place, leaders of the contending forces must agree on the rules by which they will disagree. They must become accustomed to rules that allow losers to fight again and require winners to realize that all victories are conditional. To do this, they must negotiate what Giuseppe DiPalma calls "pacts." Pacts are the work of elites, leaders who are willing to "coexist" and for whom "consenting to lose" has become a matter of self-interest because it is the "axiomatic condition for winning at other times."[2] Yet as the chapters in this book by Shevtsova and Hough show, this is precisely what did not take place. Noting that "all political actors and political institutions [sought] to *monopolize* power, instead of sharing it," Shevtsova concludes that the inability to compromise reflected above all the authoritarian personalities of both Yeltsin and Khasbulatov, and more decisively that of the former. In a similar vein, Hough argues that one of the main reasons why parties did not develop in Russia in this period is because neither Yeltsin or Khasbulatov wanted to encourage the emergence of independent power centers. In the end, democratic consolidation did not proceed in Russia because relevant elites in both legislative and executive institutions were unwilling to accept uncertain outcomes.

The importance of elites highlights another problem with the process of building democratic institutions in Russia in this period, one that may continue to plague institution-building under the new system adopted in 1993: political decision making in Russia remains highly personalized. The roots of such an orientation are not hard to find. Formal institutional arrangements under the old Soviet system hardly mattered. What mattered was who was party secretary. At the top, things were decided by the general secretary; locally, by the first secretary of the oblast committee. The research presented in this book affirms how much this way of doing things characterized Russian development even after the CPSU was abolished, not only at the national level, but locally as well. In his study of policies on the privatization of housing in Yaroslavl, Blair Ruble notes that, whatever role the city soviet's commission dealing with this issue may have played, decisions taken depended on the personal leadership of the mayor and the commission's chairman. Kathryn Stoner-Weiss describes how governmental effectiveness at the local level in the end came down to personal relationships between economic and political elites that had been formed over a long period of time. One of the key criteria of institutionalization identified in the introduction to this book was that impersonal and "universalistic" codes replace personalistic ones as a basis for conducting business. Yet in Russia, to the extent that government worked well, this occurred because of personal relations between individual players, not because established rules and procedures were followed.

Linkage Matters

The analysis presented so far emphasizes the importance of institutional and "state-centered" explanations for why democratic consolidation in the first Russian republic failed. But the fault also lies in the absence of strong linkages between Russian citizens and those they chose to represent them in these institutions. As discussed in the introductory chapter, the primary function of most of the world's democratic parliaments is not to make policy, but to represent constituent interests. Indeed, it is the successful fulfillment of this representational role that makes legislatures democratic. Strong linkages can also contribute to the process of institutionalization. As Michael Mezey points out in his chapter, "Ultimately, the institutionalization of Russian legislatures will depend on their capacity to evoke a certain level of public support, and one key to developing that support will be the effectiveness with which legislators perform their representational roles."

When public interests are clearly articulated either because of strong home district ties or through well-developed parties and interest groups, they can act as a guide to legislative activity, providing order and meaning to policy choice. At the same time, the interests of the public serve as a constraint on legislators who would otherwise act as unaccountable free agents. One of the main reasons why legislators in developed Western democratic parliaments take coherent and consistent positions on issues is because they are liable to be held accountable, either by their constituents back home or by a political party whose support is indispensable to their reelection. In short, the aggregation and communication of social concerns can provide a basis for the achievement of political accommodation; its absence leaves representatives with few incentives beyond their own ambitions. Again, to cite Mezey, "In a nation such as Russia, broad representation of this sort can have an important integrating effect and can contribute to building a degree of consensus for the new political institutions."

The evidence presented in this book suggests that the development of the kind of linkages described here did not take place in Russia during the First Republic, or did so at best imperfectly. Much of the responsibility for this lies with the way in which the "founding" elections of 1990 were conducted, elections that defined the political composition of Russia's legislatures for the duration of the First Republic. In the first place, the number of seats in legislature remained large, in keeping with past Soviet practice. Second, the election rules provided no gatekeeping device to limit the number of candidates running in each district. Third, there was no legal basis for forming political parties; candidates ran on the basis of their personal views and characteristics. Finally, election rules provided for runoffs and repeat elections, producing the possibility of seemingly endless elections. As a result, there were too many deputies running for too many seats in too many elections with too little programmatic information about the candidates' views to help even the most dedicated voter make an informed choice. Those elected in the first Russian republic nationally and locally had little reason to feel linked with those who elected them. On the contrary, they had every reason to feel quite free to pursue their own ideological agendas with little regard for what their constituents thought.

The failure to establish strong linkages between the deputies and their constituents contributed much to the failure of democratic consolidation in Russia in this period. As the chapter by Timothy Colton shows, representational activities were regarded by deputies in the Russian parliament as something of a nuisance. Most viewed lawmaking as their primary function; dealing with constituents took up more time than they expected it would or thought it should. Tellingly, representatives supported by the "democratic movement" were even less concerned with what their constituents wanted than representatives from among the more conservative deputies with ties to the old party organization. The lack of linkage also helps explain why legislative factions failed to evolve into real electoral parties. As Jerry Hough shows, by 1993, there were no nationwide party organizations related to factions within the Russian CPD with the exception of the Communists, and even then there was little overlap between the Communist faction in parliament and the national party organization. Hough, too, makes the point that the "radical democrats" were more interested in making a "revolution" than in developing strong constituencies. The result was that deputies were unconstrained. As Remington puts it: "Their party ties were extremely weak and their links to their home districts only slightly stronger. But while they had few organizational means to mobilize voter support, by the same token they were not constrained ideologically."

The fact that deputies felt unconnected to their social base encouraged them to act as free agents. In the absence of accountability to any but themselves, they could choose sides more easily in the growing tensions between executive and legislative branches. This, in turn, further polarized relations between the institutions. As Lilia Shevtsova notes in her chapter, "One of the major roots of the Russian political crisis was the widening gap between all political institutions and society itself, which had already become evident in the first half of 1992." In the absence of such linkage, the two branches of power turned into substitutes for political parties. Shevtsova cites the lack of a well-developed civil society as a major reason why linkages were not stronger. The problem of deputies acting without strong links to their social base was also important in the failure of legislatures to institutionalize at the local level. As the chapter by the editor indicates, the behavior of deputies to the Yaroslavl soviets lacked the kind of discipline that close ties to a constituency base or association with a party organization might have provided. As in the findings of Hough and Colton, those deputies affiliated loosely with the "democratic movement" seemed particularly willing to go their own way. One of the crucial roles legislatures play in the process of democratic consolidation may be to engender linkage between representatives and constituents. For legislators in developed democracies, the desire to get reelected provides an incentive for close constituent ties. The evidence presented in this book suggests that this incentive was absent for most of the deputies to Russia's legislatures.

Internal Organization Matters

In the introduction to this book, the legislative studies literature was reviewed in an effort to identify criteria by which the institutionalization of legislatures could be measured. On the basis of this review three variables were chosen that seemed helpful in evaluating whether Russian legislative institutions had developed what Loewenberg and Patterson call "a definite way of performing their functions that sets them apart."[3] The first of these was institutional autonomy—that is, the existence of definable boundaries between institutions so that the rights and prerogatives of each institution in the decision-making process are clear. Looking at Russian legislative institutions in 1990–93, there is, on the one hand, little doubt that by comparison with the old Soviet system the new legislatures, locally as well as nationally, had greater autonomy. The old soviets had no real decision-making authority and their activities were fully subordinated to the executive branch, and beyond that, to the CPSU. After the reforms of 1990, they not only obtained a real voice in policy making, but they established the principle of executive accountability in practice as well as in theory. On the other hand, as all the chapters in this book make clear, the boundaries delineating what the institutions of government could do, especially after the establishment of the presidency, were not clearly drawn. In large part this is because the rules in place (and those adopted over time) were contradictory, allowing each institution to assert prerogatives claimed by the other. The assertion of institutional prerogatives in a system that lacked clear boundaries proved to be a prescription for disaster.

The second variable discussed in the introduction was the growth of organizational complexity. As legislatures develop, their workload expands, requiring an increasingly specialized division of labor among members. This in turn leads to a greater number of committees, more professional staff, and an increase in the regulations and procedures governing the interaction of members. Organizational complexity is a sign of institutionalization. Here, too, there was progress in the legislatures of the first Russian republic. Committees were formed and sometimes functioned effectively, as the case study by Blair Ruble of the Yaroslavl Commission on the Privatization of Housing demonstrates on the local level. There was a growth in the number of professional staff in the Supreme Soviet to around four hundred, as Remington notes. Rules and procedures for the conduct of legislative business were prepared. The real problem lay not with the number of committees, staff, and regulations, but with how they were used. The chapter by Jerry Hough offers a clear demonstration of the problem. Reflecting the growing organizational complexity of the Russian parliament in 1990–93, and the consequent need to rationalize its procedures, factions were given the right to determine the order in which speakers would address the Congress in floor debates, and also to appoint deputies to "reconciliation commissions" to resolve their differences. The problem, as Hough points out, was that factions were not fixed groups, and the organizational rules of the Congress allowed members to join as many as five factions. Since participation in controlling the flow of speakers and in the reconciliation commissions was a function of how large a faction was, the result was not the stabilization of partisanship over time but its disruption.

A third variable used to gauge levels of institutionalization is continuity of norms—that is, the development over time of a consensus among the members of an institution about how to conduct business. For legislatures, this would involve, among other things, the accumulation of precedent about "how things are done," formal and informal rules of conduct, and becoming accustomed to the transfer of power across generations. While Russian legislators can hardly be held responsible for the brevity of their tenure, it is clear that part of the reason for the weak institutionalization of Russian legislatures was simply a lack of experience. In another respect, however, the leadership of parliament may have more actively contributed to this result. As noted in the introduction, Nelson Polsby argues that continuity of norms also requires that the internal business of the legislature be conducted according to "impersonal codes" rather than "personalistic" ones.[4] One example of this in developed legislatures might be the use of seniority to appoint members to committees. Yet as the chapter by Remington demonstrates, in the Russian parliament from 1990 to 1993, committees were created and filled to enhance the internal patronage powers of parliament chair Ruslan Khasbulatov. Doing so greatly contributed to the growing standoff with the executive branch, where Yeltsin was doing much the same thing to ensure the loyalty of his supporters. Far from operating according to "impersonal codes," the internal organization of parliament reflected the seemingly unlimited personal ambitions of its chair.

How Does the New System Work?

In the introductory chapter of this book, the section describing the evolution of political institutions in the first Russian republic ended with the dissolution of the legislative institutions known as the soviets in October 1993. To replace them, Yeltsin decreed that a referendum on a new constitution would be held on December 12, 1993, simultaneous with elections to a new parliamentary body to be called the Federal Assembly. The new constitution was one version of several that had been discussed during the previous summer by a constitutional assembly whose work had quickly become polarized by the conflict between president and parliament. Not surprisingly, the version favored by Yeltsin called for a strong presidential system and was modeled after that of the Fifth French Republic. Officially approved by 54 percent of those voting on December 12, the constitution establishes the new rules defining the relations among the major political institutions of the Russian Federation: the president, the government, the two chambers of the Federal Assembly, and the courts.[5]

Under the new constitutional rules, the president is clearly the dominant player. He remains head of state and commander-in-chief with the right to introduce martial law. He continues to be in charge of Russia's foreign policy and chairs the Security Council. He has the right of legislative initiative. The new constitution gives the Russian president far more power than the old one did. For one thing, it extends his control over the formation and dismissal of the government. As in the case of France, Russia has a dual executive consisting of the president and a government headed by the prime minister. The latter is appointed by the president subject to approval by the lower house of parliament, known as the State Duma. The Duma, however, may not reject the president's nominee three times without being dissolved by him. Moreover, the president appoints the remaining members of the government without having to submit them for approval as before. The constitution also gives the president the right to issue binding decrees (*ukazy*) as long as they are not unconstitutional. He has the right to introduce states of emergency, though such a decision must be confirmed by the upper chamber of parliament, called the Federation Council. Also unlike the old system, the president may introduce national referenda. Finally, while there is a procedure for impeachment, it is much harder to do than before. In short, the new constitution gives the president unprecedented power to dismiss both parliament and the government, but restricts parliament's ability to remove him.

What does the parliament do? In addition to laws they may propose, all draft legislation must be adopted by half the total members of both the 450-member Duma and the 178-member Federation Council. Of the two chambers, the lower house is more powerful; if the Federation Council fails to approve legislation supported by the Duma, a two-thirds vote by that body can override. Also, the Duma may adopt a vote of no-confidence in the government, although it runs the risk of its own dismissal by the president if he does not agree with the decision. While the power relationship between president and parliament is decidedly asymmetrical favoring the former, there are limits to the president's power. However difficult, the Duma can impeach the president and the Federation Council can remove him. A presidential veto can be overridden by two-thirds of the "total members" of both houses. While the government draws up the budget, it must be approved by both houses, a process that starts in the Duma. High-level judicial appointments must be approved by the Federation Council, while the chair of the State Bank must be confirmed by the Duma. If parliament feels that the president has exceeded his authority, it may ask the Constitutional Court to declare his acts unconstitutional.[6] In the end, however, the ultimate constitutional limit on presidential power is electoral: the Russian president is limited to two four-year terms in office.

Elections to the new Russian parliament were held on December 12, 1993, after less than two months of preparation. Since no legislature existed to enact them, the laws governing the elections were the product of presidential decrees. In the Duma, half of the 450 seats were chosen on the basis of proportional representation from party lists. As in Germany, there was a 5 percent threshold that had to be met for a party to obtain seats in this fashion. For this reason, although thirteen parties presented lists of candidates in the December 1993 elections, only eight of them succeeded in gaining representation.[7] The other half of the deputies were from single-member districts. Unlike previous practice, the winner needed to obtain a simple rather than an absolute majority, with only 25 percent (rather than 50 percent) of the eligible electorate taking part. The Federation Council consisted of two members from each of the eighty-nine federal units (*sub''ekty*) that make up the Russian Federation.[8] Although the constitution says only that the Council will be made up of one representative from each unit's executive and legislative bodies, Yeltsin's decree called for them to be elected in a two-seat simple plurality election. The overall results of the election to the Duma are shown in the first column of Table 10.1.

The most widely reported outcome of the election was the success of the Liberal Democratic Party (LDP) led by an ultra-nationalist candidate, Vladimir Zhirinovsky, whose party won about a quarter of the votes cast for party lists, more than any other party. However, because the LDP did poorly in the single-member district seats and Russia's Choice did comparatively well, in the final tally Russia's Choice emerged as the largest single party and the LDP accounted for about 15 percent of the seats (see Table 10.1). Party representation in the Duma became the basis for the organization of parliamentary factions. While there were some differences, the size of a faction generally coincided with the number of party adherents. The editor's best assessment of the ideological composition of the Duma as of 1995 is shown in Table 10.2.[9] Perhaps the most striking observation to be made about the political composition of the Duma is the absence of a dominant ideological orientation. The numbers of those on the democratic left and on the democratic right are roughly equal, with a somewhat larger grouping in the middle. Zhirinovsky's notoriety notwithstanding, the far right accounts for a distinct minority (16–17 percent). The contest for places in the Federation Council was not widely conducted on a partisan basis. Most of those elected were regional-level officials. While the partisan composition of the Council is consequently hard to assess, one report suggests that 144 of the 171 who were elected had no party affiliation.[10]

Factions were formed at the opening session of the Duma in January 1994 and, as already noted, were based on the eight parties that ex-

Table 10.1

Partisan and Factional Composition of the Russian State Duma (in numbers of deputies and percent)

Name of party, group, or faction	Party composition after Dec. 12, 1993, elections (ITAR-TASS 12/25/93)[a]	Factions registered Jan. 14, 1994[b]	Factions reported as of June 8, 1994[c]	Factions reported as of Jan. 11, 1995[d]
Russia's Choice (Gaidar)	96 (21.6%)	76 (17.0%)	74 (16.5%)	67 (15.0%)
New Regional Policy (Medvedev)	18 (4.1%) (18 elected as "Civic Union")	65 (14.5%)	60 (13.4%)	62 (13.9%)
Liberal Democratic Party of Russia (Zhirinovsky)	70 (15.8%)	63 (14.1%)	64 (14.3%)	60 (13.4%)
Agrarian Party of Russia (Lapshin)	47 (10.6%)	55 (12.3%)	55 (12.3%)	54 (12.1%)
Russian Federation Communist Party (Ziuganov)	65 (14.6%)	45 (10.1%)	45 (10.0%)	45 (10.1%)
Party of Russian Unity and Accord (Shakrai)	27 (6.1%)	30 (6.7%)	31 (6.9%)	30 (6.7%)
Yabloko (Apple) (Yavlinsky)	33 (7.4%)	25 (5.6%)	29 (6.5%)	27 (6.0%)
Women of Russia (Fedulova)	25 (5.6%)	23 (5.2%)	23 (5.1%)	22 (4.9%)
December 12 Alliance (Fyodorov)	—	—	32 (7.1%)	22 (4.9%)
Democratic Party of Russia (Travkin/Glazyev)	21 (4.7%)	15 (3.4%)	15 (3.4%)	15 (3.4%)
Russia's Way (Baburin)	—	—	13 (2.9%)	12 (2.7%)
No Faction	30 (6.8%)	50 (11.2%)	7 (1.6%)	31 (6.9%)
Totals	444 (97.3%)[e]	447 (100.0%)	448 (100.0%)	447 (100.0%)

Notes:

[a] Includes both party list and single-member district seats. As cited in Vera Tolz, "Russia's Parliamentary Elections: What Happened and Why," *RFE/RL Research Reports*, vol. 3, no. 2 (January 14, 1994), p. 3. ITAR-TASS overestimated the seats going to Russia's Choice and many registered finally with the New Regional Policy faction.

[b] As reported in *Izvestiia*, January 14, 1994, p. 2.

[c] As reported in *Izvestiia*, June 16, 1994, p. 2.

[d] As reported in *Kommersant-Daily*, January 24, 1995, p. 4.

[e] Percentages do not add up to 100 because there were twelve deputies from other parties, all elected from single-member districts.

Table 10.2

Political Composition of the Russian State Duma in 1995—A Provisional Ideological Spectrum (N = 447)

	Percentage of Seats in Duma	Economics[a] (Market/State)	Politics[a] (Liberal/Authoritarian)	Foreign Policy[a] (Western/Nationalist)	Chechnya[b] (cease hostilities)
Left (27.1%):					
Communist Party of the Russian Federation (CPRF)	10.1%	State	Mixed	Nationalist	Yes (82%)
Agrarian Party (AP)	12.1%	State	Mixed	Centrist Nationalist	No (14%)
Women of Russia	4.9%	Center	Center	Centrist Nationalist	Yes (90%)
Center (30.9%):					
New Regional Policy (NRP)	13.9%	Center	Center	Centrist	No (30%)
Democratic Party of Russia (DPR)	3.4%	Center	Center	Centrist	No (0%)
Independents	6.9%	—	—	—	No (32%)
Party of Russian Unity & Accord (PRUA)	6.7%	Market	Liberal	Centrist	No (26%)
Right (25.9%):					
Yabloko	6.0%	Market	Liberal	Western	Yes (84%)
Russia's Choice	15.0%	Market	Liberal	Western	Yes (88%)
December 12 Alliance	4.9%	Market	Liberal	Western	No (32%)
Far Right (16.6%):					
Russia's Way	2.7%	Anti-Market	Authoritarian	Nationalist	No (33%)
Liberal Democratic Party of Russia (LDPR)	13.9%	Anti-Market	Authoritarian	Nationalist	No (0%)

Notes:

[a] These catagories are adapted from Stephen Whitefield and Geoffrey Evans, "The Russian Elections of 1993: Public Opinion and the Transition Experience," *Post Soviet Affairs*, vol. 10, no. 1 (1994), p. 45.

[b] Percentage of vote in favor of a law to "cease hostilities in Chechnya" is indicated in parenthesis. Data are reported by Alexander Sobianin and Eduard Gel'man in *Kommersant-Daily*, January 24, 1995, p. 4.

ceeded the 5 percent threshold for party representation. Aside from the original eight, factions could be formed if a minimum of thirty-five members registered as one. The centrist "New Regional Policy" faction was formed in this way from a core of deputies elected from "Civic Union."[11] While deputies may change their factional affiliation (and the changes in numbers over time reflects this) they may not belong to more than one faction at a time. Although the formation of parliamentary factions has taken place only in the lower house of parliament, it distinguishes this parliament from its predecessor in an important way. Unlike in the old parliament, the internal organization of the Duma's activities was to be decentralized. Instead of decisions being made by the speaker and a presidium led by him, they would be made by a "Council of the Duma" composed of one representative from each faction. This had an important impact, especially on the formation of committees. Whereas the previous speaker, Ruslan Khasbulatov, had been able to pack committees with his supporters and to control the choice of committee chairs, the new speaker, Ivan Rybkin (a member of the Agrarian Party) cannot. Seats on the twenty-three standing committees of the Duma, as well as decisions about who will be their chairs and deputy chairs, are decided by the factions in the Council of the Duma on the basis of parity.[12] The formation of factions and their relative degree of cohesiveness over time (as shown in Table 10.1) is one of the most significant differences between the new parliament and the old.

Since Yeltsin abolished the local soviets at the same time that he destroyed the national parliament, legislatures at that level also had to be rebuilt. In the provinces, they are generally called dumas and at the city level municipalities (*municipalitety*). The two-tiered system that existed until October 1993 has been replaced by one smaller body. In Yaroslavl, for example, there are twenty-three seats in the Duma and twenty-two in the municipality. Elections to these bodies were held in most of Russia's forty-nine oblasts in March 1994. While results obviously varied by region, some generalizations seem warranted. First, turnout was low—around 30 percent and in many cases falling below the 25 percent required. A number of elections failed to produce a legislative quorum and organizational sessions had to be postponed until a sufficient number of seats were filled.[13] In Yaroslavl, for example, the turnout was 26 percent in the city and 33 percent in the oblast, about half that for previous elections. The difference between city and oblast legislatures highlights a second general point: voter turnout was higher in rural areas than in urban ones. Consequently, a third feature of the elections is the generally poor showing of the parties associated with radical democratic reforms, especially at the oblast level. In the more agricultural south, for example, Penza, candidates from the old nomenklatura did well.[14] In the more industrial north, candidates ran as "independents," but came mostly from professional backgrounds or were associated with local executive branches. The dominant institution in local politics in 1994–95, however, was not the legislature, but the executive, and above all, the governor. In 1994 the trend toward virtually unlimited executive authority (under way even before October 1993) quickened. A presidential decree of October 3, 1994, made it clear that these individuals served at the pleasure of the president, making governors a functional equivalent of the old *obkom* first secretaries. Conversely, the new local legislatures came increasingly to resemble the old soviets.[15]

Will the New System Work Any Better?

On the whole the new system, at least at the time of this writing (May 1995), has not produced the kind of confrontation between political institutions that destroyed the first Russian republic. Except for parliament's declaration of amnesty in March 1994 for those imprisoned in connection with what Yeltsin called "criminal activities" in the crisis of October 1993, the first year of operation was marked by a more cooperative spirit. After a vigorous but generally constructive debate, for example, the Federal Assembly did manage to pass the government's budget. For better or worse, the parliament was unwilling to challenge the president on his deployment of troops in Chechnya with the ostensible purpose of ensuring the integrity of the Russian Federation. Will the new system prove to be more stable than that of the first Russian republic? Can we expect to see the emergence over time of legislatures that are not only institutionalized, but representative? Answers to such questions are, of course, speculative. We can, however, identify at least some of the factors that may determine whether democratic consolidation proceeds more successfully or not.

In certain respects, the new system appears to remedy some of the defects of the old one. For one thing, the new constitution resolves the ambiguity that existed over the respective powers of parliament and the president. The fact that it clearly does so in favor of the president is considered a major drawback by Lilia Shevtsova, who concludes that "there are few reasons to believe that strong presidentialism is a good thing for Russia." Michael Mezey, however, offers a different view. After reviewing the case against "presidentialism," he suggests that too strong a parliamentary system may be a bigger problem, especially in countries facing problems like Russia's: "Ironically, new legislatures that play a subordinate role to the executive may contribute more to democratization and have better long-term prospects than those new legislatures that attempt to play an early activist role. A subordinate legislature may allow the state to deal more effectively with its policy agenda." Whichever view proves to be correct, it seems clear that because this constitution was adopted as a whole and is not the product of often contradictory amendments over time, the boundaries between different political institutions will be better defined.

The new political system addresses the deficiencies of the old one in other respects. Because half the seats in the new Duma were allocated according to a party list electoral system, a basis was established for the emergence of parliamentary factions. These factions have produced more cohesive voting patterns among deputies than was the case in the old parliament. As Thomas Remington points out, by introducing a degree of discipline in voting choices, factions contribute to the stabilization of political conflict both within the legislature, and between the legislative and executive branches. To the extent that they become the basis for electoral politics, factions may also serve to encourage greater accountability to the electorate, thereby enhancing linkage. The role of factions in the new parliament also provides evidence of another positive development: learning from experience. The internal organization of the Duma is now defined not by the speaker, but by factions. Moreover, in place of the virtually unlimited factional membership described by Jerry Hough in the previous parliament, experience has taught the deputies the value of limiting representation in factions. It may also have taught them the need to compromise on issues like the rules for new factions and the assignment of committee members. It seems clear that locally as well as nationally, deputies have begun to develop what the legislative studies literature refers to as a continuity of norms.

Despite these promising signs, any speculation on the likelihood that the new Russian parliament will prove to be longer lasting and more democratic than its predecessor cannot ignore certain continuing obstacles. Perhaps the main trend in Russian politics since 1990, nationally and locally, has been the steady tendency toward unlimited executive rule. By 1995, the dominant political figures were unquestionably the president and, locally, the governors whose positions depended on his goodwill. This tendency was under way well before the decision was made to send troops into Chechnya in December 1994, but the way in which that decision was made reveals much about the continued weakness of Russia's political institutions. The decision appears to have been made by the Security Council, a body of hand-picked personal advisers accountable to no one but the president.[16] In bypassing both parliament and the government led by Prime Minister Viktor Chernomyrdin, Yeltsin demonstrated that new political institutions could be marginalized much as they had been under the old Soviet system. As the research in this book makes clear, it was reliance on the rule of persons and not of law that was perhaps the major flaw of the first Russian republic; it could also prove to be the undoing of its successor.

Notes

1. See Dankwart Rustow, "Transitions to Democracy: Towards a Dynamic Model," *Comparative Politics*, vol. 2, no. 3 (April 1970), p. 352.

2. Giuseppe DiPalma, *To Craft Democracies* (Berkeley: University of California Press, 1990), ch. 3 and p. 42.

3. Gerhard Loewenberg and Samuel C. Patterson, *Comparing Legislatures* (Boston: Little, Brown, 1979), p. 21.

4. Nelson W. Polsby, "The Institutionalization of the U.S. House of Representatives" *American Political Science Review*, vol. 62 (1968), p. 145.

5. There have been charges that the election results were fraudulent and that the turnout for the referendum was less than the required 50 percent. If true, the constitution would be invalid. For a discussion of the charges leveled by Alexander Sobianin and an official response, see the article by Valery Vyzhutovich in *Izvestiia*, May 4, 1994, p. 4.

6. A important feature of the new constitution is the establishment of a Constitutional Court that has the right to determine if the acts of the president or parliament violate the constitution and are therefore invalid. Whether this Constitutional Court will fare better than its predecessor in the first Russian republic remains to be seen. Because of controversy over presidential appointments to the Court (which must be approved by the Federation Council), the Court was unable to be seated and hold its first session until March 1995.

7. The five that failed to make the threshold included the Civic Union, Anatolii Sobchak's Movement for Democratic Reform, Dignity and Charity, Ecolog-

ical Movement, and Russia's Future. These parties did manage to gain one or more seats in the single-member districts, with the Civic Union getting by far the most (eighteen). Civic Union, a centrist party, was the only party not exceeding the 5 percent threshold that was able to gain enough adherents in the first session of the Duma to enable it to be registered as a faction.

8. The republics of Chechnya and Tatarstan boycotted the elections, and in the province of Cheliabinsk too few voters came out for a valid election to the Federation Council. Thus, when the parliament convened in January 1994, only 171 of the 178 Council seats were filled; 444 of the 450 deputies to the Duma took their seats. By the end of 1994, all but Chechnya had held elections.

9. Table 10.2 is based on *factional* strength in the Duma as of the beginning of 1995 as reported by Alexander Sobianin and Eduard Gelman in their analysis of Duma support for the war in Chechnya in *Kommersant*, January 24, 1995, p. 4. The table is labeled "provisional" because the placement of the factions is open to different interpretations. The inclusion of "independents" in the center, for instance, may overstate that category's strength. Furthermore, the table adopts a European ideological framework to distinguish between parties of the left (liberal-socialist) and right (conservative). The justification for doing so, despite the fact that deputies from the far right and the left occasionally vote together in a "red–brown" coalition, is that while the parties of the far right appear to be anti-democratic ideologically, those on the left do not. The term "democratic" used here means that a party would come to power by "free and fair" popular elections and would yield power if defeated in them.

10. See Terry D. Clark, "The Russian Elections: Back to Square One?" *PS: Political Science and Politics*, vol. 27, no. 3 (1994), p. 524. For a slightly different tally, see Thomas F. Remington and Steven S. Smith, "The Early Legislative Process in the Russian Federal Assembly," in Philip Norton and David M. Olson, eds., *The New Parliaments of Eastern and Central Europe* (London: Frank Cass, forthcoming).

11. On March 14, 1995, a new parliamentary faction called "Stability" was registered in the Duma. Led by Oleg Boiko, a banker formerly affiliated with Russia's Choice, Stability's thirty-five members come from the factions Russia's Choice, New Regional Policy, December 12 Alliance, and two from the LDP. They are centrist in ideology and regarded as close to Yeltsin (OMRI Reports, March 16, 1995).

12. For a more detailed description of the process by which factions and committees were formed and the decision about how the work of the new parliament was organized see Remington and Smith, "The Early Legislative Process." Their chapter includes a list of the committees of the Duma by factional membership. There are seventy-one subcommittees in the Duma and none in the eleven standing committees of the Federation Council. The difference reflects not only the greater stature of the Duma in parliament, but the importance of factions as well. *Kommersant* of January 19, 1994, published a distribution of factions among the Duma's committees. See also *Current Digest*, vol. 46, no. 3, p. 18.

13. For reports on these elections, see articles by Vladimir Tores in *Segodnia*, March 22, 1994, p. 2; and Leonid Smirnyagin, *Izvestiia*, March 23, 1994, p. 1. According to Tores, thirteen of seventeen regions failed to get a quorum, while the remainder barely got one.

14. See the reports by Aleksandr Kislov, *Izvestiia*, February 2, 1994, p. 1; and by Valery Vyzhutovich, *Izvestiia*, February 3, 1994, p. 1.

15. A more detailed discussion of these developments can be found in Jeffrey W. Hahn, "Latest Developments in Local Russian Government," a paper presented at the annual meeting of the Mid-Atlantic Slavic Conference in New York, March 15, 1995.

16. For a discussion of the Security Council and its power in the wake of the Chechnya decision, see Mikhail Sokolov, "All Power to the Security Council," *Segodnia*, January 12, 1995, p. 3.

Appendices

Constitutional and Legal Foundations of Legislative Development in Russia

The Stages of Constitutional Reform in Russia

Lev A. Okunkov

What are the main landmarks of constitutional reform in Russia? It is possible to distinguish three stages of constitutional reform. The first stage included the continual amending of existing constitutional legislation and the simultaneous preparation of a new draft constitution. The second stage was marked by an intensification of the antagonisms between the parliament and the president concerning the future constitution and, especially, the balance of power between the legislative and executive branches.[1] In the third stage, starting on December 12, 1993, a new constitution of Russia was adopted followed by the development of a state and legal system reflecting the new realities of political life. After examining these stages more closely, we can speculate on what further legislative changes may be forthcoming.

The Stages of Constitutional Development

The early period of constitutional reform was characterized by numerous constitutional amendments to the existing constitution of the RSFSR, which had been adopted in 1978. While these amendments in fact created a new Russian legislative system, they nevertheless failed to incorporate certain essential features, including: the Declaration of the Rights and Freedoms of Mankind; the Federal Agreement; laws on property; and laws on the presidency and the government. Moreover, even at that time some of the articles of the amended constitution became a bone of contention between the federal branches of legislative and executive power. Examples of this include articles on the superior authority of the Congress of People's Deputies and the status of the president and the government in relation to it. In the meantime, the deepening economic crisis in Russia complicated the process of constitutional reform.

The constitutional marathon passed through many stages and obstacles. Over the course of three years, parliament and its factions, the president's team, various political parties, and scholars developed dozens of drafts of a fundamental law for Russia. Thousands of amendments offered by deputies of the Supreme Soviet were filtered through the sieve of the Supreme Soviet's Constitutional Committee, formally chaired by President Yeltsin. After broad discussion, a draft of a new constitution was completed and supported by parliament in April 1992. The main features of the new constitution included the assertion of state sovereignty based on the will of the people (democracy); giving top priority to the protection of the rights and freedoms of mankind; de-ideologizing the formation of political institutions; and creating a system for the separation of powers. By cooperating, and by coordinating their activities in 1991–92, the Supreme Soviet and the president created a new legislative base for a peaceful and democratic reformation of Russia.

However, at about this time, the president's team proposed the idea of conducting a constitutional referendum. As a result, the second stage of constitutional reform was characterized by sharp polemics among the president, the Supreme Soviet, and the Constitutional Court over how to interpret votes "for" and "against" the referendum on a new constitution. The further course of events showed that parliament was actually trying to impede the preparation of a new constitution. The legislatures of the various subnational members (sub"ekty) of the Federation decided the matter, successfully arguing against conducting a referendum because of the situation in the regions. With hindsight, the wiser political decision would have been to conduct this referendum, and to adopt a new constitution based on its results.

The standoff between the two powers resulted in the referendum of April 25, 1993, which called for a vote of confidence in the president and in his programs, and on whether to hold early elections to the federal institutions of power. The fact that the results of the referendum favored the president provided momentum for Boris Yeltsin's energetic initiatives in May–June 1993 to speed up the adoption of a new constitution. The swift action of the president caught the Supreme Soviet by surprise. In the president's version of the constitution, the prerogatives of the president were strengthened even more at the expense of legislative institutions. Nevertheless, the draft of the constitution submitted by parliament was used in revising the president's version. If the two drafts are compared, we find numerous insertions from parliament's draft in the version that was ultimately presented to the voters in the referendum of December 12, 1993.

The new Russian constitution was deemed adopted on December 12, 1993, when 58.4 percent of these voting voted in favor of it. But, doubts have been raised about whether this referendum was legitimate since only 54.8 percent of the eligible electorate voted and the existing law on referenda required an absolute majority of all voters. However, the absence of general approval can be regarded as normal for free elections held in the conditions of a political crisis. An analogous picture can be observed in postwar France, where the difference in the general number of votes for and against the Constitution of the Fifth French Republic fluctuated around 5–10 percent of all voters. It should also be noted that neither the Federal Assembly nor any constituent member of the Federation has disapproved of the lawfulness of the referendum. So, while it is possible to criticize individual articles of the constitution, it is impossible to consider it invalid. Besides, as the chairman of the Committee on Legislation of the State Duma, V. Isakov, said in considering the alternatives: "We will find ourselves in the worst situation, where the former constitution of the country has been destroyed, and there is no new constitutional basis for the activity of the institutions of power. This would seem to be the most dangerous situation." [2]

The adoption of the 1993 constitution signifies the beginning of the third stage of the development of Russian statehood. In structure and content, the document is similar to those found in developed democratic states with a presidential form of rule. The constitution consists of nine chapters. Chapter 3 deals with the federative structure, chapters 4 through 7 are devoted to the organization of state power, and chapter 8 addresses local self-government. However, it is in chapter 1, establishing the foundations of the constitutional system, and chapter 2, which assigns basic rights and freedoms, that the new constitution most fundamentally differs from the old.[3] Unlike the constitution of the former USSR, which declared the construction of a communist society to be the ultimate goal, the new constitution of Russia (in article 2) proclaims human rights and freedoms to be of greatest value. The 1993 constitution also reflects changes in the state's social policy. A class-based approach to various strata of society has been eliminated. The status of labor collectives as an active part of the political system has lost its constitutional meaning. At the same time, the institutions of private property and free enterprise characteristic of a free market economy have been strengthened.

The new constitution has also found progressive solutions to the question of federal relations. Chapter 3 provides a legal basis for the equality of rights among the various members (sub"ekty) of the Russian Federation based on a delineation of authority between them and the federal institutions of power. Many categories of legislation have ceased to be the exclusive prerogative of the federal powers and in accordance with article 72 are placed under joint jurisdiction. The eighty-nine members of the Federation have also received the right to issue their own laws, whereas before only autonomous republics held such authority. It is possible that the use of this authority could result in a "laws race" on questions not regulated by federal legislation; this could negatively influence the unity of the Russian state. However, the constitution establishes a strict hierarchy of laws depending on the jurisdiction of the institutions of power. First, the laws of the members of the Russian Federation cannot contradict federal laws that deal with matters exclusively under federal jurisdiction. Second, outside of the limits of federal jurisdiction, and of matters that fall under *joint* jurisdiction, each republic, territory, and oblast can adopt its own laws. If an act issued by a member of the Federation contradicts a federal law, the legal act of the member of the Federation takes priority within the limits of its prerogatives (article 76).

The constitution provides for fundamental changes in the organization of the institutions of power. Above all, it creates a strongly pronounced presidential form of government. Indeed, it is possible to characterize the third stage of Russian constitutional development as moving from "the absolute power of the soviets to the absolute power of the president." The Russian political elite and the new deputy corps expected this change as an inevitability, a result of the struggle for power between parliament and the president. But the qualitative differences between the new and old systems were not made clear to the general public. Many Russian political scientists and jurists consider the new constitution to be ambiguous. The main questions are: What role will the president's new constitution play in the future? Will it become a stabilizing factor in social life, or, on the contrary, will it be used as a legal cover for a regime of personal power, especially after presidential elections in 1996?

In Russian politics, constitutions have often performed uncharacteristic functions. They became an argument, "small change," if you will, in debates over power between the president and the Supreme Soviet, and between communists and democrats. In Russia, competition between powers has always carried an exceptionally personalized character. For the general population, disagreements between parliament and the president always meant disagreements between Ruslan Khasbulatov and Boris Yeltsin. Many Russian citizens do not believe that this conflict was inevitable; given good will and compromise between the speaker and the president, they could have found a compromise. Unfortunately, both lacked the necessary historical foresight. Strategic errors in forming the constitutional institutions of power are the result of this personalization of power. One need not be a psychic to predict that the practically uncontrolled authority of the president might one day become a Trojan horse in the political regime and fate of democracy in Russia. Given the success of Vladimir Zhironovsky in the 1993 elections and his intention to run for president in the next elections, many people have begun to wonder whether the constitution might not be conducive to the reestablishment of an authoritarian regime.

Prospective Legislative Changes

Legislative development in the next few years will probably involve attempts to amend individual articles of the constitution. However, the current procedure for doing so is rather complicated and hard to accomplish. The adoption of amendments to chapters 3–8 of the constitution requires agreement by a two-thirds majority of the deputies in the Federal Assembly and by two-thirds of the members of the Russian Federation. It will not be easy to reach such an agreement. One may predict that the main theme of future amendments will be to revise the system of the division of powers by strengthening the position of parliament. An even stricter procedure for making amendments exists for chapters 1 and 2 of the constitution. In this case, it is necessary to develop a draft of a new constitution, which then must be adopted by a majority of a constitutional assembly convened especially for this purpose, or by a majority vote in a nationwide referendum. Considering the former practice of making numerous and often nonconforming amendments to the old constitution, it is possible that the strictness of the new procedures for making amendments is fully justified.[4]

The logical continuation of the creation of new constitutional legislation is the adoption of federal constitutional laws, a process procedurally similar to amending the constitution. Unlike ordinary laws, federal constitutional laws are adopted by a two-thirds majority of the deputies of both houses, thereby excluding the possibility of a presidential veto. The adoption of such laws will eliminate some of the disagreements over the division of powers as currently found in the constitution. With the adoption of the constitution, the process of the revising other types of legislation will also become more purposeful and systematic. The constitution provides its own program for drafting laws, which includes a dozen federal constitutional laws and more than twenty regular federal laws. The most significant among the latter will be a package of laws on the institutions of state power, federal laws on the referendum, on elections of the president and of deputies to the State Duma, and on the guarantee of voting rights for all citizens. These laws will create a basis for the development of representative democracy in Russia.

Another likely step in the development of constitutional law is to bring all current legislation into conformity with the constitution. Much of this legislation is characterized by instability, internal contradictions, and incompleteness. Hundreds of laws, decrees, resolutions, and orders of the government, as well as instructions of ministries and government departments, need to be revoked. Cleaning the "augean stables" of Russian legislation is just beginning. Related to this problem is the need to adopt codified legislation essential for the establishment of a rule of law in Russia. We have in mind the adoption in 1995 of a civil code (often called the second constitution) by the Federal Assembly. In 1995–96, we anticipate the completion of criminal, labor, land, tax, and arbitration procedure codes as well. Once these codified acts are published, the assembly of a systematized Code of Laws of the Russian State will become possible.

Conclusions

Unfortunately, it must be said that the effectiveness of the constitution and of all Russian legislation is still not very high.[5] This can be explained to a great extent by the legal nihilism flourishing in society, and by the absence of strict strategic guidelines for the development of the economy. However, despite all the tradeoffs of this transitional period, law is one of the main stabilizing factors in the development of society. In this respect, there can be no doubt about the positive role of the constitution as a cornerstone of the entire legal system. In evaluating it, the most important thing to consider is that it has established individual rights and freedoms as the top priority for the state. Moreover, there is some evidence that the rights and freedoms of mankind are recognized in practice, that they are being implemented directly, and that they define the sense, substance, and activities of the institutions of state power and self-government. And even though the actual situation concerning the observance of individual rights and freedoms gives few reasons for optimism, the constitution does give parliament and the judiciary the opportunity to make the processes of the democratization of society irreversible.

Many Russian citizens skeptically say the following about law: "The worse the situation with respect to rights and freedoms is, the more beautifully they are described in our constitutions and various laws." In contrast to Americans' reverence for their federal constitution, the authority of the Russian constitution is extremely low in the public consciousness. Until strict observance and compliance with the constitution and the laws has become a natural norm of behavior, an obligation, and a moral duty, it is premature to speak about the establishment of legislation and democracy in Russia. Only by creating a civil society based on principles of respect and observance of the law can we avoid the dogma of contending ideologies. The priority of law, of universally recognized human rights and freedoms, can be the common point of agreement for communists, liberal democrats, and nationalists, all of whom have different beliefs. Everybody suffers from the absence of law.

Notes

1. The culmination of the standoff between these branches of power resulted in the president's decree no. 1400 of September 1993, which terminated the activities of the Congress of People's Deputies and the Supreme Soviet.

2. *Konstitutsionyi vestnik*, no. 1, vol. 17 (1994), p. 35.

3. Concrete norms and prescriptions covering the whole complex of basic rights and freedoms are guaranteed by the constitution in more than 60 of the 137 articles and constitute the broadest part of its content.

4. It seems probable that these difficulties will help to increase the role of the

federal courts in interpreting and applying the constitution. Above all, this refers to the right of judicial review (*prava ofitsial'nogo tolkovaniia*), which belongs to the Constitutional Court according to article 125. At the present time, this Court is considering a case concerning the authority of the upper house of the Russian parliament, the Council of the Federation.

5. It should be noted that the effectiveness of constitutional reform depends to a great extent on the way legislation will be formed by the subnational members of the Federation. The principle of equality among these members, the right of each to issue its own laws, and the broad scope of their legislative authority all reflect new approaches to the development of federal relations based on a two-tiered legislative system. Perhaps the main precondition for successfully conducting reforms in Russia today is to solve the problem of how to ensure unity in the system of state power while simultaneously defining the relative authority of federal and local institutions of power.

Problems of Executive-Legislative Relations in the Russian Federation

Yurii A. Tikhomirov

In recent years, there have been major revisions of the theoretical concepts on which the Russian state rests. One of the most important of these is the concept of the division of power, which has replaced the doctrine of the unity of state power and the preeminent authority of the soviets. However, the introduction of this concept has led to serious disagreements over relations between the legislative and executive branches of power. It is not easy to define what each branch may do independently of the other and what both must do jointly. If the relationship between representative and executive structures of the subnational members of the Federation are considered, then even more complex problems are created.

Relations between legislative and executive institutions reflect changes in their status. Previously, the Supreme Soviet of the RSFSR was the highest body of state power. Then the amended constitution of 1978 made the Congress of People's Deputies the highest body of state power, and the Supreme Soviet became the permanently existing institution for legislation, administrative law, and oversight. Constitutionally, the superior rights of the legislature were clear: it could consider and resolve any question within the jurisdiction of the Federation. To some extent this approach was also taken in the new Russian constitution of December 1993. As before, the representative and legislative institution of the Russian Federation is the parliament (now called the Federal Assembly), consisting of two houses—the State Duma and the Council of the Federation. What is new, of course, is the institution of the presidency. In the previous constitution the president was defined as the highest official and the head of executive power. In the new constitution he has also become the head of state. He enjoys great authority in forming and leading the activity of government.

The status of the government is also changing. In the old Soviet system, the government was the highest executive and administrative body of state power. Then it became an institution of executive power accountable to the Congress, the Supreme Soviet, and the president, all of whom participated in its formation, its dissolution, and in questions of confidence. Now, the government also carries out the executive power of the Russian Federation, but its functions have been expanded to include the implementation of financial policy, the management of federal property, and the right of legislative initiative as well as the regulatory functions of government normally entrusted to ministries, state committees, and departments. Organizational interactions between the legislature and the government have also changed. The Duma has the right to confirm the president's appointment of the chairman of the government, and to vote "no confidence" in the government. These are potentially important channels of influence.

Problem Areas in Executive-Legislative Relations

1. At the present time, a clearer definition of the authority of each institution is needed. Currently, interference of one body in the activities of another frequently occurs, or, conversely, inactivity and indecisiveness prevail. One example of the problems this creates can be seen in the sluggish response of federal institutions to economic processes in the regions. The lack of clearly defined jurisdiction in the republics and oblasts has produced separatist actions in the spheres of property, taxes, budgets, and culture, among other issues. This imprecision over what functions each institution performs is undesirable. It is regrettable that debates over jurisdiction have not yet become the subject of attention in the Constitutional Court. Also, the courts of arbitration should more actively establish precedent throughout the system.

2. The most difficult problem is delineating the spheres of functional independence and interaction between the legislative and executive branches of power. The jurisdiction of parliament is defined in two ways: apportioning the subjects of exclusive jurisdiction to each house, and assigning the right to decide other questions by legislation. The latter concerns the development of the state system, economic and social policy, ensuring the rights of citizens, and foreign relations. Institutions of federal executive power realize their authority in the area of administration. The law clearly regulates basic questions of their jurisdiction in economic and sociocultural spheres, in questions of law and order, and in relations with foreign states. Central institutions of executive power carry out functions of branch and interbranch importance.

3. Common tasks facing the legislative and executive branches require that they interact both on the basis of agreement and simultaneously on the strict delineation of their functions. But what is different about the new constitution is that programs of legislative activity are based on proposals made by the government and the president. As a result, the ministries have a greater legislative role to play. In practice, the following problems occur: First, there is the intrusion of institutions of one kind into the activity of another (either the parliament resolves operational questions, or the government adopts acts of quasi-legislative character). Second, contradictory decisions are often made concerning some questions (budget, property and its privatization, government development, and others). Third, acts are passed that are contradictory, including directions given by federal institutions to other members of the Federation.

4. Of principle significance for the relations between the legislative and executive branches is that their legislative acts not contradict one another. Establishing the supremacy of the laws is attained by various means. Previously, the Supreme Soviet of the Russian Federation had the right to rescind presidential decrees based on findings of the Constitutional Court (and until the case was decided, it had the right to suspend these acts). When an act of the president contradicted the norms of the constitution and the law, the constitution and the law would override that act. Now it has been established that the president's decrees and orders should not contradict the constitution and the laws. In addition, parliament may now introduce a motion to revoke decisions of the government by the president, who revokes them if he agrees that they contradict the law. However, in practice, there are frequent cases of the executive branch ignoring the law. This is unfortunate. Disregard for the legislative foundation of acts decreases the efficiency of executive activity and gives rise to juridical clashes. At the same time, the oversight activity of the parliamentary committees leaves much to be desired.

5. The relations between the legislative and executive branches of power in Russia are also shaped by various political forces. This helps explain the occasionally sharp opposition between these branches. Since the pressure of social movements, parties, and the press affects the course of preparation and adoption of laws and other acts, it would be desirable if social factors were not destructive, but optimizing. Solving the problem of political participation is important for the division of powers. There should be full expression in the legislation on taking public opinion into account by state bodies. This is very important, because the alienation of citizens from power has not been diminished. Reform "from above" does not generate social support if the channels of participation have become narrow.

6. Relations between legislative and executive branches, not only at the same level of government, but between different levels, are of great importance for Russia as a federated state. It is not always easy to coordinate the division of powers vertically. Can the parliaments of the Federation and its component members cooperate? How are the laws and the president's decrees to be correlated? How great is the relative authority held by the Federation and by its members in the fields of local self-administration, the judicial system, and the apparatus of administration? It would hardly be possible to divide the judicial system into two levels as this would weaken the influence of unified federal codes and undermine the protection of citizens' rights. Executive bodies in republics and oblasts exist in a unified system of executive power. Nevertheless, a strict measure of independence in their internal organization is needed since their functions may exceed the limits of federal jurisdiction. Although the governments of the republics are somewhat settled, in the territories and oblasts not all is going well yet. The head of the adminis-

tration is all-powerful, and the committees and administrative departments often form their decisions using only his acts. It is doubtful that these bodies can be called administrations in view of the multiple meanings of this term.

To conclude, the relationship between legislative and executive branches of power has two aspects: the delimitation of their authority and the guarantee of their interaction in resolving common state problems. Underestimating either of these aspects weakens the effectiveness of the actions of each institution, as well as the functioning of state power as a whole.

Legislation on Local Government in Russia [1]

Aleksandr E. Postnikov

The Legal Reform of Local Government, 1990–1993

Because the legal system of Russia was an organic part of the legal system of the USSR until 1991, the legislation of the Soviet Union played an important role in reforming the organization of local power. The first serious effort to reform local institutions of power came in 1988, when changes were introduced into the constitution of the USSR. According to article 149 of the constitution of the USSR, permanently functioning legislative entities called "presidiums" were organized in the soviets at the oblast, regional, and city levels. At lower levels (small cities, villages, settlements), the presidium's functions were to be carried out by the chairman of the soviet. Executive committees ceased being institutions of the deputies, and, on the whole, their functions became separated from the soviet. It is from that time that a real division of executive and legislative powers at the local level began.

More systematic reform of local institutions of power took place in 1990, when the USSR law "On Fundamental Principles of Local Self-Government and Management in the USSR" was adopted. The Soviet version of local government embodied in this law contained a number of innovations. First, the law recognized the relative independence of the local soviets in resolving questions of local significance. Second, relations between the soviets and local enterprises were to be built on a contractual basis. Third, the law established that taxes would go directly into the budgets of the soviets, creating a real possibility for the soviets to use their budgets independently, Fourth, the law provided greater rights to local authorities in their relations with enterprises and with higher-level institutions of power. Finally, the law established a legal basis for public social organizations, local referendums, and other local forms of direct democracy.

In practice, the implementation of this law was complicated for a number of reasons. For one thing, neither the state nor society were prepared for such a high level of decentralization of state power as proposed for the local level of government by the adoption of this law. For another, the union republics of the former USSR lacked any legislation concerning local government's conformity with federal law. Nevertheless, the law regarding the general concepts of local self-administration and local management in the USSR had considerable influence on all subsequent legislation affecting local government in both Russia and other newly independent states.

On July 6, 1991, the law of the RSFSR "On Local Self-Government in the RSFSR" was adopted.[2] For its time, this law was a fairly innovative legal act. According to it, local administration was no longer solely a function of the executive branch (*ispolkom*) of the soviets. The respective authority of the local legislatures and administrations was defined in detail. This was a serious step on the way to reforming the local soviets. The new division of labor between local representative and executive branches was not easily implemented. Nevertheless, these branches of local government in Russia gained valuable practical experience by interacting within the limits of the law on local self-administration of 1991. Chiefs of local administration (*glava administratsii*) were to be elected directly by the population in accordance with the law of the RSFSR "On Elections of Heads of Administration" of 1991. However, at the fifth Congress of People's Deputies of the Russian Federation in October 1991, a moratorium was placed on these elections, and heads of local administrations were nominated by the head of the next higher level of administration. This latter circumstance did not enhance the ability of institutions of local government to "independently solve the questions of local significance."

The reform of local government in Russia coincided with the implementation of radical economic reform. For this reason, many serious problems in forming a new system of local government were caused by the unstable economic conditions in which the activity of local government took place. The key economic problems for local communities trying to create true local self-government included insufficient financial resources, the complete dependence of local budgets on centralized state subsidies, and inadequate authority for the institutions of local government in managing land and natural resources. The way to resolve these problems lay in the improvement of legislation governing intergovernmental relations (budgets, taxation, land use, and so forth), which regulates the authority of local government in different socioeconomic spheres. One of the most meaningful legal acts for the development of the financial and economic foundations of local government was the Law of the Russian Federation, adopted on April 15, 1993, "On the Principles of Budgetary Rights and Rights to Form and Use Non-Budget Funds by Representative and Executive Institutions of State Power." This law created the precondition for the formation of stable local budgets.

Economic problems of local government were not the only obstacles. The development of local government was also held back by the continued existence of a supercentralized system of state administration in the Russian

Federation. The so-called "vertical line of executive power" often acted against the interests of local communities. And when, beginning in December 1992, a "vertical line of *representative* power" began to form as a result of opposition between the president and the Supreme Soviet of the Russian Federation, the polarization of political interests, refracted at the local level, often began to dominate the activity of local soviets and local administrations. In this way, the institutions of local government became, to a certain extent, hostages of Kremlin politics.

President Yeltsin's declaration that "the soviets and democracy are incompatible" was followed by a rather energetic ideological attack on soviets of all levels on the grounds that they were too political and failed to deal with urgent economic and administrative affairs. In the author's view, such criticism misses the point. One distinct feature of any representative institution is that the interests of the people are represented in it and are negotiated by representatives who are elected by the people. Unavoidably, this negotiating carries a political rather than an administrative character. It is precisely the democratic nature of representative institutions that enables them to restrain bureaucratic influences on the part of the executive. The absence of oversight by representative institutions can lead to the absolute power of local "chinovniks." So, shortcomings in the economic activity of local soviets were not such an absolute evil, the eradication of which would ensure harmony in the organization of local government.

After October 1993, of course, the system of local government created according to the Law on Local Self-Government in the Russian Federation was effectively dismantled; the activity of the local soviets, with few exceptions, was suspended. For students of local government in Russia the following question remains unanswered: "Could the local soviets have been reformed into the major new representative institutions of local government?" The possibility of such a reformation existed and could be seen in the practical activities of the so-called small soviets (*malyi sovet*), whose creation was stipulated in the resolution of the Supreme Soviet of the RSFSR, "On Procedures for Implementing the Law of the RSFSR 'On Local Government in the RSFSR.' " The small soviets were entities within the local soviets as a whole, and were authorized to decide, with few exceptions, practically all questions connected with the jurisdiction of the larger body. The small soviets were compact in composition (as a rule, one-tenth the total number of deputies of the soviet), and were capable of efficiently and actively solving the problems that stood before the representative branch of local government.[3] The small soviets were not inclined to produce political conflicts to the same degree as the soviets that elected them, and on the whole, therefore, they could minimize the costs of parliamentarianism at the local level. The exclusion of the full soviets from the realm of practical action by the small soviets signaled a serious shift in emphasis in the organization of power at the local level, and proved the small soviets to be a rather effective model for organizing local government.

The Legal Reform of Local Government after 1993

Despite the negation by the new Russian constitution of a number of the established forms of local government, the document does provide a framework for the legal regulation of local government in the Russian Federation. This framework coincides to a considerable extent with the outline set forth in the Federal Treaty. After the signing of the Federal Treaty and the inclusion of its contents in the constitution of the Russian Federation, the center of gravity in the regulation of local self-administration was to shift from the federal legislature to the legislatures of the subnational members *(sub"ekty)* of the Russian Federation. According to the constitution and the Federal Treaty, the establishment of the general principles of the organization of local government in the Russian Federation was placed under the joint jurisdiction of the institutions of state power of both the Russian Federation and its members.

The constitution of the Russian Federation of 1993 uses the same formula for delineating the subjects of jurisdiction of the Russian Federation and its members with respect to the organization of local government as did the previous constitution. In accordance with it, a law on the general principles of the organization of local government in Russia is to be adopted at the federal level. Until its adoption, the unitary law on local government in the Russian Federation, as amended by the decrees of the president of the Russian Federation that were published after September 21, 1993, remains valid.

The Russian practice of legislation on local government reveals certain consistent features in its formation that allow us to treat it as a specific branch of law, a branch that is sometimes referred to as municipal law.[4] These features seem likely to be repeated in the new legislation on local government as well. What must be done to clarify the function and role of legislation on local government (municipal law) in the system of Russian law that is now being formed? First, it is necessary to define its relationship to other branches of law. Most important is its relationship to constitutional law. Constitutional law in Russia defines the concept of local government and the general structure of legislation on local government in the Russian Federation. Second, the legislative acts of the subnational members of the Russian Federation will also play an important role among the sources of law on local government. The constitutions of the republics and the statutes of other members of the Federation can stipulate the most important norms related to the organization of local government among the members of the Russian Federation. Third is the great weight attached to *local* normative legal acts. In particular, the sphere of independent local regulation applicable to the organization of local government is established not only by the subnational members of the Russian Federation, but also to a considerable extent by the constitution of the Russian Federation. Thus, article 131 of the constitution states that the structure of the institutions of local government is to be defined independently by the local population. In this way, constitutional law and law on local government differ significantly in the character of their sources. The most important are the normative acts of legislatures at the federal, subnational, and local levels. Of these, according to the model for regulating local government that was set forth by the constitution of the Russian Federation, acts of the members of the Russian Federation and local legal acts will carry the greatest weight.

One of the most important problems connected with establishing legislation of local government as an independent branch of law is defining the optimal relationship between acts that enter the system of legislation on local government and acts that belong to other branches of the law (civil, financial, administrative, and so forth). A contradictory practice developed in which the powers of the institutions of local government established by the law on local government were being constantly changed by the norms of other branches of legislation, thereby undermining the reality of the legislative guarantees of local government. Conversely, the approach of local legislators, who proceed from the axiom that the norms of legislation on local government always have priority over the norms of another branch of legislation (civil, administrative, land, financial, and so on), has not proved to be correct. Without the support of detailed regulation, such an approach literally crashes into the walls of other well-systematized branches of legislation, which already have solid mechanisms for their realization. It is precisely for these reasons that many of the norms of legislation on local government that relate to their participation in such areas as financial and land relations, management of property, and privatization remain unrealized. The introduction of these norms should be accompanied in all cases by active work to systematize existing legislation.

In conclusion, it is necessary to emphasize that all the arguments introduced here for separating the law on local government (municipal law) into an independent branch of law assumes that the objective preconditions for the formation of such branches already exist in Russia. Yet to speak of the appearance of a legitimate branch of law with good grounds will be possible only in the future, when local government in Russia really develops, when its traditions take root, and when a framework for the legal regulation of local government adequate to the federal structure of Russia is achieved.

Notes

1. *Editor's Note*: In current usage, the Russian term denoting local government is *mestnoe samoupravlenie*, which literally means "local self-administration" and applies principally to city and district-level government. The concept is relatively new in Russian legislation, and until 1985 was considered by official Soviet ideology to be contradictory to the Soviet-style organization of power. This term was used throughout the original Russian version of this chapter. The term "local government" is generally used in the translation that follows.

2. RSFSR stands for the Russian Soviet Federated Socialist Republic, which was the formal name for the Russian republic during the Soviet period. After the dissolution of the USSR in December 25, 1991, most of the laws of the RSFSR remained in force, including this one.

3. *Editor's Note*: The small soviets were a subset of all the deputies and were elected from among the deputies to the soviet as whole. Whereas the body as a whole met in relatively short sessions perhaps twice a year, the *malyi sovet* operated permanently and met about twice a month. The average size of the small soviets was between fifteen and thirty deputies, depending on the level of government.

4. Without debating the correctness of this term, we note that relative to the conditions of the Russian Federation, it would be more accurate to speak about a law of local self-government. In point of fact, the concepts of "municipal" and "municipality" for the Russian Federation do not correspond either to the system of local self-government as a whole, or to any specific level of it. The concept of "municipal property" *is* sufficiently rooted in Russian legislation and in the practice of institutions of local government. However, the name of the property of local self-administration cannot be a decisive argument for resolving a controversy over the name of the branch of law now being formed, which has its own distinctive meaning.

Structure of the
Russian Federation Government

Legislative Branch—The Federal Assembly

The parliament as a whole is called the Federal Assembly and consists of two chambers: the State Duma and the Council of the Federation (much as the House and Senate comprise the U.S. Congress).

State Duma

The State Duma consists of 450 members, 225 elected according to single-member districts and the remaining 225 chosen on the basis of proportional representation according to party lists. Deputies are elected for four-year terms to the Federal Assembly (the current Duma's term is for only two years). The Duma has the power to:

- issue votes of confidence in the Russian government;
- declare amnesties;
- initiate impeachment proceedings against the president;
- approve president's nominee for prime minister;
- initiate legislation and approve budgets.

The Council of the Federation

The Council consists of 178 members—one member from the executive branch and one member from the legislative branch from each of Russia's eighty-nine units. Like the Duma, terms are for four years, but the current Council deputies will serve for only two. It has the power to:

- confirm presidential decrees regarding martial law and states of emergency;
- remove the president from office;
- appoint justices to Russia's three supreme courts;
- schedule presidential elections;
- decide on the usage of Russian armed forces outside Russia;

Executive Branch

President

The president of the Russian Federation is the head of state and supreme commander-in-chief of the Russian Federation Armed Forces. The president determines the basic guidelines for domestic and foreign policy. The President is popularly elected to a four-year term, and may serve no more than two consecutive terms. The president has the power to:

- appoint the prime minister with the consent of the State Duma;
- dissolve the Duma and call for elections to the Duma;
- issue decrees and declare war and states of emergency;
- sign and endorse all legislative acts;
- nominate justices for the Constitutional Court and Supreme Court.

The Government of the Russian Federation

This consists of the prime minister, the vice chairman of the government, and the federal ministers. The prime minister is appointed by the president with the approval of the State Duma. The government of the Russian Federation has the power to:

- create the federal budget and present it to the State Duma;
- ensure Russia's defense and state security;
- carry out measures to ensure civil rights and liberties;
- implement a uniform credit, financial, and monetary policy.

Judicial Branch

The judicial branch at the federal level consists of three courts: the Constitutional Court, which settles disputes about the constitution; the Supreme Court, which is the highest appellate court; and the High Court of Arbitration, which handles economic matters. Justices to these courts are nominated by the president and approved by the Council of the Federation. They are not subject to removal from office and they have immunity from criminal charges (article 122 of the Constitution). The Russian Federation Prosecutor's Office is the highest prosecuting office in Russia; its powers are determined by federal law. The head of this office is the prosecutor general, who is nominated by the president with the approval of the Council of the Federation. The prosecutor general is also subject to removal by the Council of the Federation.

LEGISLATIVE PROCESS FOR A BILL THAT ORIGINATES IN THE DUMA

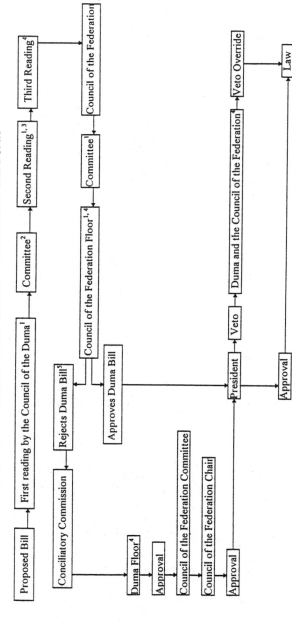

Source: By the author with the assistance of Brian Sloyer.

[1]Bill may be amended here.

[2]The Committee considers legislation and amendments and sends a report to the president and government for their views.

[3]Legal staff prepares bill and sends a preliminary copy to the Council of the Federation.

[4]Bill is voted on.

[5]The Duma may override the Council of the Federation's rejection with a two-thirds vote, thus sending the bill to the president for approval.

Election Laws

1. 1989 USSR National Elections

USSR Congress of People's Deputies, 2,250 seats—750 from single-member districts, 750 from national territories, and 750 from public organizations such as the Communist Party and the Academy of Sciences.

The nomination procedure was a three-step process. The first phase was the nomination phase; the second was the preelection meeting phase, which further screened candidates; the third was the campaign phase, which lasted six weeks.

Quantitatively, these elections were unprecedented. However, qualitatively they could have been more democratic; the nomination process was too difficult and not truly democratic, as most nominations occurred in the workplace where the party secretary had too much influence. Elections were also limited by the number of seats automatically allocated to public organizations such as the Communist Party.

To win a seat in the election, a candidate needed 50 percent of the votes cast by at least 50 percent of the electorate. Runoff and repeat elections were held in districts where none of the candidates got more than 50 percent of the vote.

2. 1990 Local Elections in Russia

Russian Congress of People's Deputies—1,068 seats elected to five-year terms—900 from single-member districts and 168 from national territorial districts.

Russian Supreme Soviet—252 seats—126 in a Council of the Republic and 126 in a Council of Nationalities.

Similar to the 1989 national elections, a candidate needed 50 percent of the votes cast by at least 50 percent of the electorate to win a seat to the CPD; deputies to the Supreme Soviet were then elected by the deputies of the CPD.

These elections were more democratic than the 1989 elections because of two major changes: first, the automatic allocation of seats to public organizations was dropped, and second, the complex nomination process that screened out candidates considered to be threatening to the apparatchik was omitted.

3. Presidential Election—June 12, 1991

Elections for the new Russian presidency occurred on June 12, 1991. To win the presidency, a candidate needed 50 percent of the vote cast by at least 50 percent of the electorate. The president is elected by the people for a term of five years and for no more than two consecutive terms. The constitution adopted in December 1993 specifies a four-year term, but when Boris Yeltsin was elected in June 1991 it was to a five-year term).

Six candidates were officially registered for the election. They were Boris Yeltsin, Vladimir Zhirinovsky, Vadim Bakatin, Nikolai Ryzhkov, Amangeldy Tulayev, and Albert Makashov.

Results: 70 percent of eligible voters went to the polls. Yeltsin received 57 percent of the vote, Ryzhkov 17 percent, Zhirinovsky 8 percent, Tulayev 6 percent, Makashov 4 percent, and Bakatin 3 percent.

4. Parliamentary Elections—December 12, 1993

Along with these elections there was a referendum calling for the passage of a new constitution that not only strengthened the powers of the executive branch, but also created a new government structure in Russia. The new legislative branch was divided into two chambers: the State Duma and the Council of the Federation.

1. The State Duma consisted of 450 members—225 from single-member districts and 225 from party lists. These were full-time positions as deputies could not hold any other governmental position. The 225 single-member district seats were based on a "winner-take-all" election system, although there needed to be a 25 percent voter turnout for the election to be valid. The party lists needed a 5 percent voter threshold for representation. Although the new constitution called for four-year terms for Duma deputies, the deputies elected in this first election would only serve two-year terms.

2. The Council of the Federation consisted of 178 seats—one member from the executive branch and one member from the legislative branch from each of Russia's eighty-nine units. Different from the State Duma, these members could hold multiple government positions. As with the Duma, members to the first Council of the Federation would serve only two-year terms. However, the new constitution does not specify the length of terms for future Council of the Federation seats, or does it specify that these seats are elected. Rather, it states that the procedures for *forming* the Council of the Federation are established by federal laws (chapter 5, article 96.2).

In this election and referendum, the voter turnout was 54 percent. The constitutional referendum passed with 58.4 percent (and it was valid because the turnout was greater than 50 percent).

5. 1994 Local Elections

A series of presidential decrees issued in October 1993 established the basis for new local legislatures among the subnational units of the Russian Federation, not including the republics. Provincial (*oblast*) legislatures were to be composed of 15–50 deputies elected to two-year terms. Most of these new legislatures were called "dumas" or assemblies (*sobranie*) although there was no regulation to this effect. Elections were to be held between December 1993 and March 1994 using a single member district system. The primary rule was that for the election to be valid, 25 percent of the registered electorate needed to vote. Thereafter, it was a winner-take-all system in which the candidate who received the most votes won the election. If the electoral turnout was less than 25 percent, repeat elections were held two months later. In fact, by April 1994, elections had been held in only sixty-seven of the eighty-nine federal units and they continued to be held into 1995.

Chronology of Reforms of the Political System

1988

May 23: Central Committee approves theses for nineteenth Party Conference.

June 28: Nineteenth Party Conference opens in Moscow; Gorbachev proposes multicandidate elections to a new parliament (Congress of People's Deputies).

December 1: Constitutional amendments implementing Gorbachev's changes are passed by the USSR Supreme Soviet.

1989

March 26: National elections for the USSR CPD are held.

May 25: First session of the USSR CPD opens; election of the USSR Supreme Soviet and Gorbachev as chairman of the Supreme Soviet. Session lasts until June.

June 3: First session of the USSR Supreme Soviet as a new legislative body.

June–July: USSR Supreme Soviet rejects nominees for ministerial positions; first independent act of authority.

July 29: Interregional Group of Deputies formed in the USSR CPD to promote the liberal-reform agenda.

December 16: Abolishment of automatically allotted seats to "public organizations" for future Congresses.

1990

February 5: Gorbachev proposes to Central Committee that the party abandon its leading role (article 6 of Soviet constitution) and accept a multiparty system.

February–March: Creation of new Russian political system; nationwide republic and local elections.

March 13: CPD approves a law creating a presidential system of government; official removal of article 6 from Soviet constitution.

March 15: Gorbachev elected as president of the USSR by the CPD; the next election is to be by popular vote.

March 24–26: Gorbachev creates fifteen-member Presidential Council as a consultative body.

May 16: First session of RSFSR CPD; lasts until June 22.

May 29: Yeltsin elected chairman of the Presidium of the RSFSR Supreme Soviet.

June 8: RSFSR Supreme Soviet declares that its laws take precedence over Soviet laws.

June 14: RSFSR CPD adopts Declaration of State Sovereignty.

July 2: Opening of twenty-eighth and last Congress of the CPSU, which lasts until July 12; factionalization of CPSU.

September 24: USSR Supreme Soviet grants Gorbachev the right to rule by decree for eighteen months.

October 24: USSR Supreme Soviet rejects the assertions by individual republics that their laws take precedence over Soviet laws.

November 17: USSR Supreme Soviet approves a Gorbachev proposal for a major government reorganization; the Council of Ministers becomes a smaller Cabinet of Ministers directly subordinate to the president; the post of vice president is also created.

November 27: Second session of the RSFSR CPD; lasts until December 15.

Fall: Yeltsin's opposition in parliament demands special CPD session for spring to discuss Yeltsin's removal as chair of parliament.

December 5: USSR Supreme Soviet approves draft law concentrating executive power in the president's hands by turning powers of Council of Ministers over to the Cabinet of Ministers.

1991

March 28: Third session of Russian CPD; lasts until April 5.

April: The Russian constitution is amended to provide for a separate, directly elected president of the Russian Federation; Gorbachev also agrees to a Confederation 9 + 1 Treaty (nine republics plus a Soviet Federation), which ultimately fails.

April 24: Gorbachev offers to resign as CPSU general secretary at Central Committee plenum, but offer is rejected.

May 21: Fourth session of Russian CPD; lasts until May 25.

May 22: Russian CPD adopts a law creating a separate Russian Republic presidency.

June 6: Law on Local Self-Government adopted.

June 12: Yeltsin elected president of Russia.

July 10: Fifth session of Russian CPD, which recessed on July 17 until the fall of 1991; political gridlock becomes apparent.

July 26: CPSU Central Committee accepts new draft Party Program that abandons key elements of Marxism-Leninism and embraces pluralism.

August 19: Coup attempt to stall signing of 9 + 1 Treaty; CPSU dissolved.

August 31: Yeltsin signs a temporary regulation defining the roles of the presidential representatives.

October 28: The fifth Russian CPD reconvenes and lasts until November 4; parliament gives Yeltsin power to rule by decree for one year.

November 1: Adoption of the resolution called "On the Organization of Executive Power in the Period of Radical Reform" giving Yeltsin the right to approve regional executives.

December 8: Formation of Commonwealth of Independent States.

December 25: Dissolution of USSR.

1992

January 1: Implementation of Egor Gaidar's shock therapy plan.

April 6: Sixth session of the Russian CPD; lasts until April 21.

July 15: Yeltsin strengthens presidential representatives by placing them directly under his control, thereby undermining the influence of parliament over them.

December 1: Seventh Russian CPD session, which lasts until December 14; Egor Gaidar resigns and Viktor Chernomyrdin is elected prime minister.

1993

February 5: Yeltsin signs Ukaz no. 186 making the presidential representative positions a permanent institution.

March 10: Eighth session of Russian CPD, which lasts until March 13; marks conservative trend in Congress. CPD moves to impeach Yeltsin but is narrowly defeated.

March 20: Yeltsin announces that he is declaring a "special regime" but later withdraws his declaration.

March 26: Ninth and final session of Russian CPD; lasts until March 29.

April 23: Compromise agreement to hold national referendum; voters favor Yeltsin, his policies, and new parliamentary elections.

June: Constitutional Convention convenes.

Summer: Anti-Yeltsin opposition assumes nearly all the leadership positions in parliament.

August: Yeltsin demands that early parliamentary elections be held; Rutskoi suspended as vice president.

September 21: Yeltsin dissolves Russian Supreme Soviet and Congress of People's Deputies with Decree 1400.

October 3: Yeltsin bombs parliament building when Khasbulatov and supporters refuse to leave.

October 9: Yeltsin dissolves local soviets.

December 12: New constitutional referendum and parliamentary elections held in Russia; creation of new legislative structure. First Russian Republic ends.

1994

January 11: First session of new Russian legislature convenes in Moscow.

January 17: Approval of package agreement that settles problems of matching demands with committee and leadership positions.

January–March: Local elections held in most of Russia's forty-nine oblasts.

March: Parliament grants amnesty to those arrested in the October crisis.

June: Yeltsin attempts to rule by decree, ignoring parliament and the government.

October 3: Presidential decree signed making it clear that the governors (presidential representatives) serve at the pleasure of the president.

December 12: Yeltsin and advisers begin war in Chechnya.

Index